Martina Burke's copy

One
CHAPTER A
Moment

18/8/18

Inspired Messages from
Mirella Amarachi &
David Richman Olayinka

authorHOUSE®

AuthorHouse™ UK
1663 Liberty Drive
Bloomington, IN 47403 USA
www.authorhouse.co.uk
Phone: 0800.197.4150

Published by AuthorHouse 04/08/2016

ISBN: 978-1-5246-2910-6 (sc)
ISBN: 978-1-5246-2902-1 (e)

Print information available on the last page.

Any people depicted in stock imagery provided by Thinkstock are models, and such images are being used for illustrative purposes only.
Certain stock imagery © Thinkstock.

This book is printed on acid-free paper.

Because of the dynamic nature of the Internet, any web addresses or links contained in this book may have changed since publication and may no longer be valid. The views expressed in this work are solely those of the author and do not necessarily reflect the views of the publisher, and the publisher hereby disclaims any responsibility for them.

Scripture quotations marked KJV are from the Holy Bible, King James Version (Authorized Version). First published in 1611. Quoted from the KJV Classic Reference Bible, Copyright © 1983 by The Zondervan Corporation.

Contents

Dedication
&
Acknowledgements

This book is dedicated to God our Father, Jesus Christ Our Lord and Saviour, the Holy Spirit Our eternal helper, Our Source and Our Strength and the Owner of our lives. To Him alone be all Glory.

We deeply also acknowledge our Biological pedigree through Chief Bello Olayinka (of Blessed Memory) & Mrs Amudat Olayinka [David's Parents) and Pastor Tony & Mrs Felicia Ejiugwo (Mirella's Parents).

Our Spiritual pedigree is also worthy of deep appreciation. I, David, got born again in March 1992 and attended Deeper Life Bible Church of Pastor W.F. Kumuyi first and obtained vital training in righteousness there, exploded into a fiery Evangelist under the Leadership of Pastor Peter. O Morakinyo (Jesus Revolution World Outreach) who in turn introduced and recommended me for training under Bishop David O. Oyedepo of the Living Faith Church Worldwide. After my return from the Training, I was released to Pastor under the tutelage of Bishop Rowland A. Peters of ICM (Then Royal Christian Chapel Ile-Ife, Osun, State). After completing my journey there, I went to serve under Bishop Francis Wale Oke of the Sword of the Spirit Ministries, Ibadan, Oyo-State from whence I came to this stage of life joined by my wife, Mirella.

We are proud enough of these two streams of pedigree from whence we came.

Many co-labourers we strive to uphold God's service together are too numerable to mention, but chiefly the pastors, Ministers, elders, deaconess, workers and members of The Power House International, and all my friends across the Island of Ireland and the world over. We acknowledge and honour you in the name of the Lord Jesus our High Priest and Redeemer.

And our Son Answer Samuel Akorede Richman, we love you from the depth of our hearts. It's been joy to hear you cry and see you also laugh during the course of working on this volume. You shall be great in the sight of the Lord in Jesus name. Amen.

Peace!

Foreword

Just like the holy writers of old who through inspiration of God put to paper their revelations, observations and experiences, we have put together this book, 'One Chapter A Moment' from the abundance of God's dealings with us over the years. To pass on the faith delivered to the forefathers from Abraham down to the contemporary ones, penning divine dealings down is of utmost importance for the coming generation(s). And that's exactly what we have done here.

My wife, Mirella, is young but imbued with the wisdom of the Ancient of Days wrote many things here under the tag **"***Word from Mirella..."**! She shared many things that will stir up your spirit from the depths as she's inspired and moved of the Holy Ghost! I have personally written the 136 chapters with all carefulness and sensitivity developed over the course of 24 years of my walk with God knowing surely that the blessings will extend beyond this generation till the end of life.

There is something for everybody in this great treatise of many colours. Some parts of it taste like the Psalms of David to bring you to your face before God, the proverbs of Solomon to make the simple wise giving life-tested tact for all dealings, others appear like the rebukes of Elijah on erring prophets and backslidden children of God, the prophecies of Isaiah with promises of salvation from God, the warning and wailing of Jeremiah to seek God again, while many parts come in like the epistles of the Apostles and the rest like the messages of the book of Revelations talking both to the church and the world.

Our clear intention is to bring you to or revive your faith again in God and inspire you to link up with God more properly to become who God has purposed you to be before your birth.

Some chapters or words from Mirella are short and snappy while others are moderate, however, some are long enough to be a mini-book on their own each. It's called "One Chapter A Moment" because once a chapter is done with, you can relax and not run into another immediately until you've totally squeezed out the juice of the present one. More so, the topics therein are so multi-dimensionally multifaceted that we can't find a more suitable name for it.

Many of the Bible quotations there are from KJV, but others are from many other Bible translations suitable for each line of its usage and a lot of them are paraphrased for the purpose of giving meaning within context!

"**One Chapter A Moment**" is good for devotional purposes, Christian Educational Classes, Bible Study Ministers' training, Retreat, Conference, Seminar or for personal growth and inspired motivation in the way of righteousness.

May our God whom we serve day and night in the faith of His Son Jesus Christ encounter and reveal Himself to you as you read through this volume any day, anytime, anywhere in Jesus name. Amen.

Mirella & David Richman Olayinka
April 2016

Chapter 1

Looking for the Truth and Standing on the Truth Only!

People who want the real truth cannot be tied down by anyone for that matter. They will not rest until they find the place of truth. No matter what any pastor or person does to tie you down in a place, it cannot suffice if you're really thirsty for the truth.

What your pastor teaches you or doesn't will not be an excuse on the day of judgement. You have many avenues to know the truth! If your spirit is comfortable where anybody can dress as they like and act as they deem fit, I doubt if you have the Holy Spirit. He is the spirit of decency and orderliness.

There's something in a child of God that refuses to rest in a place where God is not fully revered or honoured. A true child of God is not comfortable in sin; he does everything to repent out of it because the seed of God is in him. HE CAN'T REMAIN IN SIN!

If there's no joy in you where righteousness is preached, check your soul, it might not be in God yet! The church of God is a hospital indeed, but people do get well and move on in a hospital. So, when will you move from the stage of those sins everybody calls your name with?

Grace rather frees us from sin than pampers us in unrighteousness.

Don't let church people deceive you, they're enjoying their pastor that's why they're still in that church. They all know where what is, but like to be pampered in their indulgences. Even infants reject any food they don't want.

If you're able to read for yourself and you saw how they got baptized in the Holy Ghost in the Bible, but now somebody is teaching you to learn it syllable by syllable, it's because you personally enjoy deception!

Thank God for grace for by it we're all saved and not by work, but that doesn't mean the church should look like a clubhouse. New members can come as they are, old members should cover up the tattoos on their chest/breasts cleavages!

The bible is clear about everything, when we are ready to go Bible way, we will learn its truth.

"And in thy majesty ride prosperously because of truth and meekness and righteousness; and thy right hand shall teach thee terrible things." Psalm 45:4.

Peace be unto you in Jesus name. Amen.

Chapter 2

Only God Has the Key to Your Destiny

Don't use pretence to get anything from nobody, because you can never have anything, as a child of God, except it comes from heaven.

"John answered and said, a man can receive nothing, except it be given him from heaven." John 3:27.

Jacob pretended to be Esau as advised by Mother Rebecca to get the father's blessing. He spent about the next 21 years of his life being cheated by his task-master Uncle, Laban. He was cheated 10 times.

"And your father hath deceived (cheated) me, and changed my wages ten times..." Genesis 31:7.

Leah was prepped up by her father to join in conspiracy against Jacob pretending to be his wife on the wedding night. She spent the rest of her life fighting for marriage and naming most of her children after one issue or the other.

If only you know enough that the blessings of a man are just mere words except they carry the breath of the Almighty, you will stop all forms pretence immediately.

"Who is he that says, and it comes to pass, when the Lord commands it not?" Lamentation 3:27.

Many carry some false sense of humility, leaving in hypocrisy (acting) just to have that pastor pray for them or their father bless them. You should query why those who have received such time and again never became instant success! Only God blesses when your heart is confirmed right!

"The blessing of the Lord, it makes rich, and he adds no sorrow with it." Proverbs 10:22.

They've advised you, "Don't make him angry and do everything he says till he releases you with his blessing". Have you ever wondered that the most outspoken member of Jesus team was Peter? He would confront and even rebuke Jesus. He never kept quiet about what he thought to be true, yet Jesus made him the leader of the whole bunch! Why? Because God 'requires truth in the inward parts', King David submitted in Psalm 51.

Your father, Your Pastor (Bishop, Apostle or Prelate) combined with the king of your city or country can all bless you, but if God has not, you're not blessed.

God searches the heart; therefore, a child of God doesn't pretend. We're blessed already in Christ Jesus and not in search of a blessing elsewhere. Thus, we conscientiously do all we do before God and men not for anyone's favour like those who render eyes service.

"Blessed be the God and Father of our Lord Jesus Christ, who hath blessed us with all spiritual blessings in heavenly places in Christ..." Ephesians 1:3.

Hypocrisy the mother of pretence is best defined as acting. Greek word: Ypokrisía means "play-acting", "acting out". A child of God does not act pretentiously. He lives in truth. We're not men pleasers, but servants of righteousness. Don't call somebody Rev'd in his presence and call him foolish boy in your heart or while he's not there. You'll quench the Spirit of God.

Pretenders could easily attract the fancy of leaders. They speak well. They act right. They dress good. But their end shall be empty. I met many of them where I once worked. They were promoted quickly but they ended up empty! Live in truth only!

In the old testament people looked around for blessings, not so after the death of Jesus Christ. We are blessed already, as we continue to live in truth and in obedience to the leading of the Holy Spirit, we grow in grace.

God is the only one that blesses and you're truly blessed. Pharisee-like pretence only brings you mere words from humans (Pastors, Parents and People). Be real. Be true. Be truthful. Your destiny is only in God's hand. Nobody can bless you if He's not and nobody can curse you once He blessed you.

"To the angel of the church in Philadelphia (city of love: the man who loves Jesus) write:

These are the words of him who is holy and true, who holds the key of David. What he opens no one can shut, and what he shuts no one can open." Revelation 3:7.

In righteousness you will be established and far from oppression in Jesus name. Amen.

I love you.

Peace!

***Word from Mirella...

*** To all weary ministers of the Gospel: be encouraged in the LORD. Things may not have conformed to the manner you envisioned in the work of the ministry, however, one thing stands true! Habakkuk 2:2-3 declares,

"2 And the Lord answered me, and said, Write the vision, and make it plain upon tables, that he may RUN that readeth it.

3 For the vision is yet for an APPOINTED time, but at the END IT SHALL SPEAK, AND NOT LIE: though it tarry, WAIT FOR IT; BECAUSE IT WILL SURELY COME, it will not tarry."

God is not a man that He should lie; whatsoever He promises, He fulfils. Our part to play is to walk in faith and patience, so to inherit His promises for our lives.

Beloved, keep running, for the LORD sees your incessant labour of love in His Kingdom. He is a just God and shall surely repay you in awesome folds.

Cease murmuring; cease complaining! Keep keeping on, for the clouds are gathering over your life and destiny for an abundance overflow!

God is working through all and in all to bring you to His desired end for your life...thus, don't be discouraged!

Shalom! *******

Chapter 3

Trust in God Alone, but Always Also Treat Men as God Would

Humans can use you and dump you once they're done with you or better opportunities show up. Always bear that in mind! A true child of God will never do so though!

Reason why God emphasizes your trust being in Him only at all times and not on your spouse, co-minister, best friend, parent or boss is that, "...all that is in the world, the lust of the flesh, and the lust of the eyes, and the pride of life..." And anyone can yield to such anytime.

It's so painful when you speak with people whose spouses have let down without considering the sweet and lofty promises made when they first met. That's why your trust must be rooted in God alone. Don't trust in chariot nor horses, but in God alone, otherwise you may fall without being able to rise again.

God has put men and women around us not so you can rest your whole life on them for if you do, God Himself can remove them yonder from you. The way some women depend solely on their husbands as if they're God is so alarming. That's why many can't move on if such die.

"Cursed is the man that makes flesh his strength." Jeremiah 17:5.

It's God that brings men into our lives, but men must not become gods in our lives. No human is our strength and source,

7

only God the Almighty is. The life of any human is in his nostrils, he can breathe the last unexpectedly. If your trust is in him and not God, your hope dies with him.

The exit of an important figure from anyone's life can be very fatal. That's why if you relate closely with God, He would have filled the gap before it's void. He is "the fullness of him that fills all in all."

People whose total trust is in God alone don't hold too tightly to anyone or anything, not even their spouses or children. Abraham agreed with Lot when he asked out and the father of the prodigal son didn't stop him.

Life is fragile, so transient that one little sickness can change the whole landscape of your relationship with anyone. He promised to always be there, but now he's sick. But not so with God. He does not fall sick. He can't be sick. Never!

Why did Jesus teach us to pray? It's so we will build daily reliance on the source of all things, God the Almighty!

I love my wife. I love our son (God's son in our care). I love my family. I love those I work with. I love the church of God in our care. I love my friends and the country I live in... But I constantly detach my heart to dedicate it back to God because anything can finish without prior notification. Only God doesn't!

There's too much love of self, love of front line, love of money in the atmosphere than to not focus on God alone, because you don't even know what someone else is thinking. But we know the thought of God.

"For I know the thoughts that I think toward you, saith the Lord, thoughts of peace, and not of evil, to give you an expected end." Jeremiah 29:11.

There are still Nathaniel(s) around, Israelis indeed in whom there's no guile. There are still true children of God that God sends to other children of God who look to Him alone for help!

You can't be someone who wants to use others and not be used by others. "Evil men will wax worse, deceiving and being deceived", Apostle Paul warned.

The best way to have the best of anyone around you is to keep your eyes on God above them at all times!

If you check the bible very well, you will discover that through the flesh, Satan destroyed many relationships and not God! And God refused to meddle, not even when serpent was destroying the relationship between Him and Eve (plus Adam). He's not a forcing God!

Many use others to get money, get name, and get up. One man once told me, "Join that man of God (name withheld), when you make name through him, branch out. That's how everyone does it. That's the secret of success in ministry." If that's what you're doing my friend, you're labouring in vain. Your work is not in God's record.

How can a true child of God get married to another fellow just to get children, document for legal residency in a foreign country or money from them? God is not in that. No!

"An inheritance may be gotten hastily at the beginning; but the end thereof shall not be blessed." Pro 20:21.

Your relationship with humans God brings you across will determine how much of God you will have or miss out on in this life. God will not send humans to you to replace Him, for you to use and dump or to sift your focus off Him at any time. Your heart is being weighed and tested by God always. He watches all of your thoughts!

May God grant you peace all round in Jesus name. Amen.

Look up to God my friend!

Chapter 4

Notwithstanding the Situation...
You Can Live A Full Life

No matter what's breaking down, hold your life together in Him.

"In him is life and the life is the light of men. The light shines in the darkness and the darkness cannot comprehend it." John 1:4.

Joseph was in the prison, but he held his life together. Moses was in exile, but he held his life together. Paul was in many troubles and often imprisonment, but his life was intact. There's so much life in Christ that no matter what a man is going through, he can be buzzing with real life!

You can't be breaking down because your marriage is breaking down. You can't be breaking down because men are breaking you down. No! You can't be breaking down because the ministry is breaking down. No!

If you're breaking down because things are breaking down around you, it's because you're not drawing much life from Him alone who's your life. "In Him is life..."

Your life is not in your academics, so if your studies are down your life is not breaking down. Your life is before and beyond any physical activity.

Be rooted in Him alone. Let His life be your life. Let not your marriage, business, ministry or academics be your life. Let Him alone be your very life.

You're building on sinking sands and an unsure future if your life is built on your marriage, your business, your ministry, your academics or even your anything!

There are many people with broken homes but with strong life because their hope, their very life is in Christ! There are many saints with challenging health, trying ministry, unstable business and troubles all around, but with robust, vibrant and abundant life because their heart is stayed on God, therefore they are kept in perfect peace!

You can have life in abundance despite or in spite of any circumstance around you. Circumstances don't define you, you define circumstances. Our life is in Christ, because "He has come to give life and in abundance." John 10:10.

You can shake off anything with the life of God in you. Paul shook off the viper into the fire and moved on unperturbed! You can shake anything off. Brush it off your shoulders.

Your life is in Christ with God and not in things on earth. Colossians 3.

The more of His word and prayer you engage in, the more of His life is injected into your spirit. Acts 6:4. We can do all things through Christ who strengthens us. Amen. Philippians 4:13.If things are breaking down around and you're also breaking apart, you need more injection of life from Christ. Go for it.

"If you faint in the day of adversity, your strength is small." Proverbs 24:10.

May God strengthen you with might in the inner man. May you be infused with new strength and might from the very throne of Jesus Christ in Jesus name. Amen.

Peace be upon you.

Chapter 5

God IS EVER READY... to Cradle Us Up When We Are Determined to Move on with Him

Bad dreams from you do not mean somebody else should not go ahead with the project they're determined to do once all options have been weighed based on God's word. I've had bad dreams about what others wanted to do before, they still went ahead and succeeded. Determining factors change based on interplay of many forces. Things happen based on dispositional changes! God is not static. Once our trend matches His principles, there's a contraflow of what's been afore-normal! Remember evil prophesy overturned on Ahab when God saw him fasting and sorrowful!

How can you say your life has finished because you had a child outside of wedlock or without a husband? New beginning does happen when you make up your mind you're not a mistake and that no matter what it takes, you want to move on with God. God will not reject you.

"Those who come to me, I will in no wise cast away", Jesus said in John 6:37.

I know you've aborted so much that even your womb is in pain, but do you think if you're ready for God now He will say "no" to you? He will not do such to you. Those who turn a new leaf are ushered in for a fresh start. Prodigal son was not turned back! You will not be rejected!

It's man that determines how God deals with him. God already stated what He will do before we came here. He has love, He has grace, He has favour, He has wisdom and He has greatness. Whenever a man wants any of these, it's his. God's principle for taking is clear: Demand it, fulfil its course and take it. Mathew 7:7.

If you're just being tolerated in a relationship, move away from it. You have more values than to just be tolerated. You're very important to God. So, if you're in a rut, you can with Him get out of it. Luke 18.

God has always been ready even before you're ready. Move close to and move on with Him.

You have children for different men and so what? You can still have a great life with and in God if that's your desire. You can still fulfil the very plan of God for your life. The throne of mercy is open for you today.

There are more sins people commit that don't see the light of the day than the ones known to all. Refuse from your heart on the basis of your determination to move on with God to be crucified for your known sins and faults. You can still get to the very top. Dust yourself up my friend! You can make it! Yeah, you can!

Many greats rose from the rubbles!

"He(God) raiseth up the poor out of the dust, and lifteth up the beggar from the dunghill, to set them among princes, and to make them inherit the throne of glory: for the pillars of the earth are the LORD'S, and he hath set the world upon them." 1 Samuel 2:8.

You must know that not only that all your trespasses were paid for by Jesus Christ before you're born, you're totally forgiven by God. With this in mind, rise above them and move on. Be strong my friend. You're forgiven. Colossians 2:13.

It is your personal choice if you remain down or in sin, regrets or within the human definition of who you're after all that Christ did for you.

"Blotting out the handwriting of ordinances that was against us, which was contrary to us, and took it out of the way, nailing it to his cross." Colossians 2:14.

Satan can no longer hold you down once you're willed to move on with Christ, not even if you're in the prison yard. His power is broken. Christ reigns supreme and we can reign with Him no matter what our past has been. We're complete in Christ - nothing missing, nothing broken!

"As ye have therefore received Christ Jesus the Lord, so walk ye in him: Rooted and built up in him, and stablished in the faith, as ye have been taught, abounding therein with thanksgiving. Beware lest any man spoil you through philosophy and vain deceit, after the tradition of men, after the rudiments of the world, and not after Christ. For in him dwelleth all the fullness of the Godhead bodily. And ye are complete in him, which is the head of all principality and power..." Colossians 2:6:10.

Truly you're sent to school, but there you misbehaved: you got pregnant or you impregnated somebody and your whole world is thrown into a shameful spotlight...this cannot be your end except you want it so. You will still be who God has designed you to be if you're in with God the rewriter of destiny! You can move on my friend!

There's no time your life has ended except you end it by yourself. God doesn't give up on people if they don't give up on themselves! You can move on my friend!

What happened has happened leaving bad taste in your mouth: your grades are down, your life slides-back, family and friends did forsake you, talking bad about you...this doesn't mean that God has forsaken you. No! If God forsakes people like that, not many people will be great. God is for you and your future can be realised. Don't look down, look up. God thinks well about you.

"For I know the plans I have for you," declares the Lord, "plans to prosper you and not to harm you, plans to give you hope and a future." 29:11.

What people do not know about Christianity is that when a man agrees with God to move off his past or present mess, God moves him on and the past is past, totally forgiven.

"We have a high priest..."

Staying put in the mess without a heart to move out is the trouble.

No matter where you're at now if you want to start all over with God, He will pick you up. Yes, He will! He will. Yes, He will. He will. He definitely will. Yes, He will. He's always ready for you. Think of the prodigal son. God's willing to help us up. Yes, He is! Amen.

Peace be upon you in Jesus name. You're victorious in Christ. Amen.

Peace!

*** Word from Mirella...

*** Times and opportunities are so important in our walk with God. We've to understand that there are seasons and times in the kingdom of God, wherein He executes His plans! That's why Ecclesiastes 9:11 says," *I returned, and saw under the sun, that the race is not to the swift, nor the battle to the strong, neither* *yet bread to the wise, nor yet riches to men of understanding, nor yet favour to men of skill; but **TIME** and **CHANCE** happeneth to them all".*

This verse reveals the thin line between people of success and those of failure: that is, the former ride on the wings of the right timing and opportunities, unlike the latter. Thus, let's see to walk circumspectly this year, if we desire to see tangible results in our lives. Let's see to walk with God's agenda, rather than our planned calendar! In so doing, we'll avoid needless stress and heart-ache. It doesn't matter SOLELY how prepared you are... how strong...how wise you are, but ALSO how accurately timed you are, along with the right opportunity!

Beloved, let's align ourselves rightly...for the best is yet to happen!

Shalom! ***

Chapter 6

Are You in The Will of God or Just Fulfilling the Desires of Your Soul?

Many times we think we found the will of God, not knowing we just found our own desire and not His will. His will is deep inside, only the dead (to the flesh-their will, pleasure and desire) find it.

"Counsel in the heart of man is like deep water; but a man of understanding will draw it out." Proverbs 20:5.

There's a great peace that attends your soul when you've found or when you're found in the will of God that doesn't exist in the natural world of materials.

"Thou wilt keep him in perfect peace, whose mind is stayed on thee: because he trusteth in thee." Isaiah 26:3.

The first layer of forces a man battle with while in the place of searching or prayers are his own desires flashing over his face. If he can search or pray deeper, he finds the will of God, the gold of heaven.

"You will seek me and find me when you SEARCH for me with all of your heart." Jeremiah 29:13.

Even Samuel the accurate prophet whose words never fell to the ground FOUND Eliab first and would have ordained or made him King before God opened the eyes of his heart to see

David, the sent one, the will of God. Why? Because, "Man looks on the outward appearance (what the eyes desire) but God looks at the heart (His eternal counsel)", God told him.

Mistakes, misfiring and missed-targets abound innumerable in this age of pursuits of all that glitter than at any other time. Many things called the will of God or the voice of the Holy Spirit are at best "the lust of the eyes, the lust of the flesh and the pride of life."

I am young but the water of battle for significance has dried up in my soul owing to several encounters with heavens. I have seen Jesus our Lord. I have been to the very gates of heavens. Many of the fathers you see have left the will of God a long time ago and pursuing the significance of life in competition and comparison with others.

I used to think preaching around, ministering in big programs and planting churches around count you in as playing big in the scheme of heavens until I discovered that Faithfulness to His will alone makes you count.

"Now when they had gone throughout Phrygia and the region of Galatia, and were forbidden of the Holy Ghost to preach the word in Asia, after they were come to Mysia, they assayed to go into Bithynia: but the Spirit suffered them not... a vision appeared to Paul in the night; There stood a man of Macedonia, and prayed him, saying, Come over into Macedonia, and help us." Acts 16:6-9.

Why do you want to come out church? Why do you want to branch out of that church of God? Why do you want to start an independent ministry? To be called a General Overseer? To be accorded the honour of a founder or what? If yes, you will lose on earth and in heaven! God only rewards what He commands!

The things you've heard and seen around have a great influence over what your heart is established on. Many things people call the will of God are the things they heard over the television. When your body is totally submitted on God's altar as a sacrifice and you're renewed on moment by moment basis, you will see the difference very clearly.

"I beseech you therefore, brethren, by the mercies of God, that ye present your bodies a living sacrifice, holy, acceptable unto God, which is your reasonable service.

And be not conformed to this world: but be ye transformed by the renewing of your mind, that ye may prove what is that good, and acceptable, and perfect, will of God." Romans 12:1-2.

When you study the word of God profusely, not to become anything, but just to know God and His heartbeat, you will understand the will of God. The quest for success at all cost will put gleams on your eyes and give you spurious interpretations while studying the word.

The will of God does not turn you to an instant success, but it first grounds you in the faith our Lord Jesus Christ. It gives you peace that passes human understanding. I know you've found the will of God when I see the peace and stability you exhume even while every physical thing is crashing on you.

The will of God is simple for the simple-hearted but the many-sided complications of life have complicated many people's lives.

"This only have I found: God created mankind upright, but they have gone in search of many schemes." Ecclesiastes 7:29.

If you truly seek God to know His will, you will find Him!

May the Lord lift up His countenance upon you and give you peace in Jesus name. Amen.

Peace!

*** Word from Mirella...

*** Until the kingdom of God is enthroned in our heart, His will can't be on earth, as it's in heaven. God's will is to have true sons...people that bear eternity at heart; heavenly-bound people. To live heaven on earth means to align to God's will. How? It's written, no unclean thing shall enter into the kingdom of heaven. Thus, to live the Kingdom life we must seek God's kingdom and His righteousness firstly. ***

*** "People of God, there's [Grace for eternity...even to as many that seek the Kingdom of God and His righteousness, find it and press into it (Matthew 7:12-14)." ***

*** "Trust in the LORD: He is God, the only true God; unchangeable Changer, the Covenant-keeping God! He is faithful Who has spoken. He can do and does what no flesh can do, thus let the earth tremble!" ***

*** The fall of man made him confined to his physical senses, weaknesses and limitations, and broke the true communication line with his Maker. Through the eternal and life-giving priesthood of Christ Jesus, provision was made for man - to be redeemed and restored to the place of fellowship with his Maker, the almighty God.

When Christ Jesus was glorified, He sent forth the promise of the Spirit to help as many that shall believe in Him, and become sons of God. Lo, the Holy Spirit came, and set forth a new dispensation! He is come, and unto every genuine and seeking believer, the supply of the Spirit is given...yea, even the Grace of God.

The apostle Paul writes, *"Sin shall have no dominion over us: for ye are not under the law, but under grace."* This affirmation is as a result of the supply of the Spirit.

The supernatural power that convinced you, o Believer, at the time of your salvation is of the supply of the Spirit. This latter empowers us in the race of our most precious faith to walk above the power of sin and death, for indeed we have been crucified with Christ and are arisen with Him, to live unto God.

The supply of the Spirit is the answer to the limitations of the human nature.

Oh, isn't it written, in Hebrews 4:16, *"Let us therefore come boldly unto the throne of grace, that we may obtain mercy, and find **grace** to help in time of need."*

Finally, Romans 6:22-23 KJV says,

"22 But now being made free from sin, and become servants to God, ye have your fruit unto holiness, and the end everlasting life.

23 For the wages of sin is death; but the gift of God is eternal life through Jesus Christ our Lord."

Today, receive the grace of the Lord Jesus Christ to walk in holiness and righteousness!

Shalom! ***

Chapter 7

One Day It Will Be the Final Moment: Are You Always Ready?

Rapture, the return of Jesus, will be so sudden that many will be caught unawares! Are you always ready?

Programmes, good deeds or carrying out so called "visions" will be the greatest distractions of many that they won't know when death strikes or rapture takes place! Are you always ready?

The greatest surprise at the gates of eternity will not be that of unbelievers told to depart to hell but of many believers whose faith is based on what Pastors said alone without properly checking the Bible for real truth and are sent to hell.

One great trick of Satan is to make the gospel so light so everything can be permissible in it. The tough stuff folk are running from are very easy to bear for those who have truly submitted to God. "My yoke is easy and my burden is light", Jesus said.

Many people you see on the pulpit are well compromised beyond measure that you need your bible undiluted to gauge things said otherwise you will land in hell fast!

Many people you see on the pulpit are there because many churches want to grow up fast and expand everywhere. Many are not born again. Many have half-truths (which are more dangerous than outright lies). Many are forced there to hold forth. Many do it for employment purpose. And they will do everything to make people stay. Check and base your life on the Bible only!

I have met pastors who don't see why God will send them to hell because they fornicate from time to time owing to what is tagged "weakness of the body". They claim so much of grace that you'll be thinking why is your own gospel so hard. Many have given heed to seducing spirits and doctrines of daemons. Study your bible!

You always come with the guy you're sleeping with from the house to the church (while unmarried, but immorality continues unabated), this is a common knowledge to all, your pastor inclusive, but he says nothing about it nor excuses you from the choir or ushering unit you're ministering in, HE IS NOT A SERVANT OF GOD, but a hireling. He hates your very soul. Just using you for gain.

If you truly thirst for eternity with God and not to end up in eternal damnation, you will not stand only on what man says but look thoroughly through the Bible like the Berean christians of Acts of Apostles!

"Now the Berean Jews were of more noble character than those in Thessalonica, for they received the message with great eagerness and examined the Scriptures every day to see if what Paul said was true." Acts 17:11.

A supposed big pastor then in the 90's held me in a conversation, teaching me how no matter what we do we can never go to hell. He's reputed to have bedded several girls, so I think he began to read some books on the so called "super grace" to quieten his soul from condemnation. I knew better, because I was too glued to the Bible. Nothing gives peace like the truth. Repent if you sin. Tell others it's wrong. Simple!

Truth is: Many people who go to church don't go for truth but just for other purposes of that church has always been part of their life from birth or they must be there to socialise. Therefore, don't blame entertaining churches and pastors because many created their pastors and churches to be so, funding them to be so! Paul prophesied it while writing to Timothy!

"For the time will come when they will not endure sound doctrine; but after their own lusts shall they heap to themselves teachers, having itching ears; And they shall turn away their ears from the truth, and shall be turned unto fables." 2 Timothy 4:3-4.

Once your heart is totally set on the things of eternity and that every other thing is secondary, you will face such a stiff opposition among believers to such a stage you will wonder, "for what reason did they come to Christ in the first place?"

There's grace and it's by it we're saved. Functional grace makes the life of God, life of holiness liveable and eternity with Christ accessible. Grace is not to be living sinful life and expecting Christ to take us home on the final day! No!

Many people are too compromised beyond repairs (at least for now) that you need to focus your own heart on God and the things of God rather than trying to bring them along because you might slide down the slope with them if you keep being around them. "A little leaven leavens the whole lump", Paul warned!

One day everyone will turn their back on your coffin. You're left alone with God the judge of all. The sweet-tongued pastors are no longer there!

One day the trumpet will sound. Will be too late for those who are not prepared. Jesus taught this. The Apostles also did! Does your pastor do or you're just doing everyday singing and dancing?

If your husband or pastor is comfortable with you opening your breasts in your dresses and doesn't correct you on such, he's not a godly man. A true child of God should not follow such fellow!

The Gospel of Jesus is simple. Sin is sin. Righteousness is righteousness. No unrighteous person shall see the face of God.

"He that sins is of the Devil." 1 John 3:8.

There's no grace that covers people's sins. Grace deals with sin culture and implants God-culture so we can live God-life. If you habitually live in sin, you've not received grace. With repentance from dead works, grace culture will have free flow in your life.

Bottom line is: Before that day of death or rapture when you'll no longer be able to argue anymore, check and re-examine yourself bible-based, then repent if sins are found. That's grace. Ability to check yourself and repent. That's grace!

Seek the Lord while He may be found. There's a time it's too late!

Peace be upon you & all yours in Jesus name. Amen.

Peace!

*** Word from Mirella...

*** How many times we easily become discouraged in pursuing God's vision delivered unto us because of others' perspectives. Yes, how many a times we unreservedly accept the crucifying dictates of others concerning our lives. However, that shouldn't be so for us as believers and that beckons the importance of erecting spiritual altars of memorial!

It will become easy to stand firm when you base your life on God's Word and faithfulness to you-wards, because life on earth is laden with trials of faith and hurdles of discouragement. If you can't stand with and for God when everyone stands against you (rather than refusing to succumb to man's insatiable pleasure), it merely signifies that you've decided to live unto man, having chosen to forget what God's spoken unto you!

Beloved, has God spoken to you? Hold His word most preciously hidden in your heart.

Speaking from my own experience, many have been surrounding and daring situations that exclaimed in my face," Mirella, back out!" However, I CHOSE to remember the words that the LORD of hosts had spoken unto me and regained my ground! That's a secret of spiritual victory.

Beloved, decide to pursue what God's voice has declared unto you, not wavering at and giving heed to every dead echo of mortals. ***

Chapter 8

If God Will Raise You, He Will Send Humans to You: Understanding Relationships 1

God made the first ever relationship happen. "It's not good for man to be alone", He said based on His unsearchable wisdom. Genesis 2:18.

Nobody becomes great outside of good relationship!

If God will have to take you to another level, it will not only be by angelic intervention, it will also involve human connection. God uses humans for humans primarily!

God orchestrates relationships. He brought Jonathan to David, otherwise David could have died without fulfilling the will of God for his generation by the wickedness of Saul, his primary hater!

Jesus sent them two by two. There's someone who steps into your life and the light turns on!

Who God sends into your life never ever sees you as a burden. The expensive purple selling woman of Acts was begging Paul and his team to house, feed and treat them well, because God had "opened her heart" for them. Acts 16:14.

It takes many people (arranged by God) to make one man. Many great names you know are products of many names unknown to the world.

When God's favour is upon you, He causes men to serve His cause in your life.

"Jesus grew in favour with God and men". Luke 2:52.

When Satan is ready to attack you, he moves men against you. If you refuse to take the issue of human relations very seriously, you will be stranded a long haul. Don't take anyone for granted. Treat all as angels of God, because they are.

Don't worship or depend on those sent into your life. See them only as messengers of God. You don't worship messengers, you worship the one who sent them, God! Don't use or take advantage of anyone. Be a messenger to the messengers God sent into your life. All have a purpose to fulfil, not only you.

You must minister to your minister if the ministry of your minister must continue with you. Discover the need of those ministering to your needs. Elisha prayed for the woman who built him an apartment (after knowing her need) and she had a man child.

""What can be done for her?" Elisha asked. Gehazi said, "She has no son, and her husband is old." 2 Kings 4:14.

God doesn't usually bring a divine relationship to a close, humans do. Lot wanted Independence. Jonathan loved to retain his position in the palace. Paul and Barnabas had sharp contention.

If God couldn't stop the prodigal son from going away, He will not stop anyone from saying bye to a divine orchestration. He never will!

Once the heart of a man closes against a thing, even God will not force him to open it. That's why your heart must be transformed by renewing it so you may always know that which is

"...good, acceptable and perfect will of God". Romans 12:2.

You may end up divorcing a man or a woman God Himself sent into your life once your heart grows calloused!

To sustain a divine relationship, you must focus on the reason God started it and not on the things you redesigned it to be along the line.

God sent that woman to be a prayer warrior over the church, not a financier. Don't forget. Don't frustrate her out because she doesn't give much and she refuses to go on missions.

Keep yourself within the jurisdiction of the divine purpose of that relationship. God saw your wife may not be a prayer warrior, but will physically be there for you all your life. Don't force prayer mission on her. Others will fulfil that. Okay?

Your spouse may not have been sent to you for bed-purposes primarily, but to raise you up. Don't force every minute sex on her, otherwise her mission to you may be frustrated. Some people are sent into your life to help you with weightier matters of life.

You will be able to keep all your divine connections, if you make God and not man your bedrock. If you will pray for all involved with you. If you will keep to the reason of their sending and take care of who takes care of you.

Don't judge any by their mistakes around you. Show deep love. God knows they will make the mistakes before sending them to you, but their purpose in your life is a divine design that's weightier than their errors. Be wise!

If you've forgotten how God brought you together, retrace it, ask God for it and keep it in your heart. Focus on that reason always. Peter rebuked Jesus for saying He'll die to save the world and John/James wanted the biggest thrones beside Jesus on the right and left when they forgot the reason of His existence in their lives!

Don't exact yourself over none. Jesus never did. The apostles never did. The prophets of old never did. Let God alone open or close the door. Stay human. Stay loving all the time with all sincerity from a pure heart!

Your prophet is not your friend. Discern the difference. Refuse to let him be. Leave him as prophet only. Look over his humanity. The second Kings woman to Elisha remains a great example forever to the wise of heart!

"And she said unto her husband, Behold now, I perceive that this is a holy man of God, who passes by us continually. Let us make a little chamber, I pray thee, on the wall; and let us set for him there a bed, and a table, and a stool, and a candlestick: and it shall be, when he cometh to us, that he shall turn in thither." 2 Kings 4:9-10.

If a divine relationship shuts down, despair not. Revive it by love. If it stays locked, handle it in deep prayers in handling it back to God, the giver. Never give up on precious matters without a great fight.

"By faith … women received their loved ones back again from death." Hebrews 11:35.

May God restore all your lost divine contacts and bring you into greater relationships that take you higher into fulfilment in this life and the one to come in Jesus name. AMEN.

Peace be upon you and all yours.

I love you!

*** **Word from Mirella...**

*** Greetings in Christ to you,

In this season, ask for the supply of the Spirit to see tangible results of the Word of God. It is possible to live by the Word of God. Get connected to the Spirit, and see the Word of God made manifest. It's your season.

What's the supply of the Spirit? GRACE: yes, what the Holy Spirit supplies unto us is the supernatural ability to walk in the Word!

We have toiled...and toiled unceasingly by the strength of the flesh. Now is the time to hearken to and obey the Word of God - by the supply of the Spirit - and see miraculous results. There's indeed the supply of the Spirit to this very cause. Ask in the place of prayer and receive.

Philippians 1:19 KJV says,

"For I know that this shall turn to my salvation through your prayer, and <u>the supply of the Spirit of Jesus Christ</u>,"

Shalom! ***

Chapter 9

What Then Can I Do to Move on from Here, Lord?

Maybe you're locked up in a very serious issue. You've failed yourself, Family, Church, friends and God! And you're asking, "where do I start now, what can I do?" Start from repentance!

You can start anew if you start with repentance now.

Whatever will take God to happen will only take repentance first.

"Repent ye therefore, and be converted, that your sins may be blotted out, when the times of refreshing shall come from the presence of the Lord." Acts 3:19.

If your pastor cannot correct your fornicating and deceiving habit or other evil involvement any longer, you should know he's the same as you. He never repented of such. If he's any other opportunity, he'll still do it.

The difference between remorseful feeling and repentance is: Repentance comes with conversion of heart whereas Remorse is about escaping the present shame.

New beginning can start for anyone whether a backslidden believer or a rotten unbeliever if repentance is thoroughly done.

A repented soul does not care about his past anymore. The pastor can even preach about it while he's there. He doesn't feel pain, because that's past. He can freely talk about it, for he's never going to continue in it anymore.

"Therefore, if anyone is in Christ, the new creation has come: [a] The old has gone, the new is here!" 2 Corinthians 5:17.

Pastor-Deborah Sade Jones, my friend and associate of many years revealed to me on our way to Dublin to preach in late 2009 who she used to be while a non-born again. She freely preaches about it without shame. This is the same trend with anyone who's truly converted by means of thorough repentance.

If they can't truly talk about what transpired in the past, their past is still in their present flowing to the future.

The difference between confession which billions of believers the world over have done and true repentance is: Confession is talking whereas Repentance is doing.

"Whoever conceals their sins does not prosper, but the one who confesses and renounces them finds mercy." Proverbs 28:13.

Many churches are just theatres where dramas go on weekdays and weekends. People just mark register without making any mark. Grace demands growth.

If since you got born again (assumedly), you're still the same as you're used to being, you've not repented.

Repentance changes your course, path and group! A repented prostitute doesn't wear clothes to seduce people neither does she leave cleavages open anywhere anymore except for the husband at home alone, for old things have passed away.

Many people don't dress bad nor go to every party before being serious church members, but now they do all those things. They've been initiated. They're Jezebels in many churches initiating people. I see many of them in many churches. The day you truly repent, you will know the difference!

You're not forced to live righteously after true repentance, you're empowered to become servant of righteousness!

"Being then made free from sin, ye became the servants of righteousness." Romans 6:18.

Godly sorrow leads to true repentance that's for life. Shame only leads to Remorse. Remorse happens when you're caught, Repentance occurs when God touches and convicts the heart.

"For godly sorrow worketh repentance to salvation not to be repented of: but the sorrow of the world worketh death." 2 Corinthians 7:10.

God can raise anybody again once there is a true repentance.

"The sacrifices of God are a broken spirit: a broken and a contrite heart, O God, thou wilt not despise." Psalm 51:17.

Heavens cannot reject a soul who's ready to return, even the prodigal soul had another chance.

"Consider how far you have fallen! Repent and do the things you did at first. If you do not repent, I will come to you and remove your lampstand from its place." Rev 2:5.

You don't need to tell people when changes have occurred in your life, people know. You can't hide repentance, you can only pretend to be, but people know. "By their fruits, we shall know them."

The soothing words of the pampering and deceiving pastors will not matter anymore at the gate of heaven when the final day arrives, but whether you've truly repented and turned back from your sins. True grace leads to thorough repentance. David had that grace. True grace. Psalm 51.

Change is a product of repenting, quitting from unproductive past and returning to God's way. That's how we change from Glory to Glory! You need change? Repent!

In-filling of the Holy Spirit and His attendant gifts answers more to repentance than any other thing. Many people have testimony of being filled with the Holy Ghost while repenting of certain evil deeds.

If God becomes far from you, repentance will bring Him back.

"Return to me and I will return to you, Saith the Lord". Malachi 3:7.

There's no sin too thick that repentance can't break off you.

"Repent, then, and turn to God, so that your sins may be wiped out, that times of refreshing may come from the Lord..." Acts 3:19.

Neither grace nor the blood of Jesus has nullified repentance from evil works. Instead, repentance gives easy access to the blood of Jesus and grace.

Don't pile up sins to a point where you don't know where to start anymore. Ask God to forgive you. Ask man to forgive you. Repentance confers great authority over you to be forgiven.

Jesus is always at the door, get on your knees and give Him a chance today. Your sins will be forgiven, a new lease of life will be given you and you will start again on a clean slate.

You can't go wrong with repentance. Nobody ever did. Don't sear your heart with a hot iron. Don't harden your heart. That you're now the head choir or titled General Overseer doesn't matter. BREAK DOWN so God May Lift You Up.

May God today pour out on you a spirit of grace and supplication to look on Jesus, the one they have pierced for your sins (the one your sins have wounded sore), to mourn and repent for Him as one mourns for an only child, and grieve bitterly for him as one grieves for a firstborn son in Jesus name. Amen.

Zechariah 12:10.

Peace be upon you!

*** Word from Mirella...

*** As I laid down, some hours away from one of my exams, in the early hours of the day, I began to commune with the LORD in my heart.

I kept asking Him, *"why does it seem hard to tarry DAILY in the place of prayer?"*, when suddenly the words Jesus uttered in Matthew 11:28-30 resounded clearly in my heart!

"Come unto me, all ye that labour and are heavy laden, and I will give you rest.

29 Take my yoke upon you, and learn of me; for I am meek and lowly in heart: and ye shall find rest unto your souls.

30 For my yoke is easy, and my burden is light."

So clearly did He further speak, and I paraphrase: *"the place of prayer isn't for the [presumptively] strong, but the weak; it is a time and place to bring your burden unto Me, and receive strength[rest] of Me. Don't think you've to approach My presence as a tornado! I simply call you FIRST to COME; I didn't call you to COME AND PROVE STRONG. Come and I will give you rest... I will give you strength!"*

Wow, no wonder it's written that those that appear in Zion go from strength to strength (Psalm 84:7)!

Beloved, don't let your heart be cast down and over-laden with the issues of life! Don't let the burdens drive you away from the place of communion with the Father. Choose to come to the Father daily, and receive rest of Him. As long as we remain upon the earth and are involved in serving the kingdom of God, burdens will always be present and only the place of prayer can saddle them away, replacing them with the only true and light burden of Christ.

Shalom! ***

Chapter 10

Are you a David? You Must Never Be a Saul. Never!

Many people have waxed gross and grown numb to God's touch for repentance. They prefer to hold on to position even though with hands soiled than to seek for God's restoration. Leaders especially!

The difference between David and Saul is that David will never sleep overnight with a known sin, even if it will cause shame, he's ready for it.

Saul reigned for about 40 years without God's spirit and only 2 years with God's hand. David would profusely refuse to continue in life without the Holy Spirit. "Take not thy spirit away from me", he cried in Psalm 51.

The reason for the coldness in the church is the heart that's waxed gross on the pulpit. Many are career pastors who can no longer yield to God's spirit anymore.

Repentance opens the doors to God's mercy and revival. A sin not repented of cannot be purged. It's still there. Proverbs 28:13.

I see many "churches" where sins are rationalized. The leaders have soiled hands unrectified, so members are pardoned for whatever. That men forgives you doesn't mean God has. Until repentance, all sins remain unforgiven.

There are things many leaders will never want you to speak out, because honour of men is more important to them than escaping the horrors of hell.

Fornication is not a mistake or cheating. The name is fornication. Call sin by the name it bears and its eternal seriousness will hit you straight in the face. Sin is very, very fundamental in all its ramifications!

Don't line up behind a pastor who hates to repent. Don't move with people who play with sins and claim grace.

If you're caught in a sin, don't explain it away. Saul always gives excuses; David cries out in repentance!

David doesn't make himself of reputation, he will break down before God anywhere, But Saul will defend his dignity before people till death.

We have fewer David(s) and Multiplied number of Saul(s) everywhere now. Grace is seen as covering what God doesn't cover. Grace is useful only when we walk in it. David did, Saul didn't. But it's always available!

God's slowness awaiting our repentance is not a pardon for sin. Sin will be judged with death like Saul was if it's not turned from and left off completely.

"The Lord is not slack concerning his promise, as some men count slackness; but is longsuffering to us-ward, not willing that any should perish, but that all should come to repentance." 2 Peter 3:9.

"Who's not sinned, should cast the first stone" is not an excuse to remain in sin for anyone. In hell, all seek to have a chance for repentance!

Sins power gets broken by true repentance. I have sinned many times like all have, But I repented and refused to continue!

Mercy rejoices at judgement for those who truly repent without reservation.

You're following a Saul if he or she is always talking of grace, Spiritual covering and covenant of God without repenting of evil deeds.

Jesus blood is our grace and it only purges when the sinner repents. Proverbs 28:13.

If God loves us whether we repent or not, then nobody will be in hell. Be not deceived, grace is only active on those who tow its path.

If you're a David, keep your simplicity, sincerity and integrity of heart. Grace multiplied to Noah because he's a righteous man.

"But Noah found grace in the eyes of the LORD. This is the account of Noah and his family. Noah was a righteous man, blameless among the people of his time, and he walked faithfully with God." Genesis 6:8-9.

What's bad in being righteous? Jesus died to make us such. So, if you're living righteously, live on without shame or giving in to human mockery. Righteous living is strange to sin environment so it mocks it!

No unrighteous person shall enter heaven nor see the face of God. Grace turns us righteous. We can live in God's nature. Grace doesn't cover any continued sinfulness.

"What shall we say, then? Shall we go on sinning so that grace may increase? 2 By no means! We are those who have died to sin; how can we live in it any longer?" Romans 6:1-2.

When you see a man whose heart easily get broken while in error, you've met David. But when you see such who dress up sin, you're in Saul's camp. Flee!

What's the big deal in standing up to say I did what you said, please forgive me? Every chance to repent is an eternal opportunity to go higher. Amen.

Peace!

Chapter 11

There's Something You Must Do

When you get it right, heavens will move on it. Elijah got twelve stones, arranged the altar in order, then the fire fell. Struggles are less in Rehoboth. There's a place of purpose. Search for it.

"He made from one man every nation of men, to dwell upon all the face of the earth, having determined the appointed times and the boundaries of their habitation." Acts 17:26.

Zechariah might have remained childless and also ruined the destiny of Elizabeth if he'd refused to be in service the day he met the angel at service. There are places and people where and with whom miracles/answers to prayers are positioned by God. You can't change it. You just need to be at the right place with the right people. Cornelius went for prayers, met an angel there who asked him to send for Peter. You need to bisect your angles right!

The burning bush in the desert marked the turning point for the afore-planned destiny of Moses. He was not somewhere else, but leading the flock of Jethro in the back side of desert. There are appointed places!

God has just sent me to speak to somebody so your years are not wasted. Heed the voice of the Spirit.

"Wait in Jerusalem till you're endued with power", Christ instructed. There's a place of power. There are places where God encounters you, not everywhere. Don't die deceived by freelance grace. There are sacred spots.

There's something God will guide you to do and you will hit the gusher. The long-term prayers will be answered. Hannah was just led to pray to give back to God if God gives her a son. Ooops, Samuel came and his siblings. Barrenness was shattered for ever.

"Go and wait for me in Galilee", Jesus said, not Samaria. You have to search for "there" to avoid labour loss."Go back to Bethel", Jacob was instructed. Going to Mahanaim will be a waste of efforts.

There's a place you're going to meet your WIFE or other important matters of life, you must be there and on time!

Pray this: Father, order my steps and doings aright this season. I refuse to be a waste in Jesus name. Amen.

Peace be upon you!

*** Word from Mirella...

*** Only desperate people are licensed for earth-quaking interventions from above! Now, don't think the word "desperate" under a negative shade of light. Herein, *desperation connotes true hunger and thirst for God*!

Let's seek Him with all our heart, and we shall find Him.

Matthew 5:6:*"Blessed are they which do hunger and thirst after righteousness: for they shall be filled.";*

Genesis 49:10 (emphasis added): *"The sceptre shall not depart from Judah, nor a lawgiver from between his feet, UNTIL SHILOH COME; and unto him shall the gathering of the people be."* ***

*** Only the Grace of God can key a man into a realm of sweatless possibilities and realities of the kingdom of God.

Be humble enough to recognize that only His grace is the answer to every struggle, be it with sin, relationships, ministry, calling, academics, finances, etc.; and RECEIVE it.

Surrender to His priceless Grace. ***

Chapter 12

Why Not Give a Distance for a While? (On Relationships)

"To whom we gave place by subjection, no, not for an hour; that the truth of the gospel might continue with you." Galatians 2:5.

Doing same thing expecting a different result may be a sign of insanity as commonly known. To travel light and fast in life, you must learn to shed brown leaves. They may become manure. Maybe!

Many loads you've carried over the years may need to be put down. You've been trying to deal with the same issue and the same people for long, but there's no change. You may need a detour, a change of direction, change of tactics. No hating -Just taking a new stance.

Sometimes, distance may give an erring soul, a prodigal son, a change of mind. To join matter with such while they're having none of you anymore is to plunge into a destructive conflict.

From time to time, I remove hundreds of people from my Facebook friends list, phone or social media contacts to give room for new people. I created space for my wife to come in during one of such exercises years ago. I just deleted over hundreds of contacts off my Facebook list and space was created for her unknown to me.

"...a sower went forth to sow...some seeds fell by the way side, and the fowls came and devoured them up: Some fell upon stony places... they...withered away...some fell among thorns; and the thorns choked them...other fell into good ground, and brought forth fruit, some an hundredfold, some sixtyfold, some thirtyfold. "Mathew 13:3-8.

When you perceive a ground is unresponsive, don't die there. Jesus stopped going to certain places, stopped joining issues with certain people and stopped answering certain questions if you check the Gospels well.

"For this people's heart is waxed gross, and their ears are dull of hearing, and their eyes they have closed; lest at any time they should see with their eyes and hear with their ears, and should understand with their heart, and should be converted, and I should heal them." Mathew 13:15.

Nobody who's stuck to the unyielding old ever moves into the fruitful new. "You can't put new wine in an old bottle", Jesus said.

To be really effective, sometimes, you must trim down, get pruned and travel light. Especially, if a relationship has become a burden. A pain instead of a blessing. GOD IS ABLE TO STEADY YOUR SHIP. HIS EVERLASTING ARMS ARE UNDERNEATH YOU. LEAN ON HIM!

May God grant you wisdom to know the difference, strength to decide, frankness to tell the truth and the power to move on without giving or harbouring offence in Jesus name. Amen.

Blessed new season Beloved.

Peace be upon you and all yours. Amen.

*** Word from Mirella...

*** The LORD our God is the King and, so, when we approach His throne of grace, we ought to come declaring, *"...blessed is He that comes in the name of the LORD; Hosanna in the Highest!"* (Matthew 21:9 KJV).

Funnily, when believers gather, we use solely our lips to say, "Jesus, You're welcome!". Oh, if only we can peep into the realm of the Spirit and recognize the One with Whom we are come to commune with, we will cry out,*"...blessed is He that comes in the name of the LORD! Hosanna in the highest!"*

Today, approach His presence, reverencing Him as the King He alone is!

Shalom! ***

Chapter 13

What can I do next? (On Relationships)

Things are breaking apart or things are really down. There's a friction, silent war or rowdy brawl. There's a long break or physical altercation.

What should a child of God do when things do fall apart and the centres can't hold anymore either maritally, ministerially or otherwise? When a supposed divinely orchestrated relationship turns sour. A pastor turns Saul or a follower turns Gehazi or Ahithophel. A wife turns unruly or the husband becomes dodgy and prone to personal private practices!

Although pains will certainly ensue from this, but A true child of God who's given all he's to a relationship doesn't have anything to lose. You don't have my friend, so you don't have to be afraid. No form of relationship is the beginning or end of your life if you've truly given your all to it before God. All God requires in any venture is faithfulness.

"Moreover it is required in stewards that a man be found faithful." 1 Corinthians 4:2.

But beyond faithfulness, take these 3 steps:

1. Always forgive no matter what's done against you otherwise you turn yourself against God. You have to forgive whoever has done whatever against you at all time. Whatever is done against you is a test for your growth. Take it as such.

"Jesus said, "Father, forgive them, for they do not know what they are doing." And they divided up his clothes by casting lots. "Luke 23:34.

2. Never lock your heart against anyone. You can stay distant. You can keep contact to the barest minimum. You can take a different direction. You can focus on your own journey. But you must never lock your heart against anyone. You may never truly know if God wanted a gap and "allowed" the misunderstanding to be so you may be more profitable for each other later on in life. Your heart must be always to help all with all the strength, time and resources God has gifted you with whenever needed. You must live in truth-based love and never hate!

"Only Luke is with me. Take Mark, and bring him with you: for he is profitable to me for the ministry." 2 Timothy 4:11.

Mark, don't forget, caused the breakdown of the relationship between Paul and Barnabas. Acts 15.

3. You may never know why who is doing what, therefore take time to truthfully pray for such. Pray as this whole issue might depend on this.

"I urge, then, first of all, that petitions, prayers, intercession and thanksgiving be made for all people— for kings and all those in authority, that we may live peaceful and quiet lives in all godliness and holiness." 1 Timothy 2:1-2.

Jesus prayed for Peter otherwise he's gone. Permission had been sought by Satan to finish him and disrupt God's plan and Jesus ministry despite all the promises Peter made to Jesus. Paul prayed for the Galatians who started in the Gospel faith, but now turning the church to the Synagogue of Moses and his laws. Pray my friend. God listens.

May the Lord hear you when you call, may His face shine on you healing all your heart pains and giving you peace

round about. May you find comfort in the Holy Ghost. I pray that the God of heaven will visit you this season and your secret tears will be wiped away. You will find joy and comfort more than you ever did in Jesus name. Amen.

Peace be unto you!

Chapter 14

God Still Blesses and Uses People - Only That the Foundation Remains the Same

CLEANSING precedes His use! You can't build God's kingdom on worldly trends. God doesn't need our help. Just surrender for cleansing or forget the blessing!

"Nevertheless, God's solid foundation stands firm, sealed with this inscription: "The Lord knows those who are his," and, "Everyone who confesses the name of the Lord must turn away from wickedness." In a large house there are articles not only of gold and silver, but also of wood and clay; some are for special purposes and some for common use. Those who cleanse themselves from the latter will be instruments for special purposes, made holy, useful to the Master and prepared to do any good work. Flee the evil desires of youth and pursue righteousness, faith, love and peace, along with those who call on the Lord out of a pure heart." 2 Timothy 2:19~22.

God be with you.

Chapter 15

3 Keys to Sustainable Peace and Progress

Don't ever in life, relationship, business or ministry invest on, look for or give yourself over to what does not satisfactorily last when God can and He's set to give you what can be divinely sustained in peace and massive progress!

"Labour not for the meat that perishes, But for the one that endures to everlasting life (lasting till eternity)", Jesus warned. John 6:27.

I see how people ambitiously struggle for many things including growing churches,ministry,business or making name. Crap! It shouldn't be for a child of God when God has a plan of peace, welfare, hope and future for you. Jeremiah 29:11.

1. Don't physically fight over anything. "A servant of God must not strife", Apostle Paul instructed Timothy.

Why do you have to talk bad about a fellow to gain contract or have somebody come to the church you pastor? Why does anything have to become a do or die affair? If you have to sin, hoodwink or deceive to get anything, God didn't give you and it will not give you peace! When they physically strove with Isaac over a well (sustenance of life, business and future) which rightfully belonged to him via his father, he left it off because there's a Rehoboth coming...There's a space coming from God that none can fight! Gen 26. Amen?

2. Don't run too speedily, don't rush into anything, and don't be under any pressure of those doing their thing. Your life, Your race is different, so also your time. The seed that fell by the rocky place in Jesus's wise saying are those who received the word and started off without any root, stamina or experience. Satan, the fowl, rocks such very fast with no resistance. Build resistance. Get rocky. Be steady. Take time! Mark 4:16-17.

Take time with God over anything, then move on steadily. My wife and I fasted, praying for more than one year consistently from the moment I proposed to her before marriage. What we have both passed through, but with internal peace, are unfathomable. We have fought with beasts in human form with undaunted strength on the inside.

You will disintegrate without internal stamina. All maybe against you, but you will be on top with a fortified inside.

Refuse side attraction to give you direction. Focus on God.

The Angel of God in 1 Kings 19:7 told Elijah," Eat, for the journey is too great for thee."

3. Pray. If you don't pray, you may complain till death. Jesus prayed with groaning that cannot be uttered unto Him that was able to save Him and was heard. Hebrews 5:7.

Don't ever lower your guard. Pray.

Everyone around you are trying to help you or planning to help you may suddenly be attacked by a strange force, hearing strange voice, seeing strange vision and believing strange notion concerning you if don't pray. Human mind works in a very strange way. They called Jesus Elijah, Jeremiah, John the Baptist. You will be surprised Satan speaks to people in a very convincing way by voice, dream, vision and even in a fellow human's voice! Pray!

Prayer can be short and powerful. Angels do physically show up when we pray.

May you experience a physically tangible intervention of God this season in Jesus name. Peace be with you.

*** Word from Mirella...

*** Many believers reside in the plains of seeking God to obtain 'their' expected response, and not GOD'S, in the place of prayer. This attitude reveals the heart inclination of a believer!

Beloved, when we seek God in the place of prayer, let's approach Him with a heart to hear from Him, and not hear what we EXPECT from Him: that will make a whole world of difference! Then only, can we FIND Him.

That is what the Word of God means when it declares in Jeremiah 29:11-14 KJV (especially, verses 13 & 14):

"...11 For I know the thoughts that I think toward you, saith the Lord, thoughts of peace, and not of evil, to give you an expected end.

12 Then shall ye call upon me, and ye shall go and pray unto me, and I will hearken unto you.

13 And YE SHALL SEEK ME, AND FIND ME, WHEN YE SHALL SEARCH FOR ME WITH ALL YOUR HEART.

14 AND I WILL BE FOUND OF YOU, SAITH THE LORD: and I will turn away your captivity, and I will gather you from all the nations, and from all the places whither I have driven you, saith the Lord; and I will bring you again into the place whence I caused you to be carried away captive."

Shalom! ***

Chapter 16

Relationships: Knowing When to Stop Beating the Dead Horse

Relationship is so critical to divine fulfilment that God Himself created the first one - Adam and Eve.

"And the LORD God said, it is not good that the man should be alone; I will make him an help meet for him." Genesis 1:18.

God sits at the helm of affairs of arranging relationships so much that if you miss His plan for you in this area (either marital, Ministerial or otherwise), you may be an aberrant, a fugitive wanderer for life struggling to make ends meet.

Lot thought he could move on without Abraham since he'd as much animals as did Abraham. He lost everything including family, business and dignity. He became an incest inadvertently living in cave at the end of his life that started very gloriously!

Many people, ministries, marriages and businesses are like this. Jonathan died ignobly as a result of his detachment from David. There are people who enter into your life, business, church or project like Joseph and everything changes.

However, Man will never take the place of God. When man gets to this point of making you know without him you're going nowhere, he becomes a dead horse (Like Herod who's eaten up by worms and died after receiving glory due God- Acts 12:23).

Make sure you hold unto and treat as you would an angel of God everybody God brings into your life. You can't go forward without this!

"Let brotherly love continue. Be not forgetful to entertain strangers: for thereby some have entertained angels unawares." Hebrews 13:1-2.

But if they become a dead horse, stop beating it and keep leaning on God as before!

But...Do everything you can do to keep the horse alive. Live in truth with them, keep Jesus the centre of your connection. Forgive before explanation. Love even when not equally loved back. Be sincere in all manners of conversations. Don't hide truth or matters of importance. Don't be unfaithful. Don't use anyone as a stepping stone to somewhere or someone (God frowns at shady deals, imbalance scale -Judas will always not go far). Let your yeah be yeah and nay be nay. Relate with your heart out. Walk in integrity of heart/acts always and apologise if you falter as all humans do. Don't plan anyone's downfall nor use them for your ambitions. Let people always see clearly what you're doing with them and relate with them as God would to a man.

Then if the horse be dead, as humans could open up themselves for daemonic hijacking, hearsays, strange dreams or personal plans, they become delusional about you and leave you, then God will take you up far above human imaginations.

A spouse, a brother, a friend, a pastor, a fiancé, a disciple, a helper and what have you may leave, BUT GOD WILL NEVER LEAVE YOU and you will go higher AS YOU CONTINUE TO SEEK HIM WITH ALL OF YOUR HEART as always!

"When my father and my mother forsake me, Then Jehovah (God) will take me up." Psalm 27:10.

May Jehovah God reach out to you in this period in Jesus name. Amen.

Look up to Him alone!

Chapter 17

Relationships: Things Do Change

"...the Holy Spirit said, "Set apart for me Barnabas and Saul for the work to which I have called them." Acts 13:2.

In causing us to fulfil the kingdom mandate, God painstakingly chooses who partners with us in marriage, ministry, business and etc. if we let Him. Jesus sent them two by two. If you choose by yourself, many are the calamities of your journey on earth my friend!

"From one man he made all the nations, that they should inhabit the whole earth; and he marked out their appointed times in history and the boundaries of their lands." Acts 17:26.

God has everything mapped out in such a way that if you miss out any detail, you will be detailed(ly) handled by Satan. After many years of repenting and calling upon His name, you may be put back in line.

I suffered missing out on a ministerial and marital partner God clearly arranged for me in the 90s. God only restored me with such fashion about 2 decades later after suffering ills in many parts of the world. I almost became a proverb and a byword on earth.

Many are like this but never repent, stiff-necked(ly) moving on with much pain and difficulties.

When Satan enters through man-made principles, strife, over-inflated ambition, love of pre-eminence, lust of the flesh, lust of the eyes and pride of life, God-arranged relationships can nosedive!

"They had such a sharp disagreement that they parted company. Barnabas took Mark and sailed for Cyprus, but Paul chose Silas and left..." Acts 15:39-40.

Suddenly, your soup doesn't taste nice to him again. Your hard-earned money doesn't get appreciation from her anymore. Everything you do is heavily criticized. Every message you preach is taken as an attack. Your joy becomes a sorrow to such. Your accomplishment is disdained. Every move you make is wrong. You prayed, you cared, you explained, you cried, you wept and yet nothing changed. There's a lethargy, hiding away, side-planning and etc. LEAVE IT TO GOD. NEVER FORCE IT OUT. LEAVE IT TO GOD. Maintain your spirit filled-loving position.

Relationship is in the heart and once it's attacked, you can't force it to flow. Keep your environment love saturated so you don't fail God yourself.

I pray for wisdom from above for you to have dominion over all things around your life, destiny and mission on earth this season and forever in Jesus name. Amen.

Peace!

*** Word from Mirella...

*** Psalm 23:5-6 KJV declares,

"5 Thou preparest a table before me in the presence of mine enemies: THOU ANOINTEST MY HEAD WITH OIL; my cup runneth over.

6 Surely goodness and mercy shall follow me all the days of my life: and I will dwell in the house of the Lord for ever."

It is your season of fresh unction.

Shalom! ***

*** Beloved, it takes fresh unction to operate fully and effectively for every new season of life. Yes, for the old can't sustain the new!

This season can be filled with triumphs. Thus, pray your way into the heavens opening and the Spirit of the LORD overshadowing you.

Psalm 92:10 KJV says, *'But my horn shalt thou exalt like the horn of an unicorn: I shall be anointed with fresh oil.'*

Shalom! ***

Chapter 18

Supplication Is to Plead with God, Entreating Him to Do a Thing, NOT COMMANDING HIM

There's such a thing called the Spirit of Grace and supplication in the Bible whom God promised to His people. It's to such effect that if all fails, through the Spirit of Grace you can engage in supplication to the Father so an evil matter is overturned.

"And I will pour out on the house of David and the inhabitants of Jerusalem a spirit of grace and supplication. They will look on me, the one they have pierced, and they will mourn for him as one mourns for an only child, and grieve bitterly for him as one grieves for a firstborn son." Zechariah 12:10.

One thing the new generation of Christian people and their pastors will not want us to talk about is the fact that after being born again, we can still deeply hurt God to the point where other kingdom principles stop working for us except we come with Supplications.

Supplication is an action of asking or begging for something earnestly or humbly. To entreat, to beseech, to humbly implore. THERE ARE TIMES AUTHORITATIVE BINDING AND LOOSING DOES NOT WORK.

In teaching Timothy the four stages of prayers to engage to have peace all round, Apostle Paul mentioned Supplications first. Letting him know that if entreaties to the Almighty has not been made first, many other things may not work.

"First of all, then, I urge that supplications(entreaties)..." 1 Timothy 2:1.

Many are our rights and privileges in Christ and vast is our authority, but heaven is laced with principles of accessing them that all true winners in Christ Jesus have the spirit of Grace to engage supplications first before any other thing.

God is abundant in mercies and a great God of all grace, but in His abundant mercies and grace towards us He teaches us to make entreaties to Him so such abundant mercies and grace can be effective in our lives otherwise many things will go wrong.

The body of Christ has been so flogged with "Name it and Claim it" for such a long time that only a few really know how to stay put in the Presence of God with much entreaties like Daniel to do stuff that cannot be really handled by "gimme" syndrome.

There are so many times God has been hurt beyond normal even in this dispensation of Grace that only those who can make real entreaties stay His hand of wrath. We're told to not grieve the Holy Spirit nor quench Him. Hmmmn...serious one!

The old testament is littered with how people entreated God for turning points in dead end situations, but because we think we have so much authority now as children who should not be begging God, we have many dead ends that remain as they are.

Jesus painted an example of how supplications work in Luke 18 of the case between a widow and the judge that was not ready to give in to her case. She won because she stayed put entreating the unyielding judge. He told the story to tell us how to do in this world.

But God knows my need before I ask. Yes, oh yes. Why do I need to entreat Him? Maybe we should ask Jesus the reason for Luke 18 story.

There are many issues that do not involve Satan anymore, it's just between you and God. Binding and loosing will not affect God, but entreaties will do. He opened the womb of Hannah. Meaning that Satan didn't close it in the first place.

Two major things affect heavens structures like nothing else. One is His unbendable holiness and Second is His eternal principles that can't be moved. Many times we come short of these both and only entreaties to Him will move things forward.

Many of us have left our divine design a long time but we are quick to engage in quoting scriptures on God come any situation.

Read of John Osteen the father of Joel in a book. He was praying for somebody but the case remained unchanged. He went behind the Altar to enquire of the Lord, his error was shown him, he entreated the Lord, turned back to the situation and got an instant result.

If you really lay low before God a long haul in deep entreaties, you will rise higher that you ever imagined! There's something so very serious reserved for those who can really seek the face of God with supplications even though He's not far from us.

Many serious issues of life demand a check into supplications room for real time entreaties!

"And Isaac entreated the LORD for his wife, because she was barren: and the LORD was entreated of him, and Rebekah his wife conceived." Genesis 25:21.

The long history of reoccurring problem, sickness, failure or any other issue needs more than dealing with Satan. You need a real time of private entreaties to the God of all flesh. It might be Him standing in the way until a factor is in place and the plaque will stop. King David knew how to do this!

"During the reign of David, there was a famine for three successive years; so David sought the face of the Lord. The Lord said, "It is on account of Saul and his blood-stained house; it is because he put the Gibeonites to death." 2 Samuel 21:1.

May God grant you grace to seek His face, to entreat Him, to plead with Him till you truly find Him in Jesus name. Amen.

Peace be unto you.

*** Word from Mirella...

*** Won't it amaze you to know that the righteous can still tread in defeat? However, that's possible. It takes spiritual 'sanitation' to dispose of every trait and trace of the enemy within your circumference. God won't do anything concerning that, until you do something! Until Achan - the cause of the shame and defeat of Israel - was discovered and put away from among the people of Israel, defeat would have remained their daily bread!

If you ask of the LORD - as Joshua did - He will point out the 'accursed' thing within your circumference and, then, it becomes your responsibility to do away with such. Only then shall you ride upon the wings of glory and victory in Christ.

The accursed thing may be a secret fault...relationship... friendship...some gift received...some contacts made, etc.

Cry out to the LORD of hosts this day that He may point out every accursed thing in your possession and see Him take you from glory to glory - upon dealing with the stranger in your life.

Shalom!" ***

Chapter 19

Supplication Is to Plead for God's Help Passionately at His Feet

There are times in the life of a man that he comes to the end of his strength. Not because he's not been depending on God before, but there's a greater height for him to go on. Then he needs to come to God for a new strength. That's why we fast.

"Those who wait upon the Lord shall renew their strength..." Isaiah 40:31.

You will always in life get to some points where you would have exhausted all wisdom, strategies and strength yet the issue remain the same way. That's why we enter in with God in deep supplication cushioned with open-ended fasting and prayers.

"...this kind goes not out but by fasting and prayers." Mathew 7:21.

Issues of life don't just go away on their or with time, people deal with them. Otherwise they multiply. People go to God with questions and petitions asking for His help on enemies that are tougher than their capacity. That's how help comes. That's how issues fade away.

"In my distress I called upon the LORD, and cried unto my God: he heard my voice out of his temple, and my cry came before him, even into his ears." Psalm 18:6.

You cannot be vague about the situation that has come upon you. You cannot wish it away. Hannah knew if she didn't get a grip of a lifeline from God she could be barren for life. They've always come to Shiloh, but no result. She turned to pleading with God committing herself to turn back to God the victory granted if she got some. God moved and the issue disappeared.

God is not interested in what hurts any mortal man, but man is too obstinate. We go exactly the opposite of what He wants time and again. As such, doors of tough situations open against us. We must in this situation go back to Him asking questions and pleading for mercies where our feet have slipped. This is supplication.

Eventually every challenging situation can be crushed once God is at peace with you. You can be a born again child of God and not at peace with God. A challenging situation could be a warning sign and not a note of finality. Satan is not too powerful for a child of God whose life is at peace with God.

"I am the LORD, the God of all mankind. Is anything too hard for me?" Jeremiah 32:27.

Nothing will ever be bigger than pleading with God on a personal note. Everybody might have prayed for you, but it's not working until you take sometimes out to seek the face of God for yourself. There may be a correction God wants to make over your life.

I know many people pray for many people and sometime you wonder why it takes such large amount of voices crying to heaven but all seem to be falling on deaf ears. Securing God's interest in an issue takes Satan off balance. He can't contend for long on an issue that interests God.

"I will build my church (fight over my interest) and the gates of hell will not prevail against it", Jesus said.

When it seems all hope is lost (and this happens so often in all great lives), enter into a secluded time of fasting laying prostate before God both to find out why and to task His power to move things on. Fasting is powerful in that it stops most fleshly activities for a time so you may know where what is wrong. Do it often child of God, it's the way of all kingdom greats. "When you fast...", Jesus said. Not if.

If God is dealing with you over an issue, only Him then can deal with your issue. Pope's prayers, Archbishops' intercession and Apostles' prophetic declaration won't move the issue. Only God can and only God will. He will when you truly return and repent.

"For this is what the LORD GOD, the Holy One of Israel, says: "In repentance and rest you will be saved..." Isaiah 30:15.

Many nowadays Christians don't have a clue we have loads of things to repent of. They're taught to keep quoting and declaring scriptures. To be quoting and declaring scriptures on issues God Himself sits over is to stay long in the valley of delusion. Supplications open the gates for God to listen again after He's being deeply hurt and disappointed by you.

"First of all, then, I urge that supplications... that we may lead a peaceful and quiet life, godly and dignified in every way." 1 Timothy 2:1-2.

May the Lord hear you when you call. May the God of Jacob defend you, send you help from Zion and support from the sanctuary in Jesus name. Peace be unto you. Amen.

*** Word from Mirella...

*** Until God becomes the strength of your life, you're bound to be defeated by the battles of life. In Psalm 18, David said:

"the LORD teacheth my hands to war so that a bow of steel is broken by my hands."

This day, ask the LORD to step in as the LORD of hosts into your life and clothe you with strength. Shalom! ***

Chapter 20

Words on Appreciation, Worship and Truth

After thanking God, don't only look to appreciate your pastors only, thank friends, lawyers, doctors, drivers, nurses and every single person involved in your case or situation. Take gifts to their house also. Let them know you're deeply grateful! Let them know!

Worship starts from God's presence and not in front of people. If as a worshipper you don't spend quality time to worship God before leading others in worship, you're just displaying talent without His anointing. People will dance, shout and get emotional, but may never get saved, healed, delivered or edified. The flow of rivers starts from God's omnipotent presence, your private life, the holiness of your tabernacle in His presence! Amen?

I doubt you being a true child of God if the things of God, the works of God don't mean much to you, but you're so busy with your things and business. I greatly doubt you!

You must be sincere and truthful at all times from your heart. Don't hide from those around or ready to help. If your sincerity is taken advantage of, not believed or used against you, God will raise help for you. A child of God must be always straight, sincere and truthful! Always! Don't live a lie!

Why do you think judges take such a long time on cases before delivering their judgement? Sometimes two to ten years or more. One of the reasons is that what appears to be true now maybe a total lie given test of time! Don't get involved easily with tangling people, you may not know the real truth. Exercise constraint!

"In a lawsuit the first to speak seems right, until someone comes forward and cross-examines." Proverb 18:17.

One great way to pass your faith on to others is never to hide your pains, struggles, your gut and your God from them. If people know your troubles and how you're holding to God alone in the trouble and how God pulled you through, they follow without coercion. THIS IS THE TREND WITH JOSHUA-Moses, ELISHA-Elisha, DISCPLES-Jesus, TIMOTHY-Paul. Open yourself up. Ego will stop the transfer any day anytime!

Believers' relationships should never be with any deception. Be it marital, ministerial or business relationship. Truth and sincerity must be its foundation, otherwise it's godless and will be full of crisis non-stop! When I met my wife, she asked me all questions that could make a man shiver, I answered with all truth with detailed description. Her spirit could not resist such truthfulness; the result is the God-ordained marriage we're in! Be boldly truthful!

"So stop telling lies. Let us tell our neighbours the truth, for we are all parts of the same body." Ephesians 4:25.

If your truthfulness irritates somebody: your sincerity makes him or her hide from you, they like your faked self or celebrate you being a camouflage, Don't weep or die over such. One day your truthfulness will meet who God has prepared you for and prepared for you. They'll be better a million times than those who want you to live a lie. God is truth, therefore stand in truth on truth only! "...And the truth shall set you free..."

Only in search of total truth, standing in truth and spreading the truth can anyone relate with and fulfil God's purpose for his or her life. But there must be a search first. Many have lies they hold to they think is the truth.

"And the people of Berea were more open-minded than those in Thessalonica, and they listened eagerly to Paul's message. They searched the Scriptures day after day to see if Paul and Silas were teaching the truth." Acts 17:11.

If you speak the truth with all firmness with your heart out combined with very practical love, but yet some cannot stand you, those are the ones your life is not meant for. Jesus is not only full of grace but truth also.

Before the year goes out, God will visit you. This year's pain will not go with you into next. The new year will bring you into a new level in Jesus name. Amen.

Chapter 21

I Encountered God in a Revelation

I had a revelation of the gates of heaven and hell in February 2015 few minutes past 3 a.m. I saw how I will be judged. I saw many Christians doomed to hell. From then, I lost appetite for overt involvement in activities that don't foster holiness. Revelation changes us in a most profound way!

God's revelation changes a man. We know your encounter by your change. But because revelation is progressive, if real change is not obvious after an encounter, you need a second touch like the man who saw men as trees after first Jesus first touch!

True revelation of the God of heaven will cleanse and or deliver a man from ambition. There's no man who's true seen God who has ambition. His life is run by visions from heaven and not ambitions!

Revelation can turn a non-talker to a talker and a talker to a non-talker. Moses was a non-talker and Zechariah was a talker before encounter with God! Change occurs when a man has met God!

If after you claimed you've met God everything still remains the same, it's not God you've met. Change occurs with a revelation of God! You can't know God and still keep on with an illicit / immoral relationship! No!

With each encounter of God you experience, your expression changes. Your friends change. Your disposition changes. Your attitude changes. Your approach changes. Your tongue changes. Your view of life change. If this has not occurred, you've not seen God. Nobody sees Him and live. You die in yourself to live in Him!

With each encounter with God, a part of His heartbeat is released for your knowing. The more of His heartbeats you know, the less the noise of man makes sense to you. You partake of His divine nature by revelation. Your behaviours become different from other fellows around you. You begin to think different. Some people will now love you and some will hate you for this!

Revelation softens a man's stance. Your humility deepens. You're easily entreated on all matters. You're released from being a culture slave. You're better wronged. You easily understand with men because you transcend what's at stake! You forgive people before they ask for it!

If God truly brings you into His secret, like John the Beloved in the book of revelations, you will see that most of the things going on in the church and the world at large are like drama. Humans celebrate what God frowns at.

"Things highly esteemed among men are abominations to God", Jesus said!

A man with revelation from God or a divine encounter is travelling in an opposite direction of the man of earthly culture, principles, religion and policies! The more the revelation, the wider the gap. You can't keep with all the Jones's of this world!

You can't claim to have known God and your dressing has not changed. You keep up with the skimpy outfits. Your boyfriend or girlfriend remains intact. Your worldly trends are up to date. By their fruits we shall know them. A new creature emerges when a human is in Christ! Grace grammar or vocabulary notwithstanding, A cannot be B!

God's gift in you, without a proper encounter with Him, becomes a tool for entertainment! You eventually lose the anointing on it and become ordinary!

Peace is present in the life of a man who's encountered God. What brings strife is not in your life. Others want to preach everywhere, be known, ride big cars, live in big houses or be popular singers, but you just want to be in will of God.

"We brought nothing to the world and we will take nothing back", Apostle Paul said to Timothy

A revelation is an encounter with God. It's not the one that makes people shout around. A true encounter with God leaves you speechless and unable to stand or run around. You see yourself first and then your environment like Isaiah. You're totally broken. You can't have this and be looking for places to preach or sing. You look for a seclusion where you can cry in repentance.

"Woe to me!" I cried. "I am ruined! For I am a man of unclean lips, and I live among a people of unclean lips, and my eyes have seen the King, the Lord Almighty." Isaiah 6:5.

You can prepare yourself to meet God. You can create an atmosphere for encounter. An atmosphere of Purity, Peace and holiness will bring God heavy on you. "Blessed are the pure in heart, for they will see God", Jesus said and "...Peace and holiness without which no one shall see the Lord", Apostle Paul instructed. You don't have to go to Mount of Kilimanjaro for this, just purify your heart and environment!

"But we all, with open face beholding as in a glass the glory of the Lord, are changed into the same image from glory to glory, even as by the Spirit of the LORD." 2 Corinthians 3:18.

May God encounter you in an irreversible way this season. I pray you will be changed from glory to glory in Jesus name. Amen.

*** Word from Mirella...

*** My greatest testimony remains my testimony of Salvation. Nobody can snatch that away from me! When all may seem to dissipate into tiny air, that unfading & eternal reality remains. The day, the hour, the minute and the very second I bear preciously in me. The power of God was wrought mightily in me, and brought about the new Mirella. Thus, I dare not to doubt such love and most precious faith.

Jesus Christ is real, and He loves you. Words can never describe this reality, till He reveals Himself to you.

What are you struggling with presently? What's that sin that renders you powerless to conquer? Why not look unto the Saviour Jesus Christ and surrender all to Him, and – thereby - receive the free, yet priceless, gift of eternal salvation and freedom of Him? Simply believe that He so loves you, that He laid down His life for your sins, and arose to usher you into His kingdom of light. Only BELIEVE: *"for unto as many that RECEIVED Him, to them gave He POWER to become the sons of God, even to them that believe on His name"* (John 1:12).

SURRENDER YOUR LIFE TO HIM TODAY. TOMORROW IS TOO LATE FOR SUCH. GOD LOVES YOU.

Shalom! ***

Chapter 22

My Thought On Ephesians 3:20 ("God is able to do Exceedingly abundantly above what you THINK and ASK...")

The greatest of the kingdom greats only have their thoughts focused on and prayers directed at God. Thereafter they work on and walk in the inspirations derived from Him!

Keep doing all you're inspired to do. Don't stop it. Don't let anyone shout you down. I met my wife while teaching and liking others' messages on Facebook. I made my first journeys around nations connected by a man I gave a tie. I travelled to Europe on a visa I got by a programme I watched on the television in a friend's house. Don't let anyone stop your well. Keep it flowing! Follow all your word based and scripture-allowed inspirations. Don't bath an eye! Go ahead!

Don't be afraid of your mistakes sinking you. No! They only get sunk who try to be perfect outside of God. All greats make very grave mistakes, but God keeps them in "Perfect Peace (ever progressive prosperity) whose mind is stayed on Him..." Keep your thoughts and trust on God!

You only had the chance of no enemy nor harsh critics before you existed and you can have the opportunity again only if you can return to that state of non-existence. All greats deal with devastating enemies and destructive critics of untold level, but those whose face stays on God never go down, BECAUSE God keeps them!

I bet you that most parts of the night of Pastor Kumuyi, Benny Hinn, Pastor Adeboye, Bishop David Oyedepo, Kenneth Copeland, David Richman and others whose strength is in God alone is spent on their knees, on their face flat before God, Walking around in serious prayers and thoughtfulness cum study! Waking up to pray, think and study looks too late for real kingdom greats.

All books, Songs, products, programmes and moves that have made men great in God ensue from inspiration from God as they pray and think of "who else, what next, where else or how else" oh God my Father?! Do the same my friend and after a time, you will rise mounted up with wings as eagles!

God does not only answer when you start praying, He's at it even while you're thinking. So, focus your thoughts on Him and His purpose over your life. It's a type of prayer!

"But while he thought on these things, behold, the angel of the Lord appeared unto him in a dream, saying..." Mathew 1:20.

Not just in your words, but even in your thoughts, you're judged already!

Work on every God-based idea you know sincerely and diligently. One day you will hit the gusher, a big bang, an open door that can't be shut by no one anymore no matter their strength, tactics or status. Keep at what you do my friend. Keep at it!

Close your eyes away from all things and just pray. Suddenly, there will be a break!

A lot of the time I don't know what to do again, but just pray. Then, new doors, new horizons just open up. Greatest of God's servants and people are like this times and again, because only

God is God. We must all depend on Him for directives. You're not alone in this my friend. Just pray!

I pray that God's peace will rest with you. That you will be healed of all pains and made whole in Jesus name. You will not carry over the pain of this season into the next phase of life. God's plan over your life will come through and Satan will lose in all the matters, cases and files of your life. Amen.

Peace!

***Word from Mirella...

*** Judges 7:9-11, 13-15 KJV says,

"9 And it came to pass the same night, that the Lord said unto him, Arise, get thee down unto the host; for I have delivered it into thine hand.

10 But if thou fear to go down, go thou with Phurah thy servant down to the host:

11 And THOU SHALT HEAR WHAT THEY SAY; AND AFTERWARDS SHALL THINE HANDS BE STRENGTHENED TO GO DOWN UNTO THE HOST. Then went he down with Phurah his servant unto the outside of the armed men that were in the host.

13 And when Gideon was come, behold, there was a man that told a dream unto his fellow, and said, Behold, I dreamed a dream, and, lo, a cake of barley bread tumbled into the host of Midian, and came unto a tent, and smote it that it fell, and overturned it, that the tent lay along.

14 And his fellow answered and said, This is nothing else save THE SWORD OF GIDEON the son of Joash, a man of Israel: for into his hand hath God delivered Midian, and all the host.

15 And it was so, when Gideon heard the telling of the dream, and the interpretation thereof, that he worshipped, and returned into the host of Israel, and said, Arise; for the Lord hath delivered into your hand the host of Midian."

Don't be dismayed nor discouraged! You know why? Why, you've the Victory in Christ. Oh, that our sight of understanding is sharpened to know that the enemy trembles at those truly bearing Christ's identity.

You may not look it, from the human standpoint. However, it's known by powers both in heaven, on earth and under the earth that the LORD God Almighty stands over you as a mighty terrible Warrior!

Simply acknowledge that the LORD is with you, then shall your hands be strengthened to receive the victories prepared for you in Christ.

Shalom! ***

Chapter 23

This may bless you, add to or confirm your prior understanding

Being gentle doesn't make you a pastor and being aggressive doesn't make you an evangelist. Offices are designated by the anointing not attitudinal disposition. No!

Being distant from opposite sex doesn't make you more moral than who frolics with such. It's an internal matter. Yeah, matter of the heart!

Gentle face doesn't always mean humility. There are many boisterous characters that are of deeply humble soul!

There are many soft speakers that are anointed evangelists and loud ones that are pastors. Anointing, not look or disposition, determines the designation.

"God looks at the heart, man looks on the outward appearance." 1 Samuel 16:7

Humans like face value but God deals with the heart. He uses people for what He anointed them for. Don't let your looks determine what God could use you for. Your way of life could be different from your calling and anointing. Don't stand in the way. Break the box. Many fiery evangelists are the gentlest people on earth when not preaching!

More often than not, in Christ Jesus your natural disqualifications maybe your greatest springboards for grace.

"My grace is sufficient for you and My strength is made perfect in your weakness..."2 Corinthians 12:9

Sometimes when you think you've failed, you might have just won. Just like when you sometimes think you've failed in Prayers, then you discover answered prayers. God determines all these, feelings are not reliable!

A lot of time we don't even know God follows our thought lines. We think we must always shout before we're heard by Him. But many times your answer has been delivered based on your thoughts focused on God. Ephesians 3:20.

God is using everybody and everything around you to prepare you for what's prepared for you. Put your attention on the lessons to be learnt and not the hurts you're enduring! If humans don't do what they're supposed to do, God won't do what He prepared to do. Learn from Joseph.

"You intended to harm me, but God intended it for good to accomplish what is now being done, the saving of many lives." Genesis 50:20.

Pray this: Father, deliver me from myself. Let self be peeled off me and let your grace fill me up. Use me Lord and don't let me be a waste in life in Jesus name. Amen.

Peace!

*** Word from Mirella...

*** The times of failure have been and remain the ones wherein we choose to lead ourselves. Isn't it written, *"as many as are*

LED by the Spirit of God are the children of God?". The Voice is still declaring, *"FOLLOW ME AND I WILL MAKE YOU...".*

Our spirit is inhabited by the Spirit of the LORD, so that He can lead us. He solely knows the Path, and He is the only One that can lead us therein.

Job 28:7-12, 23-28 says,

"7 There is a path which no fowl knoweth, and which the vulture's eye hath not seen:

8 The lion's whelps have not trodden it, nor the fierce lion passed by it.

9 He putteth forth his hand upon the rock; he overturneth the mountains by the roots.

10 He cutteth out rivers among the rocks; and his eye seeth every precious thing.

11 He bindeth the floods from overflowing; and the thing that is hid bringeth he forth to light.

12 But where shall wisdom be found? and where is the place of understanding?

23 God understandeth the way thereof, and he knoweth the place thereof.

24 For he looketh to the ends of the earth, and seeth under the whole heaven;

25 To make the weight for the winds; and he weigheth the waters by measure.

26 When he made a decree for the rain, and a way for the lightning of the thunder:

27 Then did he see it, and declare it; he prepared it, yea, and searched it out.

28 And unto man he said, Behold, the fear of the Lord, that is wisdom; and to depart from evil is understanding."

Shalom! ***

*** *"I REFUSE to embrace a powerless named gospel. The Gospel of Christ Jesus was and is of power and authority: the ministry of BOTH doing and teaching (Acts 1:1). Sound doctrine facilitates the raw power of God. Sound doctrine is of and by true fellowship with the Father and the Son, through the Spirit."* ***

Chapter 24

Prayers over prayers is what brings answered prayers & clears off delayed or hindered answers:

Pray some more

"Pray in the Spirit at all times, with every kind of prayer and petition. To this end, stay alert with all perseverance in your prayers..." Ephesians 6:18.

After Coming to Christ from Islam in '92,I took time to wait on God in fasting and prayer, Studying Bible from Genesis to Revelation to know what it says on matters of life and eternity for myself, I besought the Holy Ghost for thorough infilling, I read tough books on Christianity(not books on get-rich-quick or so),I related with serious minded christians who talked the bible with pure conscience, got involved in grassroots evangelism(not church disco party or folks hanging out for movies and kisses),was severely persecuted but was laughing in my heart at the persecutors for I was built strong to sustain all infirmities, was rejected but it's experienced with joy, was hungry but turned it to fasting. I wonder how far you can go with banana Christianity of no strong foundation. Holy Ghost preparation is always thorough!

God still blesses and uses people, only that the foundation remains the same: CLEANSING precedes His use! You can't build God's kingdom on worldly trends. God doesn't need our help. Just surrender for cleansing or forget the blessing!

"Nevertheless, God's solid foundation stands firm, sealed with this inscription: "The Lord knows those who are his," and, "Everyone who confesses the name of the Lord must turn away from wickedness." In a large house there are articles not only of gold and silver, but also of wood and clay; some are for special purposes and some for common use. Those who cleanse themselves from the latter will be instruments for special purposes, made holy, useful to the Master and prepared to do any good work. Flee the evil desires of youth and pursue righteousness, faith, love and peace, along with those who call on the Lord out of a pure heart." 2 Timothy 2:19~22.

God be with you.

Chapter 25

Music, Entertainment or Worship?

A musician is an entertainer; he plays to the taste and liking of men. He plays to wow and impress people. People then can dress and come into the dance hall to dance anyhow. He plays to the delight of people for his pay. He collects his pay for his play. A worship leader or a worshipper is not so. He's a minister of God, the God of heaven, not the god of the belly. He's not into a business, but that of entering into the presence of the God of heaven himself first and bringing others therein. He's not an entertainer. He's not into entertainment. You cannot entertain the spirit man that connects to and fellowships with God. You cannot! Many of you have lost your calling, that's the reason for struggle. You must differentiate between who God wants you to be and who you're or who you want to be.

"God is a spirit..."

There's a difference between music and worship of God, the Almighty. Worship is not to make people jump, dance, howl or run around. Worship is to submit to God...in Spirit and in Truth! I pray you catch this!

"God is a Spirit: and they that worship him must worship him in spirit and in truth." John 4:24.

Chapter 26

God Uses Trouble to Produce

Very rare to see God using or blessing a man with no trouble or a man with no vision. Troubled and very busy people are His attraction. They produce better. Great anointing is produced from hotspots.

Check all effectively succeeding people, check all great prophets of old & contemporary on fire men and women the world over, they're all hotspots.

The troubles you're in will produce great anointing bringing massive blessing. Don't dodge them, face them head on; depend on God, pray through them: leave side talkers in the gutter. Move on. Concentrate! God is working out a grace, a future, a rare destiny from your scrutiny. I can tell you many things on this, but just move on, don't retreat. God uses trouble to PRODUCE...

"Consider it pure joy, my brothers and sisters, whenever you face trials of many kinds, because you know that the testing of your faith PRODUCES...so that you may be...complete, not lacking anything." James 1:2-4.

God is good!

*** Word from Mirella...

*** ⌈Gratitude is key in walking with God. Stagnancy begins when we cease to be thankful unto the LORD at all times. You know what? We are always at loss when we walk in ingratitude, because it definitely hinders us from the depths of God, wherein His priceless treasures reside. A step...more steps deeper and you will come to see Him brighter, day after day.

Be grateful today, tomorrow...and every day given unto you from the LORD. Shalom! ***

*** Every prevailing child of God PREPARES himself/herself. That's the part of every child of God, in any aspect of life. When you do that which is expected from you(responsibility), God will respond in turn.

With the beginning of every academic session, your duty is to study and be diligent, and God's part is to impart Grace to excel. I've seen that time and again.

I pray for you: that as you set yourself on the right course of preparation and diligence, God will impart exceeding Grace upon you in the name of Jesus. Shalom! ***

*** ⌈Wisdom is revelation: until divine mysteries of the kingdom of God are unveiled to a person, he/she is bound to struggle in any area of life.

Wisdom is light: one of the dimensions of wisdom is the Word of God. Lo, the entrance of the word of God gives light (Psalm 119:130). This dimension establishes a man on the path of the fear of the LORD. This dimension of Wisdom is truly lacking in our age and that's why iniquity abound in the present Church world.

Let's therefore ask the LORD for wisdom to walk uprightly before Him this day, praying in the Holy Ghost.

Shalom! ***

Chapter 27

God's Calling is Sacred: Only God Calls People and Titles Don't Bestow Status!

You don't become a pastor because your husband or wife is one. No! Only God's personal calling qualifies you. Many churches do this, but it is a fallacy. Very wrong. Peter's wife didn't become Apostle Mrs. I don't become lawyer because my wife is one. If you're about falling into this trap, STOP!

God's calling is not in title; it is in the divine entitlement given you of God.

A servant of God, a man with a divine call, does not and cannot find himself comfortable doing any other thing than what the call is about. In 24 years, I tried working something else once, but I sank to the lowest ebbs of dryness. I ran off.

All these running up and down all week doing other things only to go to church on Sunday to mumble some words and prayers with people, and they're calling you Pastor or Pastor Mrs, stop letting people fool you. Also, don't fool yourself! Check Acts 6 to know what the called do majorly.

What preoccupies the heart of a man called of God 24hours a day is not making money or living comfortably, but doing that which God calls him to do.

If opportunities of life make you quickly abandon what you claim God calls you to do, then God didn't call you to do it. You just personally liked it. The calling of God is your whole life! Your whole life. Yes, your whole life!

I am yet to see a truly called of God man who does not abandon his personal pleasure or business to fulfil the call!

"Moses preferred to suffer afflictions with God's people than to enjoy the pleasures of sin or the palace in Egypt." Hebrews 11:25 paraphrased.

Inconsistency of character kills God's calling. You must be stable to have a table! "Unstable as waters, thou shalt not excel", Patriarch Jacob told Reuben his first son in chapter 49 of Genesis.

What's bad in being a normal person, committed to Christ, serving the Lord without the titles that leave you confused? Priscilla and Aquila didn't have a title, but very effective disciples of Christ even though tent makers.

Don't make a call because it will break you. Just be normal following Christ and let Him make you. "Follow me and I will make you", Jesus said in Mathew 4:19.

Calling is what you do and not what people call you. They call you Apostle or Evangelist, but you only teach once in a while in the church. Apostles and Evangelists are on the forefront in the field. Ask Paul the Apostle or Philips the evangelist!

It's by your fruits they will know you not by your title.

All called people I see have spring not just in their heart but also in their feet. They're like gazelle! They're restless to carry out the mandate.

People who have God's call pursue it and titles look for them. If anybody looks for titles to fulfil ministry, they're compromised. Something fundamental is missing in their lives!

If anyone is called of God specially for an assignment, you will see the changes in their face and activities! God's calling changes outlooks!

The calling has a way of making a way for itself without forcing things once you keep working on it. You don't put people in calling, God does.

"Nobody takes this honour to himself except him that's called as Aaron was." Hebrews 5:4.

If God didn't call your spouse but you force titles on him or her, they will frustrate you. Let them go to school, become teacher, lawyer or whatever they find suited for their lives so your life and home could be peaceful and progressive. Don't put a square peg in a round hole!

Faithful is God who called and who also will do only what He commanded on whom He calls alone. Don't live a frustrated life. Don't frustrate your spouse. Don't frustrate your children. Don't frustrate everyone around you. Don't frustrate yourself. Be normal. Just be a child of God doing what God clearly commands in His word. Don't push things out of order.

Everybody doesn't have to be on the pulpit preaching. Who then will be engineers? Who will be builders? Who will be Pharmacists? Not all callings are to preach. Many are to do stuffs for the environment without talking. There's a calling to be a public administrator like Joseph. You can be called into politics. What's then the need for titles?

There's a purpose for your life, personally find it out. Don't let anyone play you around. Personal discovery stabilizes focus.

"Wisdom and knowledge shall be the stability of your times..." Isaiah 33:6.

If you know how much tittles irritate people when they know they're just for camouflage, you will rather go around with your name and your normal life!

Calling is what is in your heart, not what people are pushing you to do. God's calling on you is the main joy of your heart. It's meat for you. It's your anchor of strength. You live each moment to see it done. You're high and dry without it. "My meat is to do the will of him that sent me", Jesus said in John 4.

Peace of God be with you my friend!

*** Word from Mirella...

*** Will You Be Willing to Sacrifice Your Isaac When The LORD Commands So?

Blessed day Guys,

It is easy to promise God so and so, but when the promise lands into our possession, it begins to occupy such priority in our heart(sometimes!). Whatever the case may be, God can ask you to sacrifice that long-awaited Isaac to Him. Let me concentrate on a very known aspect: financial breakthrough.

Initially, it is easier for you to sow the little you have, but when an enormous sum or contract hits your account, what shall you do? People, at this stage, find it hard to give to God. Listen: if you won't give to the LORD at His commandment, know that carnality and greed are crept into you. For God to confirm His promise unto you as an oath and - ultimately, an eternal covenant - you must be willing to sacrifice your given Isaac; that which fills your heart with such laughter, you should be open-handed about it to God-wards for He is the Author of such!

Beloved in Christ, don't hold tightly to any ephemeral paraphernalia, property or resource. The truth of walking with God is that the closer you desire to draw and be with Him, the eternally farther you must be cleaved from the world and its lusts. In fact, He will personally set the tests to proof your desire for Him and Him alone. God seems to rarely make a covenant with His people - in this age - due to their high affinity with and attachment to ephemeral lusts and ambitions in their heart and consequent pursuit.

The fact that one blissful door stormed opened before you doesn't mean that you will reside therein forever. The life in Christ is from glory to glory. So, God has planned and prepared further doors ahead for you. For every door God unlocks, there are things that must be locked behind in your life for further doors to open before you. Amen?

Every test is to proof that God is our all in all. It takes a heart that holds nothing back from God, to provoke an eternal covenant unto such a man:

Genesis 22:15 -18 says,"*15 And the angel of the LORD called unto Abraham out of heaven the second time,*

16 And said, By myself have I sworn, saith the LORD, for because thou hast done this thing, and hast not withheld thy son, thine only son:

17 That in blessing I will bless thee, and in multiplying I will multiply thy seed as the stars of the heaven, and as the sand which is upon the sea shore; and thy seed shall possess the gate of his enemies;

18 And in thy seed shall all the nations of the earth be blessed; because thou hast obeyed my voice.";

Psalm 105:7-11 says, "*7 He is the LORD our God: his judgments are in all the earth.*

8 He hath remembered his covenant for ever, the word which he commanded to a thousand generations.

9 Which covenant he made with Abraham, and his oath unto Isaac;

10 And confirmed the same unto Jacob for a law, and to Israel for an everlasting covenant:

11 Saying, Unto thee will I give the land of Canaan, the lot of your inheritance".

Shalom! ***

Chapter 28

Only God Truly Helps... Look to Him

"My boss is not helping me, My mentor is letting me down, My pastor is not there for me, My friends are distant from me..."

You have an emptiness in your soul, a void that needs to be filled. And only God can fill for you. The issue is that: Your God is not helping you because you've given His place to someone else.

If you keep looking on the hands of man, you will be stranded a long haul! Those who look for God's help are helped even by their enemies. Seek for God's help. Get alone with Him alone! Amen.

"This is what the Lord says: "Cursed is the one who trusts in man, who draws strength from mere flesh and whose heart turns away from the Lord. That person will be like a bush in the wastelands; they will not see prosperity when it comes. They will dwell in the parched places of the desert in a salt land where no one lives.

"But blessed is the one who trusts in the Lord, whose confidence is in him. They will be like a tree planted by the water that sends out its roots by the stream.

It does not fear when heat comes; its leaves are always green.

It has no worries in a year of drought and never fails to bear fruit." Jeremiah 17:5-8.

May God's face keep shining on you from now till eternity in Jesus name. Amen.

Love you.

Chapter 29

Be Focused

Don't Be Distracted - Leave Martha(s) with Matters

Life is too beautiful to answer everyone's side talks. Since you can't correct everyone's notion of you, hold unto God's hand for higher revelations of the higher life. A deeper life; a greater phase! Greater is He that lives in you than him and them that are in the world. God's good!

You give credibility to what riff raff say when you condescend low to argue with them. Ignore them; don't give them space, not an inch. Focus!

When God settles you after a period of turmoil, He sometimes shrouds it in mysteries that baffle humans and are unable to unravel them. You will be dragged in the mud to keep explaining what revelation delivered. You might lose the essence if you get involved. Flow! Psalm 126

When you've defeated their master, Satan himself in the spiritual battles, he puts side talks and fabrications of lies in the mouths of his human cohorts so they can break your grip or focus from what God is doing next. Don't shift ground; stay on in prayers and walking in the word. There's a next phase coming! Amen.

Hot heads get easily influenced by Satan. He picks them first when he needs people to make the rantings of an ant.

They're his easy targets, busy bodies, lazy bones, fault finders, glory belittlers, curse attractors. Clouds without water. They know everything going bad somewhere else except their lives! They never celebrate good because they can't discern it. From such turn away. They pass away with time and trend. They're transient like sinking sands. Keep your focus unbroken!

To know you got really victory and Satan was truly crushed, watch the mouths of analysts, the referees (Satan's extension cables). They know what God should and shouldn't do. Their ego is bruised, their predictions have failed, the cage they put you is broken. Watch them discredit your joy. It's because their master's purpose is defeated! Look for a new step to take so to run them out of ideas and out of town.

Every single thing that goes on in town is discussed in your home. Why won't curses stay on your home, setting your spouse against you, making your children wayward and stopping you seeing good. You hiss at the mention of your pastor's name? Your children know of your disregard for spiritual authorities. You will soon fall in the pits you're digging!

Don't be mad at nonsense talkers, they're being used to open your next levels.

"It is true that some preach ... out of envy and rivalry...they preach out of selfish ambition, not sincerely, supposing that they can stir up trouble for me while I am in chains. But what does it matter? The important thing is that in every way, whether from false motives or true, Christ is preached." Philpians 1:15-18

'You will never reach your destination if you stop and throw stones at every dog that barks.' - Winston S. CHURCHHILL.

"Beware of the dogs! Beware of the evil workers! Beware of the mutilators!" Philipians 3:2.

All Satan wants to do is paralyse your focus through unsubstantiated side talks and fabrications of lies so you could let go of the pressure you have had on him. Keep the pressure on. Leave matters for Martha(s)!

I like doers,they make talkers feel as if they exist not. Samballat and Tobiah would always call Nehemiah,the builder,for discussions;he always ignored them. They're talking the same old story to make everyone remain on the same spot. Ignore rattling babblers!

One great thing I observed in highly effectively successful people is: Having considered all truths from all angles and dimensions, they move on resolutely firm on the conviction of the truth they now know without a blink in their eyes over wailing distractive wailers. You surely won't be anything listening to everything everybody says!

"To whom we gave place by subjection, no, not for an hour; that the truth of the gospel might continue with you." Galatians 2:5.

May God's face shine on you from now till eternity in Jesus name.

Peace!

*** Word from Mirella...

*** Only a man HELPED by the LORD can be a voice and a spring of living waters for Him to a hungry people.

John 3:27 says,

"John answered and said, A man can receive nothing, except it be given him from heaven."

The help that God gives unto a man - which is supernatural and tangible - is His Grace, making such one a blessing! Today, look unto Him and be lightened. You are yet to see brighter days in God; don't give up!

Say this hour: "Father, help me." ***

*** Having been called to be living witnesses of the glorified Christ Jesus, let's not allow human traditions introduced into the Body of God by whosoever to deviate us from the raw living Gospel, the very power of God. Our testimony is eternal: Jesus lives and reigns forever more!

The apostles of old didn't need anything to be living witnesses…only the ministry of the Word and prayer! Let's follow their footsteps, inspired by the Holy Spirit. Shalom! ***

*** Only the Grace of the LORD can make the apparently impossible possible…the difficult easy. It will, thus, take grace to withstand the darts of the devil and, after all done, STAND! It isn't by power, nor by might, but by the Spirit says the LORD of hosts. Yes, it is by the Spirit Who supplies the Grace needed.

Don't give up for greater is ahead, even in God! ***

Chapter 30

Thoughts of My Head

As a true child of God, you can't be living with your spouse to be or having sex together before marriage. No, a true child of God does not do it. It's not in the nature of God his Father. God is holy so also is a child of God.

"No one who is born of God will continue to sin, because God's seed remains in them; they cannot go on sinning, because they have been born of God." 1 John 3:9.

Check your list of friends, companions and acquaintances if your life is not going the right or expected direction. Change! You can!

"He who walks with wise men will be wise, But the companion of fools will suffer harm." Proverbs 13:20

Sometimes you will have to leave the group you belong to so to belong to another level. Some folks will never change, but will continue to use up your life time. Spiritual,Mental and then Physical Separation...The decision is yours. New level or same old group?!

"Come out from them and be separate, says the Lord." 2 Corinthians 6:17.

When God really needs you, He might just dispossess you of all you call yours so you may link on Him who's the possessor of heaven and the earth alone. He will bring you to a point where you will not be able to call anything "mine" except Him alone.

"...the life that I live now,I live by the faith of the son of God..." Galatians 2:20.

As you grow up (nothing to do with age anyway, but maturing), you learn to overlook things, more so if you've made the truth known.

"Do not pay attention to every word people say, or you may hear your servant cursing you." Ecclesiastes 7:21.

Great products need great process and all processes need great deal of patience. You can't have any great product or fulfilment in a hurry.

All God's promises are appropriated not just by faith but also a great deal of patience. If you don't receive grace for patience in the process God or life has initiated for you, you will not just fail to receive the promise but you might waste the promise and your destiny.

Don't run another person's race by comparison of their levels with yours. In the spirit realm,God only looks on faithfulness and not fame. When you understand this like I learnt overtime, you will lose all your fleshly youthful exuberance and focus on your walk of faithfulness to God's moment by moment basis.

"Enoch walked with God and he was not because God took him."

"You should not be lazy,but followers of them (Abraham, Isaac,Jacob,David,Jesus & etc) who through faith & patience inherited the promise." Hebrews 6:12.

God is good!

*** **Word from Mirella...**

*** John 5:19-20 KJV says,

"19 Then answered Jesus and said unto them, Verily, verily, I say unto you, The Son can do NOTHING of himself, but what he SEETH the Father do: for what things soever he doeth, these also doeth the Son likewise.

20 For the Father loveth the Son, and SHEWETH him all things that himself doeth: and he will shew him greater works than these, that ye may marvel."

Brooding over the above verses bore a cry in my heart unto God! Jesus confessed he isn't able to do anything, save what He SEES the Father is doing. Thus, Jesus's source of spiritual effectiveness sprung forth from setting His sight on the Father. This reality reveals that divine power generates from spiritual sight/revelation of divine realities!

Of uttermost importance is setting our gaze on the Master so to KNOW His deep things. Then only can we be effective!

Psalm 19:2 KJV declares,

"Day unto day uttereth speech, and night unto night SHEWETH KNOWLEDGE."

Tonight, God's willing to show His deep things to you by His Spirit. Thus, pray in the Holy Ghost: "LORD, I look to You. Show me great and mighty things I don't know, that I shall be effective in Your kingdom"

Shalom! ***

Chapter 31

God is the Only Lasting Possession of Any Human

Never hold too tightly to anything...nothing in this world is really ours...houses, children, money, church or anything physical...not even you belongs to you!

"For we brought nothing into the world, and we can take nothing out of it." 1 Timothy 6:7

A young Christian guy got to a church and found a very pleasant lady. He was a guest at the church. They soon got talking. The guy had a liking for the girl, and she also didn't mind the process of things unfolding. The Christian guy had another occasion to see the pastor and told him, "Sir, I like that girl from your church", to which the man bluntly responded, "Look for another person far away [He also said other words summarily meaning "she belongs to our church & will always be"]."

Years later, the young man met the girl again and they shared pleasantries. Then, he asked of the PASTOR, to which the lady responded, "I don't know. I am not a member of his church anymore. I DON'T HAVE ANYTHING TO DO WITH HIM and many of us have left, having nothing to do with him anymore".

Nothing belongs to you, not even your own soul. Don't hold anything too tightly to yourself. Don't be possessive of anything, not even church members as a pastor, for they might not have gotten to their final destination. It's witchcraft to want to control everything. You will be deeply hurt being possessive when what you hold tightly disown you to move on!

"A rich man had a fertile farm that produced fine crops. He said to himself, 'What should I do? I don't have room for all my crops.' Then he said, 'I know! I'll tear down my barns and build bigger ones. Then I'll have room enough to store all my wheat and other goods. And I'll sit back and say to myself, "My friend, you have enough stored away for years to come. Now take it easy! Eat, drink, and be merry!"' "But God said to him, 'You fool! You will die this very night. Then who will get everything you worked for?'" Luke 12:16-20.

Chapter 32

Two Quick Thoughts

1. The word of God in you is first for you. Use it for your life. Let it work on you first before preaching it to or expecting others to respond to it. It's for you first.

2. Goose bumps (goose pimples or goose flesh-medically termed "cutis anserina or horripilation") and emotions running high don't have anything to do with the Holy Spirit. It's just your feelings & they don't do nothing but make you happy for such moments and leave you the same. The Holy Spirit comes on you to change you. Thus, if what came on you through the message or music you revelled in at church is the Holy Spirit, as claimed, then change would have resulted.

"And when he is come, he will reprove the world of sin, and of righteousness, and of judgment...Howbeit when he, the Spirit of truth, is come, he will guide you into all truth: for he shall not speak of himself; but whatsoever he shall hear, that shall he speak: and he will shew you things to come." John 16:8;13.

Chapter 33

Be Reachable, Touchable and Teachable

"Whereas thou hast been forsaken and hated, so that no man went through thee, I will make thee an eternal excellency, a joy of many generations." Isaiah 60:15.

God can fully Restore and you can be ever forever Relevant in the scheme of things in God's kingdom. I have observed many who were once down but now up and doing. I have seen people who have been on top of their game for years and still continue to be relevant in God's kingdom and the scheme of things in this life.

"I will restore the years..." Joel 2:25.

It's a commonly known fact that "Failure is never final & success is never ending".

Searching the scriptures and observing life in practical terms will give you an understanding that people who get restored from setbacks, knockdowns or blatant failures and people who stay at the cutting edge for long have one thing in common: Humility. They're Reachable, Touchable and Teachable.

"But he giveth more grace. Wherefore he saith, God resisteth the proud, but giveth grace unto the humble." James 4:6.

Successful people in God's kingdom and great fathers have Humility that will baffle you when in close range with them.

They're quick to ask for or receive help for what they don't know or have.

"All rivers run into the sea, yet it's not full..." Ecclesiastes 1:7.

Many stuck people have very sharp, biting and pompous principles that can even resist the angels of God. Everything must fit into their orders and statues otherwise it's turned down or out. Not everyone is taught in the way of your denomination and your sect is not the greatest on earth. There are other streams! Make room...large room in your heat! Large room my friend! Large one!

"Where no oxen are, the crib is clean: but much increase is by the strength of the ox." Proverbs 14:4.

People don't call you Mr, Mrs, Daddy, Mummy, Pastor, Reverend, Apostle or Bishop and issues ensue. My friend, you have a long way to go.

The recovery of Naaman, the Syrian Army captain was a product of calming down to listen to a slave girl even when his ego rose at the "dismissive" way he thought Elisha dealt with him. He would have remained a leper till death.

Many times God has sent people and situations just to change your status, but your man-made set-standard rebuffed them each time.

God does restore and makes relevant when man humbles himself under the mighty hand of God which necessarily involves his dealings with men from various walks of life.

"Humble yourselves therefore under the mighty hand of God, that he may exalt you in due time." 1 Peter 5:6.

There's more God wants to do with you than you probably have now. They're other frontiers sirs and mas. They're other territories in the horizon. Braze up beloved!

It's man's responsibility to humble himself, God doesn't humble people except you want Him to humiliate you.

Why can't you be in a service without being recognized? Why can't people call you sister? Why can't common people talk you freely and feel normal without the pressure of adding the accolades all the time? Why can't common people hear you gladly as they did Jesus?

There's a higher height for the meek for they shall inherit the earth.

Thank you Lord Jesus!

Keep in mind: Reach=ability, Touch-ability and Teach-ability.

Peace be unto you!

Chapter 34

More Than a Conqueror

Confident people are mostly fortified on the inside! Internal strength, internal courage and conviction of what they know; not what people say, do or circumstances suggest.

Don't be brought down under the power of any. Look at people in the face with the knowledge of who God has made you in Him. Don't look down! No. Stand!

It is not about what you have, own, possess or not, but about who lives on your inside and how fortified you're in the knowledge of Him. Don't be a slave of anybody or circumstances because what you need or who they're. No! "Christ in you is the hope of Glory." Be confident in Him. There are many feared or great people who lack confidence e.g. The children of Israel (we are like grasshoppers before the giants) and Gideon (Even with all the great solutions of the angel and encouragement from God, he's still the least and unable to do anything in his own estimate).

You're more than a conqueror in Christ. Stand!

You're not a wimp. You're God's very image. You're the head only and never will be the tail. Stand! No matter what has ever happened to you or what has been said about you or the report you've been given, STAND. You're more than a conqueror through Him (God, Jesus and the Holy Spirit) who loved you even before you came here. Hallelujah. Praise the Lord.

Keep moving!

"That the communication of thy faith may become effectual by the acknowledging of every good thing which is in you in Christ Jesus." Philemon 1:6.

Chapter 35

Are You Always Discouraged? Ask Why!

"Hast thou not known? hast thou not heard, that the everlasting God, the LORD, the Creator of the ends of the earth, fainteth not, neither is weary? there is no searching of his understanding. He giveth power to the faint; and to them that have no might he increaseth strength. Even the youths shall faint and be weary, and the young men shall utterly fall: But they that wait upon the LORD shall renew their strength; they shall mount up with wings as eagles; they shall run, and not be weary; and they shall walk, and not faint." Isaiah 40:28-31.

One serious thing people don't do in discouragement is finding why! People are often told why downcast, "hang on there", "be strong" or "it will happen". While these encouraging points are not bad on their own but they are only for those on the right course of life.

I've spent all of my adult life in Christ, with church folks, pastors, doing ministry since age 17 and I've observed many things, chiefly how people use good theology on a wrong course, thereby making people blatant failures.

Discouragement could be a voice to be heeded. It could be a notification for a divine detour. It could be an intervention from heaven. You need to find out why! Very important.

So many people are in place, project or with people where it's other things that put them there but not God's divine placement for their lives.

Many are in the ministry or relationship where men or personal liking have put them and from time to time God in His mercy allows discouragement so they could wake up and not spend the rest of their lives labouring with nothing to show, not even eternal rewards.

I've encountered people who told me their spouse or pastor put them where they're and not God. Many are the reasons why people are doing what they do and God only supplies strength in the area of His choosing. He only could make a way to be out of what He never puts you in the first place.

I was used to encouraging people a lot when it comes to the things of God. Somebody stops going to a particular church or dropping off from a kingdom-related project. Oh, I will be on your neck. Until God stopped me from the childishness of my thinking. He plainly told me, "People should not do what I've not put in their heart".

"And no man taketh this honour unto himself, but he that is called of God, as was Aaron." Hebrews 5:4.

Many are designed to be horse-like but they're in a place where they're being trained or forced to fly like eagles. It's not your calling my friend. Don't die trying. There's a supernatural strength that goes with what God designed you to do. Even if you're faced with the greatest Pharaoh combined with Goliath and Herod, you're unperturbed. You're totally backed up from heaven. You've peace that passes all understanding. Praise the Lord!

I see how many pastors are forcing their spouse to preach or do ministry by force just because they're in the ministry. Hunger may kill both of you soon. Peter's wife was not a preacher. Deborah's husband was not a father in Israel. Your husband is a business man but you've forced pastor's tittle on him. Laughable! Your wife is care worker, but you gathered others pastors to make her Apostle. They don't make people apostles, apostles emerge with moves that cannot be doused, quenched or doubted. Many people are just kidding around.

What you're going to counselling around for may not need this toiling you're doing. Just be sincere enough within yourself when you go to enquire from God by yourself without any prophetic involvement of the professionals around. Ask God, "please Father, where's my place in your kingdom?" He will talk you if there's no idol in your heart. Jeremiah 33:3.

Who told you or where did you read that a pastor's spouse must be able to counsel people,lead prayer or be a church group leader by force? You're wrongly informed. Many have been training or forcing theirs to preach! May this not lead to your marriage breakdown my friend!

This is the reason for a lot of awkwardness on the pulpit. I sat somewhere listening a pastor's spouse teaching others the very opposite of the Bible and I felt so much pain that I told myself, "Look at people who should be under a teacher but teaching around".

The leading of Holy Spirit and the pure love of Jesus Christ must be the sole reason for anything happening in the life of a believer and nothing else.

"So when they had dined, Jesus saith to Simon Peter, Simon, son of Jonas, lovest thou me more than these? He saith unto him, Yea, Lord; thou knowest that I love thee. He saith unto him, Feed my lambs."

John 21:15.

I love you still!

*** Word from Mirella...

*** David prayed that the LORD shall open his eyes to behold wondrous things out of His law (Psalm 119:18). What a petition! This is because ONLY then can he observe and do the commandments of the LORD.

Consequently, the [Blessing of the LORD shall come (Deuteronomy 28:1-2) !

Pray this day in the Holy Ghost: "LORD, open my eyes that I may behold wondrous things out of Your Word this day and ever in the name of Jesus". ***

*** The covenant of Circumcision - delivered unto Abraham - preceded the visitation of God, concerning the manifestation of seed of promise(Isaac) according to the time of life.

Signifying that, before God delivers His blessing unto you, He surely will give you a test...meant to prepare, fine tune and sharpen you, cutting out the unnecessary and unwanted off you!

When Abraham went through the test that initiated the covenant of God with him - on a new level - obediently, the LORD visited him and spoke of the soonest arrival of the long-awaited promise.

Oh, there's a lock you need to unlock in your walk with God that will bring about the release of God's promises unto you!

There's something that MUST be cut off before God can pronounce the manifestation of His promises unto you.

Turn on the light of the Holy Spirit within you and know what needs to be known to step into fruitfulness.

God bless you, shalom! ***

Chapter 36

Do All to God's glory Alone

The reason why we soon get tired and weary is: We think "all these I do for them and yet... "I started the church to cater for them and yet...", "I run the orphanage to care for them and yet...", "I worked for money to sow into their church, ministries or lives and yet...", "I stay in this marriage to save his face or raise the kids and yet...". No, no, no! Wrong way to live!

We humans, with our attitudes, will run you out of steams, energy and strength if all you're doing is solely because of us. Ask Moses or Elijah. We got Moses angry that he missed the promised land. We ran Elijah out of town that he asked God to take his life. Many police officers were killed by the same people they're trying to save. Jesus was crucified by the people He came to seek out for salvation. Many pastors have committed suicide being dumped, duped or defaced by people they so much loved and cared about. That's how humans are. Even you must have made some people doubt if God ever called them at one time or the other. I must have probably been a pain in the neck of some fellows who truly loved and catered for me at some point in life. It's just being human!

But...if all you do is for Him alone who never forgets nor loses count of your deeds for His name, He will supply you with new streams of energy on moment per moment in this life.

"For God is not unrighteous to forget our labour of love..." Hebrews 6:10.

This is why Peter, James, John and Paul were beaten, jailed and despised but they yet loved counting it all joy for the excellency of His name. This is the reason Francis Wale Oke is still on after 40yrs of labour in the Kingdom. This is why Mike Okonkwo, E.A Adeboye, Morris Cerullo, David Oyedepo, W.F Kumuyi, Paul Jinadu, Benny Hinn and even me, David, are still on after many years of oppositions, confrontations, frustrations in the Kingdom. Because in Him is a place of refuge, strength and peace.

If you're not on this pedestal, you've not started living as He lived. You've not started the real life of God. He lived in love not counting people's sins on them, because He's love.

Smile!!!

Do everything because you love Him and refuse to do anything if it's not based on the love for Him alone. If it's based on love for Him, close your eyes to all the pain, disappointment, despising shame and do more.

Do more not even because you're looking for reward from God but because you love Him for He first loved us. Oh the depths of God's love to-us-wards that when we're His enemies, He died for us. Blessed be the Lord God our Saviour. Amen.

"So when they had dined, Jesus saith to Simon Peter, Simon, son of Jonas, lovest thou me more than these? He saith unto him, Yea, Lord; thou knowest that I love thee. He saith unto him, Feed my lambs." John 21:15.

God's good. God's great. God's gracious. Hallelujah!

Chapter 37

Two Lines of Thought for Your Day

One is...you can't please everyone's intention. You can't fulfil everyone's desire of you. You cannot...you cannot satisfy everybody's curiosity. No way! But you can satisfy God by being in "Holiness and at peace with all men (at least in your own very heart)". Hebrews 12:14.

Another is...

WHATEVER IT IS, you can go above it...

"Whatsoever is born of God overcomes the world; this is the victory that overcomes the world, even our FAITH." I John 5:4.

The move of faith seemed to be taking over the holiness movement just after I came to Christ. Faith stuff was at the centre of everything whether Healing or Prosperity. I read many books, listened to tapes and watched videos of many faith exponents like Smith Wigglesworth, John Osteen, Kenneth Hagins, K.C. Price, Benson Idahosa and so on. If the emphasis on faith was that much, you needed to know what it's and I went for everything I could get.

I soon discovered that many people hanging on faith didn't not understand much of it; they were making faith confessions with descriptions of what they wanted and their faith soon expired once things didn't manifest quick enough.

"If ye have faith as a grain of mustard seed, ye shall say unto this mountain, remove hence to yonder place; and it shall remove; and nothing shall be impossible unto you." Mathew 17:20.

The Bible verse above was misconstrued for a quick fix. Therefore, many fell by the roadside when they could not quickly obtain the end of their faith.

Whatever situation you're found in, you can truly go above it & whatever God promised in His word or personally to you can be delivered if you exercise the true faith.

True faith is to keep doing whatever you can possibly do over the matter without throwing in the towel or calling it quit while you still have the breath of life. Conviction must necessarily go through testing all the time. All the time! Sometime for a long time! Faith holds on till the reality breaks forth. Amen.

"To him that's alive there's hope..." Ecclesiastes 9:4.

I sat down in a church not too large - mid 2005 in London on a Sunday morning - listening to Pastor E.A. Adeboye narrate how God told him that He will give him 3 jets since 1979. As at the time he was talking he'd none. I am sure he's one now and if what's in the media is anything to go with now, he's two now running under Emmanuel Aviation.

It not just about confession but deep-seated conviction and persistence in what God has said also.

"Faithful is he(God) who called you and who will also do it." 1 Thessalonians 5:24.

One day, you will strike it deep while cultivating the vision without retiring. You will heal your own mad man of Gaddara where the people don't want you and he'll take Decapolis - ten cities - for you effortlessly. You will train one Philip that will take whole Samaria that Jesus promised you and bring joy to the city. You will prophesy to a Samaritan woman that will bring a whole city to you.

Faith is continuity in the conviction, not just confessions for a season.

God is good!

God be with you and strengthen you with might in the inner man. Your faith be ignited again and the end of it be delivered to you speedily in Jesus name. Amen. Hallelujah!

Peace be unto you.

***Word from Mirella...

A true return to holiness is so needed in our generation. In as much as we long to see the power and glory of the LORD, such ONLY come by genuine hunger and thirst after righteousness!

"Blessed are they which do hunger and thirst after righteousness: for they shall be FILLED"(Matthew 5:6 KJV).

Our God is GLORIOUS in holiness!

The highway of righteousness and holiness must be re-habited in these last days, so to see the raw power of God.

Shalom!" ***

Chapter 38

Think on This

You can have a busy schedule running around doing good works that's not God's schedule. When you don't allow God to have pre-eminence over your goings and doings, you'd remain a shadow. Check it: are you driven around by God, gold, glory, zeal/passion (devoid of God's direction) or just habits of being busy? You need to know what drives you! You need to know! Examine yourself! Only God's directives have His support!

Blessed day ahead!

Chapter 39

What Remains Would Be More Than Enough...Work on it!

"Truly, truly, I say to you, unless a grain of wheat falls into the earth and dies, it remains alone; but if it dies, it bears much fruit." John 12:24.

I hope I can really encourage somebody. I like to get to the depths of your heart...the very inner recesses of your being.

My father operated two main businesses: transportation and farming. The two of them were main businesses because he made much living, money and name through both in Ile-Ife(Osun), Nigeria. However, he majorly got us the children involved in farming, joining forces with tens of workers employed to work on his large farms in various part of the city yearly.

I hated farming then [so did all of my more than 20 Male siblings], more so because in the 80's while alone with dad planting new cocoa farm, he told me "this is your work". I only wanted to obtain enough education to live on and not farming. I hated the rigors we passed through. I hated the way people looked at farmers and their children. However now, I love farming. Thinking of doing some in Ireland soon, God willing.

I know somewhat of farming and God drew a parallel between it and painful experience of life for me yesterday while meditating alone at home. The word is: "WHAT REMAINS WOULD BE MORE THAN ENOUGH...WORK ON IT."

Here is it:

We would harvest cocoa crops or orange fruits every now and then from the mother-trees. The harvests would be taken too far and wide for the enjoyment of many. Many did fall down when ripe and might sprout up wanting to become other mother-trees, but we did cut them down [99% of the time] while weeding. Many also would be eaten off by animals and ants, thereby causing them to waste; and some we would use ourselves, not minding what pains the mother-trees went through to bring them forth. Howbeit, sometimes my father would take us to the farm to plant new seeds from the mother-trees on new grounds [maybe far or near the original mother-trees]: we would be made to cater for the plants, weed grasses and other parasites around or over them till they would start bringing forth fruits and harvests.

Oh boy...when fruition or the harvests would start, JUST ONE SEED from a mother-tree would give fruits more and above what the mother-tree might have lost over the years.

"A farmer went out to sow his seed. As he was scattering the seed, some fell along the path, and the birds came and ate it up. Some fell on rocky places, where it did not have much soil. It sprang up quickly, because the soil was shallow. But when the sun came up, the plants were scorched, and they withered because they had no root. Other seed fell among thorns, which grew up and choked the plants. Still other seed fell on good soil, where it produced a crop—a hundred, sixty or thirty times what was sown. Whoever has ears, let them hear." Mark 13:3-9.

My friend, there's still that seed with you that will announce your destiny. I know it pains for your fruits and harvests to be scattered everywhere but yet your destiny never comes to comeliness. It pains really deep; very bad pain! But hear me beloved, there remains a seed with you that will announce you and deliver your lost harvests and more back to you.

Keep the faith. Keep the confidence. Keep the hope. Keep the diligence. Don't lay down. don't frustrate the grace. Keep the grace alive. Keep hope alive. God restores. Hundredfold. A thousand times more. God restores. Work on the seed. Don't cast out...Harvests are coming!

I write with tears of pain...

You will laugh! Amen.

I love you...

*** Word from Mirella...

*** The blessing of the LORD doesn't locate the untried fellow; rather, it comes upon the one whom the LORD has tried the thoughts and intentions of his/her heart. God so blessed Abraham because He was tested...tried and not found wanting!

God tries and keeps trying us - by examining our hearts - till the end that we be pure in heart with clean hands so to receive His blessing (Psalm 24:3-5).

We can vividly see such in the life of Joseph: indeed, he was TRIED, even the Word of the LORD tried him...till his word came and stepped into the blessing of the LORD! (see Psalm 105:16-22 KJV).

"The words of God are pure words: as silver tried in a furnace of earth, purified seven times" (Psalm 12:6 KJV).

"And I will bring the third part through the fire, Refine them as silver is refined, And test them as gold is tested They will call on

My name, And I will answer them; I will say, 'They are My people,'
And they will say, 'The LORD is my God.'" (Zechariah 13:9 KJV).

Only the word of the LORD that enters into our heart gives us light and, thus, life by *"...piercing even to the dividing asunder of soul and spirit, and of joints and marrow, and is a discerner of the thoughts and intents of the heart "(*Hebrews 4:12).

The entrance of God's Word, that triggers faith, is enforced by praying in the Holy Ghost upon giving heed to the Word (Jude 20) !

Oh, the Word of God means the totality of the heart of God: ranging from holiness to eternity, righteousness to kingdom service.

Why don't we pray as David prayed, to dwell in the Beauty of God's Word?

PRAYER OF THE DAY:"LORD, open my eyes of understanding, that I may behold wondrous things out of Your law in the name of Jesus"(Psalm 119:18).

Then, pray in the Holy Ghost; shalom! ***

Chapter 40

Build Yourself

You could waste all your life explaining yourself to a wrong person. Save your breath & put your total trust in God alone!

Be yourself, build yourself and leave the rest.

"Building up yourselves on your most holy faith..." and "That the communication of thy faith may become effectual by the acknowledging of every good thing which is in you in Christ Jesus." Jude 1:20; Philemon 1:6. Amen.

Chapter 41

It Is Around You

After you have looked above calling on God, look around for what He might have put there, and be wary of looking abroad because what God wants to do doesn't have to come from far. Many overlook those around them to look far for help when God has touched their surroundings to help them.

"They said, "Is this not Jesus, the son of Joseph, whose father and mother we know? How can he now say, 'I came down from heaven'?" John 6:42.

*** Word from Mirella...

*** "The resurrection of Jesus Christ is the conquering force over the kingdom of darkness! He was utterly bruised, crucified, buried and resurrected in power and glory to deliver mankind from sin and death. He is alive, and liveth forever, that you would have life and have it in abundance. Alleluia! For He came to destroy the works of the enemy Satan.

Beloved, acknowledge and receive fully Christ Jesus and see the powers of darkness loose their deadly grip off your life! Come forth into the Light that shines and darkness can't comprehend nor defeat it!

"I am the Way, the Truth and the Life - Jesus said - no man can come to the Father except through me" ***

*** "What shall it profit a man to gain the whole world and lose his soul?

When eternity-unconscious, a person is vanity-conscious.

"LORD, that our heart be sanctified so to be set on things above, amen" ***

*** "The reality of every genuine believer is: he/she is dead and crucified in Christ, and yet as long as he/she abides in his/her earthly tabernacle, there is a call to WATCH and PRAY, to deny self and follow Christ, lest he/she falls into sin. Why? Because this corrupt world is under the influence and dominion of sin, thus the regeneration obtained in Christ emancipates a believer to put sin under subjection. Thanks be to the Lord Jesus Christ!" ***

Chapter 42

Don't Be Distracted by Humans

When much is not happening through you, your life or ministry, they say, "God didn't call him"...but when God's power breaks forth and much manifestation of His glory and riches show forth, then you're a daemonic, fake prophet or a manipulator. In any case, be strong and of good courage in all situations.

"And Jesus answered and said, Verily I say unto you, there is no man that hath left house, or brethren, or sisters, or father, or mother, or wife, or children, or lands, for my sake, and the gospel's, But he shall receive an hundredfold now in this time, houses, and brethren, and sisters, and mothers, and children, and lands, with persecutions; and in the world to come eternal life." Mark 10:29-30.

Be strong, push and dig through in the spirit until you reach Rehoboth! Learn to allow God Himself to respond how He best knows... with results from Heaven that man cannot fight. Focus on Him and let not your hand be weary. God's good!

"Abandoning that one, Isaac moved on and dug another well. This time there was no dispute over it, so Isaac named the place Rehoboth (which means "open space"), for he said, "At last the LORD has created enough space for us to prosper in this land." Genesis 26:22.

Peace be unto you.

*** Word from Mirella...

Instruction Is Vital

*** Thanks be to the Omnipotent God for such honour to serve Him another year. Let's see to walk upright before Him. A little story and, then, its subsequent morale.

Not long ago, I tried operating a gadget however it didn't function...even 'cause I presumed that it were a mere and simple electro-domestic and it wasn't a big deal to operate it. However, it didn't work. Well, it wasn't my first time of using it, and it looked so bizarre why it wasn't working! Then, I said, "Holy Spirit, help me!" as I kept manipulating every button and co., to no avail. Exasperated, I opened the cupboard directly in front of me, picked up the first thing I saw and headed for the closest couch to rest. As I set my gaze on the thing I took, it was a manual...the manual of the gadget I was battling with. I opened it, turned some pages and my eyes fell on exactly where I had missed it!

So, I stood up, took the correct steps and, lo, it began to work.

On that spot, the Holy Spirit ministered to my heart:" many a times, My people expect Me to rush in and "fix" issues, not considering the fact that I can choose to lead them to the path of INSTRUCTION. There are things that you will need instruction to gain victory; instruction to succeed and instruction to stand".

What a lesson I personally learnt. So, Beloved in Christ, let's see to accept dynamics of the Holy Ghost unto us: it isn't every time that He will do the "fixing", but may choose to lead us onto the path of instruction (the Word of God). There are things the Spirit of the LORD won't force down on us, but will merely lead us onto the right paths. Blessed are those that obey His bidding.

Isaiah 30:20-23 says,

"20 And though the Lord give you the bread of adversity, and the water of affliction, yet shall not thy teachers be removed into a corner any more, but thine eyes shall see thy teachers:

21 And thine ears shall hear a word behind thee, saying, This is the way, walk ye in it, when ye turn to the right hand, and when ye turn to the left.

22 Ye shall defile also the covering of thy graven images of silver, and the ornament of thy molten images of gold: thou shalt cast them away as a menstruous cloth; thou shalt say unto it, Get thee hence.

23 Then shall he give the rain of thy seed, that thou shalt sow the ground withal; and bread of the increase of the earth, and it shall be fat and plenteous: in that day shall thy cattle feed in large pastures."

Proverbs 4:18: *"But the path of the just is as the shining light, that shineth more and more unto the perfect day."*

Proverbs 8:33-35: *"33 Hear instruction, and be wise, and refuse it not.*

34 Blessed is the man that heareth me, watching daily at my gates, waiting at the posts of my doors.

35 For whoso findeth me findeth life, and shall obtain favour of the LORD."

This year, let's see to keep our heart set to receive directions[instruction] from the LORD, even by His Word: therein, we see light in His light (Psalm 36:9). Shalom! ***

Chapter 43

Take It to God

Talking from today till next September to a fellow whose mind is made up about you in a certain direction is like multiplying 0 by millions of 0's, you will be back on the same spot. Save your breath. Resolve to take it to God and leave it there. #Chillax!

"Speak not in the ears of a fool: for he will despise the wisdom of thy words." Proverbs 23:9

God's good!

*** Word from Mirella...

*** Matthew 3:16-17 KJV declares,

"16 And Jesus, when he was baptized, went up straightway out of the water: and, lo, the heavens were opened unto him, and he saw the Spirit of God descending like a dove, and lighting upon him:

17 And lo a voice from heaven, saying, This is my beloved Son, in whom I am well pleased."

Beloved, until the heavens are opened, the Spirit can't descend upon you; and until the Spirit descends, the Word of God can't come unto you!

Oh Beloved, there's a Word for you, your family, that pressing situation...whatever it may be!

When the heavens open (speaking of the spiritual "atmosphere" around you), your word of deliverance will come! Jesus was praying when the heavens TORE open: do the same.

Thus, take out time this day and pray in the Holy Ghost, asking the LORD to open the heavens over you, breaking in sunder every gate of brass!

God bless you; shalom! ***

Chapter 44

Sit Over It in Prayers

Sit over issues just praying and don't let go. Pray with all of your heart out and don't give up. Pray! Luke 18:1.

No matter where the devil has you, you can always show the devil red card. You can dislodge him. You can always have victory over him in all things everywhere. Just submit your all to God and kick Satan out. He was defeated long time ago. This is for someone out there.

You have total victory in Christ, take it!

"Submit yourselves therefore to God. Resist the devil, and he will flee from you." James 4:7.

Chapter 45

Three Quick Points to Living a Life Pleasing unto God

1. Forgive close people talking nasty about you.

    Everybody has talked something nasty about someone else, yourself inclusive at some point in life. There are many people who love you and will do you good, but will at sometimes make very hurting comments about you. Forgive humans because you, too, are a human!

    "Do not pay attention to every word people say, or you may hear your servant cursing you; for you know in your heart that many times you yourself have cursed others." Ecclesiastes 7:21-22.

2. Do not even wish with the slightest thought in your heart that an evil dream about someone's else come true. Do everything within your power to make sure that an impending danger over a fellow's life is stopped. Don't laugh at people's calamity. Refuse to be in the place of God over people's life. Don't be another Jonah who wanted God to bring negative prophecy over Nineveh to pass to confirm his prophecy, but got angry because God forgave them and the prophecy didn't run through. Do everything to help anybody you can. Warn, Teach, Talk to and pray for them. Cancel the evil. Do everything God will want a go-between, an intercessor or an advocate to do.

"Don't rejoice when your enemies fall; don't be happy when they stumble. For the LORD will be displeased with you and will turn his anger away from them." Proverbs 24:17-18.

3. The degree of your love for humans determines the extent of your love for God. Don't be too spiritual about it. Don't get lost in feelings, prayers and tonguing. Just practice it. People will run you hot, dry and high, but that's where love is needed.

    "Whoever claims to love God yet hates a brother or sister is a liar. For whoever does not love their brother and sister, whom they have seen, cannot love God, whom they have not seen." 1 John 4:20.

God be with you and give you peace all round.

Chapter 46

Take Responsibility Over Your Life

If you will personally sit at prayers, you'd be more prophetic than most prophets you're running after everywhere. God never intends your life to depend on somebody else.

"Call unto me and I will answer you and show you great and mighty things which you know not." Jeremiah 33:3.

Men of old, men of substance, all men who move the hand that moves the world round, even the very hand of God, bend their knees in the place of deep prayers connecting to God and thereby connecting to all who God needs in their lives. However, many in our age run around to connect to men via lopsided packaging and branding that have no landing point. Prayer is still the way to connect to Him who connects all things together." ...the fullness of him that filleth all in all..." Amen.

Keep at word study and doing it. Keep at prayers all the time. Love all without holding back. Be very, very truthful at all times. Give with all your heart. Live circumspectly in holiness all the time. Use all the platforms to make God and His kingdom known deliberately.

He will perfect all that concern us in Jesus name. Amen.

*** **Word from Mirella...**

*** Until His Word comes unto you, faith isn't come yet: *"so then faith cometh by hearing, and hearing by the Word of God"*(Romans 10:17).

Only His Word that comes unto you is Spirit and life.

The Word of God comes unto a man by the Holy Spirit, for He's the One that quickens...that gives life: *"...the letter killeth, but the Spirit giveth life"*(II Corinthians 3:6b); *"it is the Spirit that quickeneth; the flesh profiteth nothing: the words that I speak unto you, the are Spirit, and they are life"*(John 6:63).

Thus, until the Holy Spirit comes, our words and confessions are lifeless. It's only His presence that brings and gives the words of Life: words of salvation, healing, deliverances!

No personality other than the Holy Spirit can glorify the Word Jesus Christ: for He takes of Christ and reveal such unto the Church.

May the word of the LORD come unto you this day; may He fill your mouth with His words, even as you open it unto Him in the name of Jesus!

Blessed week ahead; shalom! ***

Chapter 47

Three quick points to moving forward in life

1. Don't engage in any form of immorality at whatever level in whatever shape either as a single, engaged or married person emotionally, secretly in your heart or otherwise, for it casts people back to yesteryears. You may never meet up again. It messes up precious destiny. It confuses purpose without mercy! Expose it if it's rearing up anytime. Don't give it a moment!

   "For she (spirit of immorality) has cast down many wounded: yea, many strong men have been slain by her." Pro 7:26.

   The immorality you don't stop, will stop you!

2. Never forget where you met people at first in your life, especially your benefactors (helpers, pastors, leaders or senior partners). Don't turn such to your friends even if you begin to climb higher or they lower their guards for you to be yourself around them. Never turn a ladder to a hanger. No! Keep your eyes on the purpose of your divine connect. Those who despise the steps of the ladder may remain on the floor for life. There are people in your life that are not your brothers, sisters or friends (as it were) but your benefactors. Fast progress is made by recognizing

people for whom God made them to be in your life. Don't joke with this.

Jesus said," *Wherefore, behold, I send unto you prophets, and wise men, and scribes..."* Mathew 23:34.

Recognize them and honour them as such that the oil may keep flowing. You need both God and those He sends to your life to be really successful going through life. God establishes you but He anoints His prophets to prosper you. 2 Chronicles 20:20.

Many have lost sight of this and have made shipwreck of their destinies like Ahithophel and Judas.

"Now David had been told, "Ahithophel is among the conspirators with Absalom." So David prayed, "LORD, turn Ahithophel's counsel into foolishness." 2 Samuel 15:31.

3. If you're not moving forward, you're going backwards because others behind are pushing past you. Link with higher knowledge that drags forward at all times. Don't be stationary otherwise you're retrogressive! Something new must be added to you daily to stay relevant and upbeat in God's plan. Many are only referred to as leaders today, not because they're entitled to it, but because they have titles and ceremonial positions for it. People have, in a way, moved off them. There's a new thing God can do and He's doing, gun for it.

"Brothers and sisters, I do not consider myself yet to have taken hold of it. But one thing I do: Forgetting what is behind and straining toward what is ahead..." Philippians 3:13.

Peace and progress be unto you in Jesus name. Amen.

Chapter 48

Beware!

Sometimes the devil keeps you under sustained feelings of lust (that may not be physically consummated) for a long time, then he strikes from the back side to scatter, stop or topple a ministry, home or business/organisation. Don't feed lust!

If you cannot handle the monster called sexual libido by allowing the Lordship of the Holy Spirit over the sex instinct, you do not have a future in Christ Jesus, more so in the call of God.

"For she hath cast down many wounded: yea, many strong men have been slain by her." Proverb 7:26.

*** Word from Mirella...

Philippians 4:6-7 KJV commands us,

"6 Be careful for nothing; but in everything by <u>PRAYER AND SUPPLICATION WITH THANKSGIVING</u> let your requests be made known unto God.

7 And the peace of God, which passeth all understanding, shall keep your hearts and minds through Christ Jesus."

Then, Matthew 6:7-8 KJV goes on to declare,

"7 But when ye pray, use not vain repetitions, as the heathen do: for they think that they shall be heard for their much speaking.

8 Be not ye therefore like unto them: for your Father knoweth what things ye have need of, before ye ASK HIM."

Beloved Daughters of Zion, I would to exhort you about casting ALL your cares on Christ: for He cares for you (I Peter 5:7). Praise the LORD! What does that plainly mean? It signifies that He has the responsibility to provide your very needs. Awesome, isn't He?

Let these following concepts be established in our heart:

1. God KNOWS our needs;

2. God wants us to MAKE KNOWN unto Him our needs;

3. God SUPPLIES all our needs (according to His riches in glory in Christ Jesus).

Thus, bearing all these at heart, quit thinking and believing that God doesn't know nor supply your needs! All you have to do is ASK Him: "ask and it shall be given unto you..."(Matthew 7:7).

"What things soever ye desire, when ye pray, believe that ye receive them, and ye shall have them."(Mark 11:24 KJV).

Take out 15 minutes of this day and pray in the Holy Ghost concerning your needs(read Romans 8:26-27) unto the Father.

...and, in the name of Jesus, I agree with you that every need in your life is supplied!

Amen; shalom! ***

Chapter 49

Overcoming Forces of Darkness (Handling Dreams, Visions and Revelations or Prophecies)

*"Blessed be the LORD my strength, which teaches my hands to war, and my fingers to fight..."*Psalm 144:1.

Not all negative revelations are from Satan and not all good dreams are from God.

God can reveal what negative trends and traps the devil plans to bring on through dreams and the devil can bring on good visions to deceive further.

But when God reveals, it's not to put fear in our faith. No, that can never be God's intention. God reveals to redeem. God reveals to prepare you for what the enemy intends to do which can be quenched by the shield of faith always. The devil is no Match for the power of God.

"Now thanks be unto God, which always causeth us to triumph in Christ, and maketh manifest the savour of his knowledge by us in every place." 2 Corinthians 2:14.

Satan will want to hijack a warning revelation to put you in bondage. If you fear, you will fall. Fear is the devil's territory. Fear tells God, "You're not mighty enough, Satan is too powerful".

God and Satan are not on the same page. Fear not!

Also if you're on the side of God's anger, He can reveal to warn you like in the time Jonah was sent to Nineveh. And once you repent and run to Him in humility, the anger will cease. He doesn't delight in punishing the repentant or cause Satan to afflict the righteous. No!

Three quick things to do when you're having negative revelations:

1. Run to God with everything in you. "The name of the Lord is a strong tower, the righteous run into it, and they're safe". Proverbs 18:10.

2. Be a functional righteous one and not just a confessional one. Many confess the imputed righteousness of Christ without living in the active one. It's the greatest undoing of this generation. Too much talk and no action. The righteousness of God in Christ Jesus doesn't continue to live in known sins. *"He that doeth righteousness is righteous"*. 1 John 3:7.

3. Give yourself to the word of God and prayers as a matter of course. Satan doesn't have power anymore on a child of God, but he's got wiles. With profuse injection of God's word into your spirit, soul and body combined with much prayers, all of the devil's wiles and snares can be dealt a deadly blow by God's manifold wisdom.

"To the intent that now unto the principalities and powers in heavenly places might be known by the church the manifold wisdom of God..." Ephesians 3:10.

Don't ever be afraid. Satan is always a counterfeit! The blood of Jesus has him surrendered all of the time. Stay under the blood cover.

God's a good God. Praise the Lord!

*** Word from Mirella...

Beloved Daughters of Zion,

Thanks be to God for another day! Judges 5:6-7 KJV says,

"6 In the days of Shamgar the son of Anath, in the days of Jael, the highways were unoccupied, and the travellers walked through byways.

*7 The inhabitants of the villages ceased, they ceased in Israel, UNTIL that I Deborah arose, that **I AROSE A MOTHER IN ISRAEL**."*

God would have us to be mothers in His kingdom. Women bearing at heart and bringing forth His purpose. He's seeking to overshadow us with His power so to birth purpose.

Destinies are birthed by the power of the Holy Ghost: God's plan for you with signs following!

He's seeking to raise you up to His desired plan for your lives. However - firstly - yieldedness unto Him is needed.

Until you arise, you cannot shine (Isaiah 60:1). Until you arise as a mother in Zion, you can't bring forth! Only mothers travail and bring forth: substantial impact and authority, commanding divine overflow and fruitfulness.

To arise means to pray to be and until endued with the power and wisdom needed and, thus, be set ablaze for the cause of your mission on earth!

It's only when you arise, that you will walk in the light given to you from above of the LORD, for Psalm 36:9 KJV says: *"For with Thee [O LORD] is the fountain of life: in Thy light shall we see light."*

Tip for the Day: pray in the Holy Ghost that the power of the Highest shall overshadow that you shall bring forth God's purpose for your life in this season.

Shalom! ***

Chapter 50

Dynamics of Life & Ministry: Way Forward in the New Season

1. Be prayerful. Prayerlessness will always lead to futureless-ness!

   "I know the thought I think about you saith the Lord...but you will come & pray unto me." Jeremiah 29:11-13.

   No matter what, just keep praying and never stop. Pray! Anyhow, pray to the God of heaven. Pray!

   "And he spoke to them that men ought always to pray, and not to faint..." Luke 18:1.

2. Leave behind those you're done with. It's sometimes painful but you've to leave some people, places or projects behind if you will not be left behind in Life.

   "Leaving those things behind...", Paul said in Philippians 3:13.

3. Be diligent at what you do. If you're a pastor, pastor; if you're a missionary, be on missions. As a pastor of almost 500,000 members church, it's very rare not to meet Bishop Oyedepo in church every Sunday. I trained under him and lived in the house rented for his Pastors besides the church. He's in church before most of us at any given day! If you're primarily a pastor who wants a growing church, but most

Sundays you're on mission somewhere else, you will wake up to reality maybe at 70 years of age.

"See a man diligent in his business (his purpose), he shall stand before kings and not among failures." Proverb 22:29 paraphrased.

4. Obtain the appropriate knowledge. You want fresh oil from heaven and you're reading Donald Trump's books to run the ministry. Judge for yourself! Pastor Adeboye's books are there. Dr Francis Wale Oke's meetings and messages are there. Morris Cerullo's, Benny Hinn's and Reinhard Bonnke's materials are there.

    "Be circumspect, redeeming the time for the days are evil", Paul Admonished in Ephesians 5:15.

5. Give yourself over for the service of God with all you have within you and at your disposal without waiting for anyone to praise you. If you fail, rise up again. If you're discouraged, turn to God in deep prayers to find strength again. If you're despised, look up to God. Cry out for help from God always and never give up serving Him.

    "Seek first the kingdom of God & his righteousness, and all these things shall be added to you." Mathew 6:33.

Blessed new season, Peace be upon you and all yours in Jesus name. Amen.

Love you all!

Chapter 51

Dynamics of Life and Ministry - God's Calling is Sacred (You Cannot Call Yourself - God Does the Calling)

"For every high priest taken from among men is ordained for men in things [pertaining] to God, that he may offer both gifts and sacrifices for sins...And no man taketh this honour unto himself, but he that is called of God, as was Aaron." Hebrews 5:1,4.

You cannot call yourself and you cannot hijack the calling of God. It's sacred and only God earmarks people for it. Everybody in Christ can be involved in active Christian services. Nothing different much from calling though, only that calling is a divine preoccupation. It engages you for life. It's a mantle! You can't put it off!

I am sure every member of the body of Christ is called to serve God and if anyone is not in the service of God, I doubt if the life of God flows in their veins. However, things have been greatly muddled up in this age and this is the greatest undoing of many whose precious destinies have suffered great shipwreck as a result of venturing into what God never designed them for and will never help them to do. God chooses who to do what! He blesses what He plans and not what man organises! Please note that. Selah!

Not everyone is called into the fivefold ministry gifts of Apostles, Prophets, Evangelists, Pastors and Teachers; and also, not everyone in the fivefold is called to be in the front line.

You cannot impress God by being or doing what He didn't design you for just like you cannot be laughing with a goalkeeper who likes to leave the goalposts to striking for the strikers.

If you're only involved in the kingdom service and your Parents, Pastors or Partners want to use it to impose a calling or pastoring a church on you, reject it vehemently. Those called of God to handle a church find joy in doing it. They may not be strong in their ability to handle it, but there's a spiritual willingness to do it.

"In the day of thy Power, your people shall be willing." Psalm 110:3.

Five Reasons that must not push you into the calling:

1. *"All my friends are ordained and honoured as Pastors."* Can you start flying planes just because all your friends are pilots? A lot play with their lives like the seven sons of Sceva in this generation. Acts 19:11-20.

2. *"I went to Bible college or school of ministry like others did."* Bible school doesn't validate God's calling. As a matter of fact, most front line servants of God have never been through any Bible school except the ones they founded. Bible school does not provide nor prepare you for the call of God. Rather, Bible school prepares you in the call of God.

3. *"My parents are Pastors or any serious Christian in our church can go and start another church."* If you love to have life in abundance and not sorrow through life, hear God for yourself before you undertake a venture with or for God. Calling of God is not infectious. It's a pre-planned

155

arrangement of heaven. God has a specific plan for each person on earth.

4. *"We fought them there and started our own ministry because we're not being treated right."* You have just dug your own grave and those of your followers my friend. If you're not treated right, are there no other churches where you can fellowship without opening a new one you're not called to do?

5. *"I felt I needed to be on my own because I can preach very well and have better results than where I was serving."* It's not about feeling my friend, it's about His choosing. He is the commander in chief and He gives all marching orders otherwise you will be marched over!

May your life and destiny be preserved. If your life has been misdirected by any means, I ask God for a touch of redirection and restoration over you now in the name of Jesus. Amen.

Chapter 52

Take Responsibility for It

If your sin will be purged thoroughly of God and you'll enjoy times of Refreshing from the Holy Spirit, tell the whole truth about it. For instance: don't say, "he made me do it". Tell what you did that brought you in it. Tell how you anticipated it. Tell how you're ravished in it. Take responsibility and take burdens off others if you're into it with full intention or attention, anticipation or desire (no matter how faint).

David took responsibility for his sin without blaming any and he obtained mercy. Saul blamed his failing on people and he lost his throne and grace.

Only God truly forgives sins and once He acquits you, you're forever free. But if you paint yourself righteous before men and demonize others, you will be bound in that sin for life eternal.

It's the nature of man to defend himself and play blame game, but the new creation in Jesus has a heart of flesh and can't retain sin in its nature. If it does, the new creation has not taken place.

Don't pretend to be who you're not before men. Covering of faults denies people of true prospering in life. Mercy is only obtained from God and only when there's a true repentance with no cover up!

Many parents wouldn't have made the mistakes made over others if their children told them detailed truth before they took the actions taken. Many men and women would not have jumped into the actions they took if the details of what transpired with their spouse were well known.

I have counselled many and taken sides many times until I knew the truth from the other side. Now I know better. I exercise patience till all facts are on the table.

As a child of God, tell pure truth from your side and look forward to God's mercy alone.

"By mercy and truth iniquity is purged: and by the fear of the LORD men depart from evil."(Proverbs 16:6).

Peace be upon you. God's favour will always rest on you for ever. Amen.

***Word from Mirella...

*** Navigating in the Spirit by praying in the Holy Spirit and gaining progress occur gradually. However, persisting and continuing therein generates greater rushing waves of the Holy Spirit. Then, can you tell by revelation the mind of the Spirit, praying therein by faith!

Keep pressing in till the banks of your inner man overflow with rivers of living water! Only then can you gain ascendancy into the heart of God.

Keep pressing in till your utterances are by the Holy Ghost, speaking Life and bringing down every wile of the devil!

Keep pressing in till your utterances break open the heavens above and the earth beneath!

Keep stirring up your spirit by praying in the Holy Ghost and you shall prevail by the mercies of the Lord: *"for it is not by power, nor by might, but by My Spirit"*, saith the LORD of hosts.

God bless you; shalom! ***

Chapter 53

Dynamics of Life and Ministry: In All Thy Getting, Get Understanding (Knowing Appointed People, Projects and Places)

"Fools wear themselves out with hard work, because they don't even know the way to town." Ecclesiastes. 10:15.

Great understanding amplifies efforts, but lack of understanding buries skills and efforts underground.

Everyone in life has a calling but today I like to address those who have sensed or are sensing God's call over their lives or those already in it.

Calling is for God's divine purpose and not for man's desired targets. Can I say that in a more simplified way? Calling is for God's agenda and not man's pleasure.

Many in the so called 'calling' today are totally out of tune with God. Most in it today assumed from the beginning that 'It's for an independent adventure and Must involve having a church'. The reason is simple. They see church superintendents and their large congratulations as the models of real calling of God. Therefore, they labour in vain on earth and miss out totally with God eternally. After 14 years of being an evangelist and pastor, God spoke to the late Kenneth Haggins, "I don't have any record of all you did so far". Subsequently, God told him he's to be a prophet and teacher.

Many today are not just running rat race like the Bible-time Ahimaz, but they're just overtly fleshly ambitious. God is not in all these.

God wants us to talk to Him on clarifications of our purposes otherwise we will have to run on our own fuel and may struggle all lifelong.

"Call upon me, I will answer you and show you great and mighty things that you know not." Jeremiah 33:3.

There are many great and mighty things "that you know not" and God wants you to know if you will take out time to ask Him. We don't have to go through life with pains and struggles that never end.

"We don't want you to be foolish but understanding what the will of God is", Paul wrote in Ephesians 5:17.

Major questions to ask about the calling:

A. *"If nobody else believes me, do I know am really called without shadow of any doubt?"* Ministry is a lonely path and most times you're on your own. So, to thyself be true!

B. *Who am I to be with or to go out?"* Many giants of faith are with other giants. Bishop David Abioye with Bishop David Oyedepo, Silas with Paul, Rev Tom with Pastor Chris and many others. You don't have to go solo to be important. Your relevance is in your assignment. God doesn't need masters but seekers.

C. *"Am I to be on mission or in a church?"* If you plant and pastor a church while you're supposed to be on mission and vice versa, you labour in vain!

   "Except the Lord build the house, the builders labour in vain." Psalm 127:1.

D. *"Where is the place, Lord, and who are the people?"* There are appointed places and appointed People. To understand the level of delusion of this generation, observe where people rush to with their calling: UK, America, Lagos, Abuja, Port Harcourt- Tarshish instead of Nineveh. Mega city instead of low-graded areas.

E. *"When is my Divine timing?"* If you Miss out on this, you may struggle for ever.

Many other questions you should ask the Father if your family will not one-day kick against God and leave you dry.

May God direct you with precision henceforth in Jesus name. Amen.

Chapter 54

Two Great Thoughts

1. If you do things without the breath of the Almighty (Meaning without God moving you to do it) and backed up with deep prayers, you will struggle with such for as long as it exists in your life! God does His own things in His own way! God is great! Hallelujah!

   "But there is a spirit in man: and the inspiration (the breath) of the Almighty giveth them understanding." Job 32:8.

2. Cheer up, God has His mind full of you and thoughts of peace, goodness and good news for you. He thinks about you and thinks on you a lot. He always also steps into or visits whatever encroaches on you and your liberty even before you have knowledge of it. God is good. A great shepherd of your soul. Praise God.

   "What is man, that thou art mindful of him? and the son of man, that thou visitest him?" Psalm 8:4.

God bless you.

Chapter 55

Dynamics of Life and Ministry: You Must Be Strong and Firm while Holy and Humble

"For it is we who are the circumcision, we who serve God by his Spirit, who boast in Christ Jesus, and who put no confidence in the flesh." Philippians 3:3.

In dealing with humans to get the best of God from them, I have observed some turn themselves to "bullies" while some cringe to "wimps". While God does not want you to be a bully, a proud one looking down on everyone and making yourself the king of the jungle in your relationship with people, God also has not created you a wimp, a beggarly creature unable to stand but blown around by every wind like pendulum!

In relating to superiors, contemporaries or those coming behind us, we must not turn to Pharaoh neither must we be the beggarly Lazarus at the rich man's gate. God resists rude people, but nobody can also fulfil God's purpose on earth a fearful one whose will is submerged or subjugated by those around him.

Paul told Timothy, a young preacher," *Do not let anyone despise your youth (your inability or inexperience) ...for God has not given us the spirit of fear (You're not a wimp), but of power (strength of purpose), of love (holiness and humility for service) and of a sound mind (firmness of purpose)."* 1 Timothy 4:12 & 2 Timothy 1:7.

If you can be easily swayed, then you can be easily led astray. Paul said," *We should not be foolish but understanding what God's will is*".

There are overpowering bosses, friends and followers that can act as the old prophet that led the young prophet astray to his early death in the book of Kings. He made him turn back to eat and against God's word to him. He died uselessly.

I have had people shouting me down from writing as I do now on social media, just because it's not their line. Nobody is immune to this, but you can be firm in your purpose while holiness and humility are not jettisoned. I met my wife doing this.

Many take connecting to people overboard that now they don't even know who they're or what God asked them to do in life anymore. Although you should also be careful so your firmness is not Pride. There's a thin line in-between.

Before you can be of use to anybody, you must know who you're and be firm in your purpose.

You cannot stop people looking down on you. You cannot stop being discouraged also but you must know what you're for in life and stand very firm in God's word and your purpose.

"...but the people who know their God shall stand firm and take action. Or they shall be strong and do exploits." Daniel 11:32.

Peace be upon you.

Chapter 56

Dynamics of Life and Ministry: Killing Pride and Connecting to Others' Graces

I have been awake to righteousness and started out preaching the gospel of Jesus Christ since 1992 and I've observed the following:

I've seen many who care less about anybody's experience. To them, they have enough revelations at their disposal. I've also seen many who care less about anybody's revelations. They're sure they have enough experience and technical-know-how.

To move on steady, strong, stable, speedily and safely into God's plan for us, we need everything available! I mean everything. Whether they be called experience or revelations.

God has so much of deposits in everyone that to despise any is to short-circuit your grace, your destiny. Satan will do everything to make you ignore, despise or totally block out what God could use to speedily bring you up.

Experience can become a pitfall and revelation can become an oversize cap that makes you fall unawares. I've had to endure much agony from the experienced time and again; also I've had my intelligence insulted by those of revelations times without number. However, you can't be without the two.

Experience can swell you and revelations can over inflate you beyond your size, but staying on the word will put you in balance always.

What is the word to stand on? Humility and simplicity at all times.

God is too infinitely multi-dimensional to be compressed into anybody's experience and His revelations are too progressive to be confined to what anybody knows.

Experience is needed, don't throw it away because there will be some Samuel that will need the instruction of how to respond to God's voice via the experience of Eli. Revelations are definitely the live wire of the Christian faith. Without it, Christianity will become outdated and unneeded!

There are people who have more experience than us. We need them. Every Moses needs a good Jethro. But Moses will bring the new move.

I will that every pastor will look among friends and in their congregation people of credible experience; people of fresh oil, connect properly with them to move on more speedily. I will that every believer relates well with those noticed to be of good track records in areas you're not too conversant and also people with new ideas to progress on without much hitches in life.

The best principle is to open your heart and never ever close it.

"But Naaman went away angry and said, "I thought that he would surely come out to me and stand and call on the name of the Lord his God, wave his hand over the spot and cure me of my leprosy. Are not Abana and Pharpar, the rivers of Damascus, better than all the waters of Israel? Couldn't I wash in them and be cleansed?" So he turned and went off in a rage. Naaman's servants went to him and said, "My father, if the prophet had told

you to do some great thing, would you not have done it? How much more, then, when he tells you, 'Wash and be cleansed'!" So he went down and dipped himself in the Jordan seven times, as the man of God had told him, and his flesh was restored and became clean like that of a young boy." 2 Kings 5:11-14.

Don't kick off experience, very dangerous. Your whole life, marriage, business or ministry could depend on it. Don't look down on revelations. God does nothing without revealing it first to His friends the prophets (the fresh-fire believers). Rather open up and connect!

David didn't kill the dying Egyptian he saw in the field while chasing after those who ransacked his city neither did he kick him off, rather he fed him, allowed him to lead him to pursue, overtake and recover all.

Connect!

Chapter 57

A believer is Different

If the way unbelievers live is how you now live and all your desires or pursuits are not those of eternal value as such, then probably you're a child of God before but now you're no more.

"Examine yourselves to see whether you are in the faith; test yourselves. Do you not realize that Christ Jesus is in you--unless, of course, you fail the test?" 2 Corinthians 13:5.

"Little children, let no one deceive you. Whoever practices righteousness is righteous, as he is righteous." 1 John 3:7.

Also always Return to God, report to God, resort to God and repent of anything He places His fingers on, then resist the devil. He will flee from you! Isaiah 30:15.

Tough though, but we have to keep moving. No alternative! God is good!

Chapter 58

Two Sides I Have Observed About Subtle and Sublime Pride

1. The obvious - those who are ahead who look down on others. This is the major one many shout about. Not good, for sure, to be like this. Very bad, God hates it!

    "God resists the proud but gives more grace to the humble." James 4:6.

But then...

2. The hidden - those who are coming behind or just rising, or just coming up or not measuring up yet, but who refuse to accept the stage they're and respect those in advantage. Many have this but refuse to recognize it. It's a sublime sort of pride not to recognize nor honour those God honours or has put ahead in any facet or level. You may never move forward in life being like this! Many are in front of each of us that must be addressed as such. Many have what we don't have and must be recognized for such.

    Bishop Francis Wale Oke once said, *"If you honour whom God has honoured, your own honour is knocking at the door."*

    "Render therefore to all their dues: tribute to whom tribute is due; custom to whom custom; fear to whom fear; honour to whom honour." Romans 13:7.

Chapter 59

Step Out of the Generational Box

You said you've set standard for yourself as a young person that until 3 years from now or when you will have finished your degree or master's degree before marrying (maybe because of what your parents, pastors or guardians told you), but now your immorality knows no bound and you can't do without being with someone. You've set trap for yourself and not a standard. You're shooting arrows and firebrands into your future. You will only get to the future to find out nothing is there anymore. All burnt out!

You've forfeited your future like Esau without knowing. You set a standard that pleases men while your breasts are being fondled around like football or your penis is shooting around like fuel station nozzle. If you enjoy the company of opposite sex enough to be fondled by them or like to share bed with them for nights and you can't stop it by whatever means (including prayers and counselling), then it's time to formalise it by marriage to put an end to your mirage or else you're finishing your future before you arrive there. Many are crying with no comfort now, don't join the list.

*"But if they cannot control themselves, they should marry, for it is better to marry than to burn with passion."*1 Corinthians 7:9.

Rather follow God's word instead of Google map or man's standard and traditions of elders that ruined the people of Jesus' time.

"See that no one is sexually immoral, or is godless like Esau, who for a single meal sold his inheritance rights as the oldest son. Afterward, as you know, when he wanted to inherit this blessing, he was rejected. Even though he sought the blessing with tears, he could not change what he had done." Hebrews 12:16-17.

Just step by step, if you follow God with your heart out, everything people have said negatively about you will be sorted out by God. People must have really said many things, but heavens will smile on you. Cry to God!

"This poor man cried to the Lord, the Lord heard him and delivered him out of all his troubles." Psalm 34:6.

If you're under this siege, may your life and destiny be rescued and put in right direction today in Jesus name. I break the hold of immorality off your life. You're free in Jesus name. Peace be unto you now and forever. Amen.

Chapter 60

Did You Miss It? Did You Fail God? You Will Be Back! God Does Restore Bigger and Better!

Millions missed it before you and many multiplied millions will still miss it, but God remains the same-The Restorer of lost hope!

Painful to miss it. Very painful. Everyone wants to get it right, on time, spot on, no repeat, no retrogression. But flaws happen. Slipping does occur. We're all doomed in this life if God just leaves us all alone in our falling, failing, faltering and fainting!

But no...

"So I will restore to you the years that the swarming locust has eaten, The crawling locust, The consuming locust, And the chewing locust..." Joel 2:25.

I remember how I missed it marriage-wise in 2001. God did everything to reach out to me but I didn't know He was the one, so I stood against every move of His unknown to me. This led to a loss of wife and two children just like a dream. Some told me I should just wait for my own death too. Many believed I was down and out for life.

Three quick points to restorations –(I did three things to move on)

1. Acknowledge your error: I recognized I was in a deep mistake and Satan already got me in a corner. Satan was ready to finish me off. I fell in the error sincerely but ignorantly. I told both God and humans that I was in error. I needed help. Knowledge of mistake, right and obligations in Christ is always a winner.

Israel did not know they're to spend 400 years in captivity, so they spent 30yrs more. Daniel was made to know the period of their servitude in Babylon. That made the ordeal easier.

"If I had not confessed the sin in my heart, the Lord would not have listened." Psalm 66:8.

2. Don't make light of what's gone wrong. Some make light of their errors as if it did not upset any of God's plans. That's one-way road to being down for life. Our failing always puts God's plan in an awkward situation. You might think you're too insignificant for this, but no. Nobody in God's plan is insignificant. We're not in-disposable but we're occupying a very significant corner of God's eternal plan. Moses and the children of Israel who left Egypt all died in the wilderness because they upset God's plans in almost an irreparable form. They're extremely important in God's scheme of work but they never really knew. They're the church in the wilderness.

Don't start quoting grace scriptures when things have gone wrong, face the enormousness of what's happened. It's heavy. David knew this as contained in Psalm 51 responding to his disappointing failing. Many get stuck at this stage and never move out. You're so important, so is your error. Satan knows this and that's why he sets all traps to get a hold of you. He plans every day to get you. You're that important. Satan doesn't attack unimportant elements!

3. Pledge and give all your life and love to God for whatever He could do with it. I remember kneeling down in my room in London around July 2005 telling God, "Lord, if you save me from all these, I do not have anything else to do with my life any more than to serve you alone." I knew enough that if my life was spared, it's no longer mine but "a borrowed life". So, I told God if He gave me, He should also use it for whatever He wanted. That's why all ambitions, aspirations and plans I was used to having were all put down at the foot of the cross. I remind myself constantly now in case any flesh wants to get in. I tell myself, "David, you lost your life, what you have now is God's totally".

When you get to this juncture of life, God takes all your mistakes, failures, falling and etc. to use all to His glory. It doesn't mean He enjoyed the errors committed but He's God. He just stands there telling Satan, "I have this one, hands off him or her".

"And we know that in all things God works for the good of those who love him, who have been called according to his purpose." Romans 8:28.

There's no problem or person that God cannot turn around if His hands have them.

Bible Case study:

"Then he showed me Joshua the high priest standing before the Angel of the Lord, and Satan standing at his right hand to oppose him. And the Lord said to Satan, "The Lord rebuke you, Satan! The Lord who has chosen Jerusalem rebuke you! Is this not a brand plucked from the fire?" Now Joshua was clothed with filthy garments, and was standing before the Angel. Then He answered and spoke to those who stood before Him, saying, "Take away the filthy garments from him." And to him He said, "See, I have removed your iniquity from you, and I will clothe you with rich robes." Zechariah 3:1-4.

Peace be unto you in Jesus name. Amen.

Chapter 61

Just ONE MOMENT

Just like one moment of brilliance could seal a man's fortune for all of life (Like Joseph's moment of dream interpretation for Pharaoh, King of Egypt), so also one stupid moment: a brief time of madness, one second of anger display, lustful indulgence; a little slip or dip in form could bring a man down and put him in obscurity for all of life. He might struggle without any headway anymore FOR ALL OF LIFE! Many examples abound all around us. Endless list of victims...

King David just walked around and cast a glance on Bathsheba. Samson just branched into Delilah's house. Somebody just slapped his or her spouse. Somebody just got angry with a trigger-happy police officer. Somebody just revealed his heart to a devil-reloaded. Somebody just ignored the nudging of the Spirit to take a detour from a dangerous route or trip... That's it!

Thus, most of the prayers and preparations you've been doing, the teachings you've been listening to, the counselling you've been having, the Bible you've been studying, the laying on of hands you've been receiving and what have you, could have all been preparing you for that ONE MOMENT!

"Look carefully then how you walk, not as unwise but as wise, making the best use of the time, because the days are evil.

Don't act thoughtlessly, but understand what the Lord wants you to do." Ephesians 5:15-17.

Prayer Point: Father, in the name of Jesus, I receive grace and wisdom of and from you not to fail the moment for which you've been preparing me all of my life. If I have failed of that moment (like Esau) and my birth right is sold, please restore me right now by the blood of Jesus. Amen.

(Take 5 minutes to pray in the spirit or pray any other way alone to God).

Peace be unto you in Jesus name. Amen.

Chapter 62

Moving Forward Steadily and with Great Balance in The New Season

1. Don't move around without having people who know everything you do. You must have accountability team. People who know everything about anything you do.

   There are liars. There are false witnesses who rise up from time to time to waylay and put people's names, family, ministry into disrepute. But with people who truly know you and can answer the enemies at the gates, like Jesus disciples who had true accounts of all things to put the records straight, you have less of a problem.

   Never get to a point in life where the only one who truly knows you is God. If this happens, you're in an evil matter fuelled by deep foolishness, ignorance or perhaps pride (paraded as deep revelation or spirituality).

   "By the mouth of two or three witnesses a truth will be established", Jesus said in Mathew 18:16.

2. Never ever come to a point whereby you're the only one who understands the principle, revelation or policy by which your life or a project is run. If you do this, you will fall.

   God gave Jesus and Paul many mysteries of the kingdom. Very hard for many around them to understand but they kept explaining to others until some understood so they ran together having seen eye to eye on the matter.

Apostle Peter writing about Paul and his revelations said,

"Bear in mind that our Lord's patience means salvation, just as our dear brother Paul also wrote you with the wisdom that God gave him. He writes the same way in all his letters, speaking in them of these matters. His letters contain some things that are hard to understand, which ignorant and unstable people distort, as they do the other Scriptures, to their own destruction." 2 Peter 3:15-16.

Paul's teachings were difficult to understand for the people of his generation especially those who never bothered to understand before jumping into conclusion, but because he went to Jerusalem to table these revelations before some, explaining the details of them in definite terms, the apostles who were the pillars of the church then, understood them and supported Paul's missions the world over.

3. Don't do anything under the cover of the dark or in your heart/head alone.

    God lives in the light and no darkness around Him at all. Don't hide in the dark to do marriage or run ministry. Don't run a venture in the dark. Don't get involved in a project or relationship in the dark. If anything cannot stand light, don't be a part of it. Satan likes darkness. Don't let him see your end.

    Subject all you see to light. Let people in the light judge or weigh them carefully.

"Two or three prophets should speak, and the others should weigh carefully what is said (Let the prophets speak two or three, and let the other judge.)" 1 Corinthians 14:29.

Don't keep a dream, revelation or vision in your heart alone. You may not have a correct interpretation of it. Don't start kissing in the dark. You may be kissing a devil saying bye to your destiny like Samson.

Gossip thrives in the dark. Expose it. Refuse to be among Datha, Coral and Abiram who got swallowed up in the ground.

Many have many things written down in their diaries thought to be God's directives but explicit Satan's deceptions.

"A backslider in his heart is full of his own ways." Proverbs 14:14

"The man that wanders out of the way of understanding shall remain in the congregation of the dead." Proverb 21:16.

God's light shall guide your feet this new season in Jesus name. You won't fall, faint, fail or falter. Amen.

Peace be unto you.

*** Word from Mirella...

*** The best set of Christians need to pray still! Have we really wondered why great servants of God are men of prayer? It's because no man is immune to obstacles in life! Prayer activates our spiritual sensor to discern good from evil; it quickens our inner man to perceive the heart of God per time. No wonder Proverbs 20:27 KJV says, *"the spirit of man is the candle of the LORD, searching all the inward parts of the belly"*. Great!

Our spirit is enlightened in and by the atmosphere of prayer, whereby we're able to receive the deep things of God searched out by the Holy Spirit, even as we pray in the Holy Ghost (being the will of God).

Beloved, if we don't want to be preys of the enemy, let's watch and pray! Prayer sets in line the necessary pathways to keep us from the snares of darkness. So, pray!

What really enhances spiritual senses is a life of prayer, during which, these former are gradually, but definitely, developed.

Pray in the Holy Ghost for it enlightens your spirit so that the Word of God will be Life unto you, for only the Holy Spirit gives life, by causing God's Word to enter into your heart (Psalm 119:130): *"Thy Word is a lamp unto my feet, and a light unto my path"* (Psalm 119:105 KJV).

Then, shall the light of the Word order your steps and iniquity shall not have dominion over you (Psalm 119:133).

Pray, pray and pray...then shall your path shine brighter day after day unto the perfect day (Proverbs 4:18): that's the way to spiritual triumph in Christ Jesus.

...and thus saith the LORD of hosts, *"the heavens are opened: thus, cry unto Me and I shall hearken unto you"*

God bless you; shalom! ***

Chapter 63

Two Major Lessons I Learnt Today as I Journeyed Through Ireland

1. I entered into RCCG National headquarters in Dublin, Ireland around few minutes to 1 p.m. only to find its National Pastor, Wife and all staff observing an hour of serious prayers. From there. I also went to a friend's church (Acting Faith Ministries) in Blanchardstown around 6 p.m. and the church was in deep prayers.

   The Lesson: behind every growing or thriving church and ministry is a strong, steady and stable prayer intercessions done with all seriousness.

2. I was coming out of Ghana either 2003 or 2004 and we got to either Republic of Togo or Republic of Benin on our way to Nigeria, then we got to a large cemetery I saw many people converge to do some stuff over there around the graves. I think it's a yearly thing. I told myself upon seeing that, "African people could be so blindfolded". To my great surprise as I drove through Naas town in Ireland today, I saw many cars parked over a quarter of the whole town. I thought there's a football, Gaelic or rugby match was going but - alas - it's a convergence of people at the town's cemetery!

   Lesson: same activities take place the world over in different versions. Anywhere humans are, they have the same lines of activities, although some could be more civilised one than another.

Also know that God will not bless what's half world's and half His. You're running a business, putting out a musical album or concert, starting out a ministry or family, you must set out whose it's from the start. The gospel of this generation is messed up for reason of people attempting to do God's business with the ideas of this world or worldly figures. Nobody can help God. He is the one that helps us! God wants to help, but will help only His own purpose and business.

Chapter 64

Overcoming the Forces of Darkness: Light is the Key

The forces of darkness (Satan and his cohorts) pretend to be who they are not a lot. Remember, 'he roars around **LIKE** a lion', but he is not.

Satan's power was broken by the death and resurrection of Jesus Christ. He has no power left.

"They overcame him by the blood of the lamb..." Revelation 12:11.

If you don't build your faith up, you may live under the fear of Satan for as long as you have breath.

I can't forget early in my Christian life when Bishop Rowland Peters showed me this light by God's revelation: "He has delivered us from the power of darkness and translated us to the kingdom of his dear Son..." Colossians 1:13.

I had gone to him for prayers because of some demonic attacks I was having. He clearly told me, "This thing is by faith". That's all I needed to show the devil the way out!

You can't face Satan fearing him. Many pray in fear. Many live all their lives fighting Satan as a result of the fear he's put in their heart. Refuse to be afraid if you've truly surrendered your all to God. Just resist him steadfastly in your faith.

"Submit yourself under the mighty hand of God; resist Satan and he shall flee from you." James 4:7.

Three quick power points for your use:

1. Live within the confines of Holiness provided by the blood of Jesus. Hebrews 12:14.

2. Stay on the word of God to feed your faith. "Faith comes by hearing the word of God"- Romans 1:17.

3. Pray all manners of prayers in the spirit with authority that comes from God. Ephesians 6:18.

Above all, be not afraid. You can't overcome Satan in fear. Take him to the height he can't survive, that's the place of the word of God in faith. Eagles take serpents to the air to deal with them.

Fear is a cycle that never ends. As you're coming out of one, another shows up. Break the cycle; step out of it. You've been down enough, step out! Take back your territories: your peace, health, home, relationship and finances in the name of Jesus. Take back your ministry! Your glory! Hallelujah!

Faith honours God, so God honours faith. Fear God only and not what Satan can do. He has no power over you. He lost it when Christ stopped him at the cross.

Praise God!

"Above all, taking the shield of faith, wherewith ye shall be able to quench all the fiery darts of the wicked(Satan)." Ephesians 6:16.

Satan is quenchable. Don't be afraid. Resist him!

"Whosoever is born of God overcomes the world and this is the victory that overcomes the world, even our faith." 1 John 5:4.

Chapter 65

Knowing and Fulfilling God's Mandate, His Calling Over You

Although I first committed to church in 1986 but I was still my normal self...The moment I left my house to step into Deeper Life church in March 26th 1992, I knew what I would do for life. I lost taste for all my prior ambitions and aspirations. The moment you get truly born again, your assignment for life will be made known to you, to your spirit man. It's there.

The least task in other things looks so burdensome whereas the most tedious uphill task in your mandate looks exciting to your spirit. I will feel dead to work an hour in the bank even if I'm paid $1,000 per minute. Jesus said, "My meat is to the will of him that sent me". Your divine assignment is a meat while others are a mess!

There are many callings in a call but you will not discover any of these more than the initial one if you don't step out first. The burden of sitting still can age you more quickly than any ageing sickness. Stepping forward in the call brings such a joy that you'll never be able to describe with words! 'Peace that passes all understanding... joy unspeakable, full of glory'.

The anointing and glory promised of the Lord to you will never 'come on' unless you 'go on' with the trend. Elisha only became a mantle receiver after a tedious follow up of the trend!

"If we follow on to know the Lord...then former and later rain will come", Hosea said in chapter 6.

You may not be Smith Wigglesworth in the 1st year of your calling!

No matter how near and dear you're to God, even if you're Abraham the friend of God, David the man after God's heart or Jesus the son of God, you will be made to pass through certain tests or circumstances that you can't explain and which will make people to mock you. You will only lay a hold of God's glory if you pass them...No jump over!

"You made men ride over our head, we passed through fire & water...then you brought us to the wealthy place", David wrote in Psalm 66.

You may not fulfil God's call if you're not ready to submit your 'thuggery' to His 'surgery'. He will break you to remove your ego. Almost Everyone I've come across (myself inclusive) has it and God cannot use you much with it. "God resists the proud".

When you're really ready for God friends, you'll on your own submit your thuggery to His surgery. He wrestled with Jacob, broke his leg and made him own up to his duplicity and deceptive sort of a lifestyle before the Israel(ic) blessing! He needs to break you, otherwise you're on your own!

May God's face shine on you in Jesus name. Amen.

Chapter 66

My Decision to Follow Jesus

'Will I be able to continue my education and Sing Fuji music around?'. These two issues were of paramount concerns to me which I was preoccupied with day and night without asking anyone while normal activities of life continued. It was late 1991 and we just concluded the leaving certs months earlier. Like every other growing adult I also had ambitions and all of them centred around the university education.

I wanted to go and study political science at OAU, Ile-Ife, form a student-Fuji music band and be able to sleep with girls free without the fear of impregnating any. My father warned me since I entered puberty that once I did anything with a lady and she's pregnant, that'd be the end of my education. Oh,I hated to hear that for I was lazy with any handiwork except education. Thus that kept me virgin all secondary school days. Girls had their field days getting stuff from me and I couldn't touch even any with the longest pole!

I loved to be a big fuji musician as I have been singing it well from age 7(Fuji is a popular genre of music from my tribe), but many people involved in it then were seen as ruffians so I was planning to carve a niche for myself setting up an elite band from the university campus.

I had my life all mapped out as a youngster without telling anybody. The choice of courses fell on Political Science or Mass

Communications. I loved and still love reading, writing and TALKING!

God's decision may be silent but will from time to time agitate you.

Anytime I passed by (Pastor W. F. Kumuyi)Deeper Life Bible Church's December Retreat Posters or banners, something serious would flash my heart, 'YOU WILL GIVE YOUR LIFE TO JESUS AND BE A PREACHER'. I was *Wakili* (a Muslim), a gyrating boy well known around AND I wasn't even considering Christianity. Thinking about this could sometimes make me absent minded for moments. But I knew there's a decision on me such that my ambitions for Education, Fuji music and anticipated Romps with girls will be truncated once I stepped into Jesus.

It took me months to agree in my heart. Many times of personal mumblings and sleepless nights. It turned out same way in March '92 when I turned myself in at a Deeper Life Bible church for Altar call after a sleepless Saturday night/Sunday morning. I immediately became a preacher and forgot about Fuji band and women issue. But I struggled with my educational ambition. I prayed and fasted that I wouldn't be denied. I did everything my colleagues were doing to go in to the university but all mine proved abortive or got seized by University Matriculation Examination Authority. I was pro-actively growing in grace and for years was without the kind of education I desired except the ministerial ones. I thought such were not fanciful for my age, but I was wrong. They built the very foundation of the life I live now and all of my open doors.

In the process of time, when God had properly established my feet in the ministry, He gave me a more fanciful education on foreign soils on higher levels.

When God intercepts, it's because He is intervening!

God's good!

*** Word from Mirella...

*** Except the keys of the [Kingdom are given unto a man, he can't operate in authority nor gain any spiritual progress: for keys are access links to the deeps things of the Father by the Holy Spirit. Thus, pray that such keys shall be delivered unto you from above. Shalom! ***

*** In all your dealings, grieve not the most precious and treasured One of the Godhead, the Holy Spirit! ***

*** In the school of the [Spirit, humility is the first door that one is firstly ushered through for other spiritual doors to swing open. Thus, be humble; let all things be done as unto the Lord. ***

*** The mind of the Holy Spirit is ALWAYS the will of God; and ONLY the will of God expressed through the unutterable groanings of the Holy Spirit through us - in the place of prayer - is RECOGNIZED and, thus, RECEIVE answers. Thus, pray in the Holy Ghost!

Romans 8:26-27 KJV states,

"26 Likewise the Spirit also helpeth our infirmities: for we know not what we should pray for as we ought: but the Spirit Himself maketh intercession for us with groanings which cannot be uttered.

27 And He [the Father] that searcheth the hearts knoweth what is the mind of the Spirit, because He [the Holy Spirit] maketh intercession for the saints according to the will of God. "(emphasis added)

Shalom! ***

Chapter 67

The Man God Uses

To get to the place of a mighty move of God in your generation, you will cross many hurdles and barricades such that if there's no resolute determination or strength in the inner man within you, you will turn back.

"If God will use you greatly, He will first hurt you deeply." A.W. Tozer.

There are some servants of God you must connect with and not let Satan rob you of what God placed on them for you like some who are trapped by physical closeness to God's vessels of functional oil, some have very distractive spouses, while others look at either age or physical-ness of such servants of God. Paul's presence was deemed 'contemptible' by the Corinthians, Elijah didn't have a home, wife nor children, Peter was called uneducated by the Jewish elite circles, Jesus was seen as one of them in Mathew 13 and He could do no miracles. Elijah and Elisha passed through Israel according to Jesus' words and they could only help a few because they're despised or looked down on, called mad prophets!

Real mantle is not for boys...but for the spiritually rugged because the Flesh, the World (humans and affairs of life) and Satan will tempt you sore; God also will try you deep as it were in the process!

God doesn't consult nobody to anoint a vessel for His use when he/she has passed the test! People like Joshua, Ruth and Elisha will weather all storms to carry the mantle! Amen.

This is a spiritual matter for only those who understand. Jordan easily parts when mantle is secured. Many run around with no mantle putting everyone around them in deep trouble!

Wait until you have it! You can have it!

"When God would take away Elijah, Elisha went with him to Gilgal (place of circumcision to roll off the reproach of Egypt) ...to Bethel (the gates of heaven; a place of total surrender to His reign) ...to Jericho (warfare centre where God's power to break barriers is heavily put to test and use) ...to Jordan (arena of baptism of boldness by means of terrifying challenges) ...And he took the mantle of Elijah that fell from him..." 2 kings 2:1-14.

Are you about giving up? Don't! There's a mantle ahead. Amen.

Chapter 68

The Functional Righteousness

If you can continue to be happy while living in any known sin as a believer and everything is still normal, it means the very life of God, the breath of the Almighty has left you for good or you never had it! You have become apostate!

"Take not thy Holy spirit from me", David cried to God in Psalm 51!

Confess your faults and sins to your friends, Christian brothers and sisters or your spouse, so your prayers are answered clearly. Don't hide away from your flesh!

"Therefore confess your sins to each other and pray for each other so that you may be healed. The prayer of a righteous person is powerful and effective." James 5:16.

You may be dying away hiding away. Come clean.

Jesus is Lord!

*** Word from Mirella...

*** ...We tend to end in the flesh, whenever we try to comprehend the paths of the Spirit. Lo, it's beyond any human comprehension and operation...in vain we seek to fully understand the ways of the Spirit in the flesh!

Too many teachings...doctrines...rigors! All this contending with the undefiled Word of His power in us. Oh, that we "unlearn" all human-made doctrines introduced into our race of faith. Oh, that we return to the very simplicity that birthed us into life eternal, even in Christ.

...And I say it again, "the ways of the Spirit cannot be unveiled by the human mind!" All we need, and it takes, is GOD...and GOD alone.

Church, let's get back to the true foundation and the very life in the Spirit: total surrender and obedience.

I wish to give an amazing example, from my walk with the LORD: the baptism of the Holy Spirit, with evidence of tongues. Now, many doctrines on this topic merely clog the flow of the Spirit, and make desperate believers - seeking the infilling of the Holy Spirit - so hopeless...that they end up thinking the gift of the Holy Spirit isn't for them.

I distinctly remember the day it all happened: that fateful Sunday morning, after such few glorious weeks that I was born into the Kingdom of God, just about to begin worshipping the LORD in the congregation of the saints; desiring solely to thank the LORD for bringing purpose and joy into my life... joy unspeakable! Then, I heard Him speak to me clearly...so clear that I couldn't deny that Voice, right in my heart, saying: "haven't I given you another language to worship Me?" At those Words, my vocal chords gave way to a heavenly language. That's how I began speaking in tongues and never ceased.

Now, this all looks so supernatural that I can't explicitly describe the details and the process of the Spirit that yielded such glorious baptism of the Holy Ghost. So, how dare we humans try to found doctrines on how believers ought to receive the Holy Ghost? Oh, our God is "many-sidedly" wise!

Never use your experience as a standard for other believers: for the Holy Spirit, the Word and the Father is the Standard (that is, however They wish to operate, they do so).

It's time pull down those human-based psychological teachings of the Word of God and yield totally to the Holy Spirit and the Word. Else, the Church will be so powerless and lifeless...with no acts of the Spirit in and through us.

Ezekiel 2:1-2 KJV states, *"And he said unto me, Son of man, stand upon thy feet, and I will speak unto thee.*

2 And the spirit entered into me when he spake unto me, and set me upon my feet, that I heard him that spake unto me."

Shalom! ***

Chapter 69

Pray but Based on, in, with and by Revelations (Matthew 16:16-19)

Jesus said," I will build my church and the gates of hell will not prevail against it", but not without saying, "I give you responsibility (the keys) to bind and to loose". To wage war in effectual prayers.

The church Jesus will build is your life, your home, your calling, your career, your future, His Ministry in your care, your health, your finances, your children and what have you...but not without your involvement in serious prayer warfare. Yes, prayer warfare!

There are so many things God has done or that He could do but won't happen without serious prayers by the receiver.

Jesus said," whatever you bind on earth will be bound in heaven". Meaning, if you bind zero on earth because you're too busy, you have nothing bound in heaven, but if you bind a million things on earth because you created time to do it, a million will be bound in heaven for your sake.

What you will discover about all effectively and or successful believers and ministers is that they take much time in serious prayers. Even Jesus prayed! He took time out to really pray.

If you slack in prayers, the space will soon be there for all to see that things are wrong in your life.

"You can do more than pray until you have prayed", an unknown author said.

There's always something glorious and inexplicable in the life of a prayerful fellow. That can be you. Get in prayers.

And although Jesus said we should bind and loose, but He also said, "I will give you the keys of the kingdom." You need revelations to pray effectively. Ask for it.

God teaches our hands to war and our fingers to fight otherwise we may be losing all the time.

If your prayers seem not working, ask God to lead you to pray. Pray in the Spirit, with the Spirit and by the Spirit!

Elijah said, "let them know I have done this thing at thy word" and the fire fell! Nothing can be more powerful than to pray as led or as revealed.

I prayed for a woman with an overdue pregnancy years ago. I saw a monkey-like daemon on her tummy while praying for her in my house. I headed for what I saw in my vision and asked it to move. That's it. The baby must be more than 20 years old now. Praying by revelation.

You need revelations to follow Jesus victoriously. Ask Him for it.

"So Jesus had compassion on them, and touched their eyes: and immediately their eyes received sight, and they followed him." Mathew 20:34.

Only God knows how many more hours Jesus would have used after exhausting three while asking the Father to take the cup away from Him, but for the fact that He was clearly hearing and seeing the Father. Then, He prepared Himself for the will of the Father. Revelations soften your hardship and remove your burden.

Prophet Isaiah in 38:21 clearly instructed Hezekiah's wards prophetically to prepare "lump of figs and lay it on the boil" and the king recovered. You need revelations in prayers. You need divine marching orders.

There are certain words, gestures and scriptures God will want you to use in prayers that will get the job done. Listen for them. Don't be a reckless prayer warrior. Listen to Spirit-given instructions. Romans 8:26.

God is willing to reveal many things to us while praying so as to do it very effectively for results that can't be thwarted. Ask Him. Elijah's secret was that "He stood before God in prayers, received instructions of what to say, said it accordingly and rain stopped, or it rained". Read 2 kings 17 & 18.

In gunning for effectual results in prayers, pray for revelations, pray in revelations and act on revelations all the time. The keys of the kingdom will open and lock any door. Satan is no match for God. All his wiles and darts can be quenched. We are more than a conqueror in Christ. Amen and praise the Lord! God is good!

May God speedily answer your prayers with result that cannot be doubted henceforth in Jesus name. Amen.

Peace be unto you and all yours now and evermore. Amen.

Chapter 70

Dynamics of Life and Ministry: Propriety in Relationships

"Let nothing be done through strife or vain glory; but in lowliness of mind let each esteem others better than themselves." Philippians 2:3.

I have so much to say on this issue than there's time and space to as I am learning and unlearning over the years on this.

There's a way to properly relate with humans and you both will revel in what God has in store. The first rule is to esteem others better than you. Seeing yourself not in this light is the opposite of humility: Pride of heart. It's very hard to accept we're proud, but with this scripture in place, you can know your measure.

Once you cannot see what makes others better than you, you've buried your progress and future. No matter how wise, anointed, holy, spiritual or accomplished you're, anyone standing around you must be esteemed better. This is a statutory order of heaven. If you always see yourself better than everyone, that's Pride.

Three ways to go about this:

1. Look at the person's grace -spheres of influence and strength of courage. Queen Sheba saw this in Solomon and bowed to connect. Don't denigrate grace. Life is all about it. Don't

look down on grace. Never! Good thing is, everybody has grace that someone else does not have. Don't die a village head, honour grace. The apostles acknowledged the grace in Paul. Don't turn your head looking elsewhere when you see grace, esteem it.

"...when they perceived the grace that was given unto me, James and Cephas and John, they who were reputed to be pillars, gave to me and Barnabas the right hands of fellowship..." Galatians 2:9.

2. Don't ignore age because you're graced. Normally anyone older than you must be honoured by you. Many older ones may not be that wise, but your part is to do what's proper. People consider their age a lot while with you. You need to always be conscious of this and give due respect. Very important! Paul told Timothy to see elderly women as mothers and men as fathers even though he's their pastor and probably had more anointing than them.

"Thou shalt rise up before the hoary head, and honour the face of the old man, and fear thy God: I am the LORD." Leviticus 19:32.

3. Never desecrate anybody's experience. Never ever! He may not have money or influence, but a veteran values his experience because it took his life time to earn. Many treat with a wave of hand others' experiences. No, you can get the best this way. In moving forward in life, always acknowledge others' track records and past dealings. Humans are funny. They tell you, 'Oh, let's forget the past.' As for you, always bear it in mind, if you want the best of anybody. If he has been there before you, no matter your accomplishment, anointing, position or grace, always acknowledge him for that. Apostle Paul consulted with Peter, John and James with his calling, revelations and ministry referring to them as, 'James, Cephas and John, those esteemed as pillars...'' Many of us will say, 'only God is my pillar.'

It costs nothing to acknowledge others and esteem them better than yourself, but you can be in a cubicle for life if you lack this concept.

"Salute Andronicus and Junia, my kinsmen, and my fellow-prisoners, who are of note among the apostles, who also were in Christ before me." Romans 16:11.

God bless and peace be unto you.

Chapter 71

Dynamics of Life and Ministry: Drive for Personal Gain (an Unknown Deep-seated Intent in Many)

"For the word of God is alive and active. Sharper than any double-edged sword, it penetrates even to dividing soul and spirit, joints and marrow; it judges the thoughts and attitudes of the heart. Nothing in all creation is hidden from God's sight. Everything is uncovered and laid bare before the eyes of him to whom we must give account." Hebrews 4:12-13.

We need to examine the reason we do what we do. Many run like the Bible-time Ahimaz who's not given any assignment but yet ran for nothing. It takes a one-on-one with God for any man to be truly naked. He is the true mirror that brings our true picture out.

Recently I ruminated a lot on the reason why we do what we do. I observed that many are running after personal gain of being known, popular, loved or financial gain while under the guise of Kingdom pursuit of any colour. Many also don't know that the dreams they're chasing are not of God. As good as the dream of wanting to be like one great man of God or singer may be, it may be down to personal gain and not God-inspired. Did you ever hear of anyone wanting to be John the Baptist or the stoned-to-death Stephen yet?

One great mark of the end time is that, "Men will become lovers of themselves, lovers of money, lovers of pleasure more than lovers of God", as Paul put it in 2Timothy 3.

Why do you want to write that book, bring out the album or build that church, do that programme, or even become a pastor? Ask yourself the sincere question and to thyself be true before God!

Things have really mixed up and the church is filled with loads of mixed multitudes that each of us has the responsibility of asking ourselves very truthful questions if we will truly walk with God and not be unnecessarily working for God (which is not His intention).

Posters everywhere. CDs everywhere. Church planting everywhere. Programmes everywhere. Dreams everywhere. Yet, fights, quarrels and malicious talks everywhere against others if things don't go according to plans.

"If you are wise and understand God's ways, prove it by living an honorable life, doing good works with the humility that comes from wisdom. But if you are bitterly jealous and there is selfish ambition in your heart, don't cover up the truth with boasting and lying. For jealousy and selfishness are not God's kind of wisdom. Such things are earthly, unspiritual, and demonic. For wherever there is jealousy and selfish ambition, there you will find disorder and evil of every kind. But the wisdom from above is first of all pure. It is also peace loving, gentle at all times, and willing to yield to others. It is full of mercy and good deeds. It shows no favouritism and is always sincere. And those who are peacemakers will plant seeds of peace and reap a harvest of righteousness." James 3:13-17.

God rewards what He wants us to do, but great waste before God are the resources used on drive for personal gain in the guise of Kingdom pursuit whether known to us or not.

Go back to the inner chamber to run some new checks. Run checks!

Peace be upon you!

Chapter 72

God Will Answer You on That Issue... Pray My Friend, Pray!

God loves to hear your voice. Whether you're feeling He's far from you or not. Feeling is not it. Just talk to Him now.

Rolling off that big trouble is just a prayer away from you.

When a child of God calls Him in prayers, He's attentive to their to them, to respond and give them peace!

God has seen the trouble before you did. It's been handled for you. Your prayers are to give permission to remit it off. Pray!

Don't play with prayers,no matter how short,it has power to detonate massive issues.

You can read many books on prayers and many teachings can be done on it,but that's not prayer yet. Prayer is done praying. Do it!

Every great grace carrier is a product of answered prayers. They carried great grace in Acts 4 after intense prayers.

What to say in the place of prayers is already in your heart. Don't be dismissive of yourself because of how somebody else prays. Pray your own telling God what bothers you.

Hannah may never have gotten a child if she's waiting for people to pray for her. Maybe many had even prayed for her before but to no avail until she prayed herself.

Separate yourself, go to God, pray for yourself and the issues will be solved quicker than you thought!

The challenge you're facing is not greater than God. Face God with it and pray your heart out. You will be heard, helped and healed! Go to Him.

The words you use in prayers are not as important as your heart. That's why an empty mouth but with a broken heart prostate before God will get the job done like Hannah!

I don't know how prayers work, but prayers work. Jesus prayed, the apostles prayed and I have also prayed many times and the problems were moved away. Pray!

God does reveal what you need to do in the place of prayers which He may not if you're not praying. Daniel prayed and God revealed the dream of the king and its interpretation to him. Pray.

I don't know what anybody can really become in Christ if he does not take prayers seriously. Jesus took it very seriously! Take it serious my friend!

Take some time out each day to really pray about you. Don't let things pile up.

If your work, marriage or academics seem to get in your way of prayers, just know Satan is already using them to siphon your strength. You will soon become too weak to face Satan in battles. There are battles of life my friend and you need to be strong in the Lord!

What will take God to happen most times will only take prayers. Pray!

In the place of fervent prayers of the righteous, tremendous power is made available.

Don't leave yourself defenceless, pray on every issue. Pray with all your heart out. Don't leave any stone unturned!

That issue is only waiting for your prayers. It will go. Pray. God will do it. Pray. You will rejoice and have testimony. Pray!

"Call unto me,I will answer you and show you great and mighty things you know not." Jeremiah 33:3.

May the Lord God almighty hear you as you call unto Him today and forever in Jesus name. Amen. Peace be upon you greatly henceforth. Your Faith will work. Your life will move forward. Your grace will be seen and your glory will arise this season in Jesus name. That sickness is killed in your body and your darkness is over in the name of Jesus. Receive your peace, glory and grace back in Jesus name. Amen. Amen. Amen. And Amen. Amen.

Praise the Lord!

Chapter 73

Fresh Revelation and Encounter with God

God will never discourage a willing person neither will He ever force an unwilling one, so, don't too!

The mother of all preparations is the one done to see and be with the Lord on the last day. Satanic subtlety has taken many people's attention off this. Many who were once born again with the urgency of heaven in their souls have now exchanged it for how their ministry, business or personal lives will grow. Strategically, Satan has blinded many with good deeds or progress they're making & have forgotten that "Nothing profits a man if he gains the whole world and loses his own soul". Let preparation for heaven be urgent and heavy over your soul. All these things shall end. "Men shall become lovers of themselves more than lovers of God", Apostle Paul said. "Because iniquity shall abound, the love of many shall wax cold", Jesus warned.

Was struck this morning about Moses and Joshua being told to remove their shoes as they're standing on holy grounds which they knew not.

God needs to bring us new awareness in our life and relationship with Him. Until then, we will be so perfect in our deeds almost un-correctable thinking we are in our best.

When you've not truly met with God or if you don't encounter Him from time to time, you could be making mouth about anything especially that you know Him and that your walk is great with Him. But then anytime you see Him again, you will fall to His feet and without strength again like John the Beloved in Revelations, Daniel and like Job who immediately started repenting in ashes or maybe like Isaiah who though had been prophesying many years and to many people before a new encounter with God said,

"In the year that King Uzziah died, I saw the Lord, high and exalted, seated on a throne; and the train of his robe filled the temple... "Woe to me!" I cried. "I am ruined! For I am a man of unclean lips, and I live among a people of unclean lips, and my eyes have seen the King, the Lord Almighty." Isaiah 6:1,5.

You will mellow and your words will be few when you encounter Him often because He will first reveal "yourself" to you! If you really get to know yourself in the light of His knowledge of you, you will plead for mercy nonstop till the end of age.

Pray this: Father, let me have a new encounter of you from now on in Jesus name. Amen.

Chapter 74

You Need God-based Relationships to Live

Don't force a relationship to happen. Be it marital, ministerial or just ordinary friendship or even family ties. Initiate appropriate momentum, but don't force.

No matter how vibrant or useful a relationship may be, it may expire divinely. Just be sensitive! Sometimes God may want you to be out that city, nation or circle because there's a new thing He's decided to do with you like Abraham. If you don't then step forward, you may be pushed out!

If you want God to take you higher, be very faithful in every relationship you find yourself as a friend, church member, pastor, worker, employee or what have you. If you're unfaithful, you're digging your grave.

Don't think evil, don't think evil, don't wait for evil to catch up with any one. Don't be Jonah, the prophet, the Christian, the friend that waits for evil revelations to come true. Pray for people with a bleeding heart no matter what brings them in the mess. Compassion!

There's no other way for God to test our heart and prove that He can rely on us for His use except through our private thoughts and public action or inaction in relation to the people, church, city and community He brings us in contact with.

If you're not going to be faithful to God and other human fellows wherever you find yourself, step out of the place. You will be judged over every contact you make with humans.

You must have relationship with other human fellows, you must have friends, you must have people around you. It is a must. Those are the people who attend to your tears and joys first. Life is too overwhelming not to have people who can carry your burdens with you and celebrate your testimonies.

Any friendship, church, city, or relationship where no one hurts no one is not for humans, by humans or from humans. As humans, we hurt ourselves, but

"faithful is the wounds of a friend than the kisses of an enemy", King Solomon said in Proverbs 27:6.

I have never been anywhere or accomplished anything that has not involved human agencies, especially people of my circle. I have hurt and have been hurt, but I have discovered that God shapes us into His image by those He surrounds us with.

"Open rebuke is better than secret love." Proverbs 27:5.

There is no one who will truly love you that never will rebuke you either sharply or correctional-wise. So, stop running away from stern people, churches, pastors or friends. It's for your future.

"Those whom I love I rebuke and discipline. So be earnest and repent", Jesus said in Revelations 3.

In regards to your spouse, friends, church, place of works and etc., God Himself is the one that rewards faithfulness. It's for His sake you must be faithful in relationship.

"A faithful man will abound with blessing." Proverbs 28:20.

It's not how people treat you that counts but how you treat people. Don't secretly try to bring your friends down because God will repay you accordingly in time.

"God who sees you in secret will reward you openly." Mathew 6:4.

God tests your heart with your relationship to His creation to know how He should deal with you.

"Blessed are the merciful for they shall obtain mercy." Mathew 5:7.

All humans rise or fall on their relationship to other humans.

Never get to a point where no human knows better than you where you're, because then you're already in a free fall. "Count others better than you", Apostle Paul Admonished.

Pray with those to be prayed with or for with your heart bleeding for an intervention from God. Rejoice greatly with those in triumph with all sincerity. Mourn with those who are broken hearted. "Owe no man nothing except to love."

Rush to help those in need. Never take your eyes off the broken hearted. Stand in the gap between God and man to see a divine exchange take place in time of need. God loves those who have a heart of compassion.

"If you can help your neighbour now, don't say, "Come back tomorrow, and then I'll help you." Proverbs 3:28.

It's your duty to size up the content of the human fellows, the church or pastor to whom you're in affinity or revolve around. Eve lost Adam's authority by relationship with serpent. One key ingredient of a helpful companion is "Fear of God".

"He that walks with the wise will be wise, but companions of fools shall be destroyed."

God will bring people around you to whom you must be committed. One great sign that somebody is sent of God to be your friend, spouse, pastor or business/ministry partner is "unwavering fear of God". Jehoshaphat lost many things because of his relationship with kings who treated God and His prophets as a joke.

I pray God to send you more of godly companions in all areas of your life & to deliver you from relationship with people, church, organisation & places that have become a trap & snare around your life in Jesus name. Amen.

Peace!

Chapter 75

God Talks to All of Us

"For God does speak—now one way, now another—though no one perceives it. In a dream, in a vision of the night, when deep sleep falls on people as they slumber in their beds, he may speak in their ears and terrify them with warnings, to turn them from wrongdoing and keep them from pride, to preserve them from the pit,their lives from perishing by the sword." Job 33:14:18.

Dreams, visions and revelations are ways God talks to us. Satan and flesh could use them too, but God speaks to us all through them. You might end up in very big problems if you always treat them with levity.

No matter how dreams, visions and revelations come to you, maybe through others or even Satan and Flesh, some actions must always be taken each time. Very important! Never ever deride them no matter how they come to you, just take appropriate actions. Some to be rejected, some to ponder upon and some to be prepared for, but none to be joked with. Pray over them all the time! Very important!

God can speak to or with anybody (believers and non-believers alike) or through them. Abraham, Isaac, Jacob, Pharaoh, Joseph, Paul and etc. all had them. God can speak in the dreams to an unbeliever to give you a message. He can use anything or anybody. I had accurate dreams that guided my life even as an unbeliever.

One of the easiest ways for God to get to all humans is by the dreams of the night when our body rests from most struggles of life. Take your dream life seriously. God talks loudly through them. Don't shut people down from giving you dreams; you may be shutting your life down by doing so. No matter how terrible or flippant, listen up first my friend! If God could speak through Balaam's donkey, He does speak to you and through you too, especially through dreams.

Some people may be as stern as Herod, but never keep the dreams you have of somebody without telling them. Somebody's whole life might depend entirely on it. Serious! Tell them! You may never forgive yourself if something serious goes wrong with a person to whom you've been sent in the dream if you never warned them. Speak out.

Cultivate a very clean atmosphere spiritually before you sleep by means of prayers and holy living so your dreams may be sharp and uncorrupted at night. Many wonderful things are revealed in the night. Very true! Many strong prophetic ministries start with dreams. No dream is mere. All dreams are coded communications. Taking over the reign of Egypt and making Jesus escape the terror of Herod; fulfilling the prophecy of Him being brought from Egypt started with dreams to Joseph of Old Testament and the one of the new testament.

If there are clogs in the way of your dream life, you can fast to subdue the fleshly activities and repent of all sins, humble yourself again before God. Then, in no time clear channel will be activated again. You can always clean up the valve! Yes, you can!

Dreams are not to terrify us but to sensitise or sanitise us. God reveals to redeem. God is good! It is not unusual to come out of dreams sometime shivering and terrified, but put yourself together on God's word and go back to God.

When there are no dreams, visions and revelations to you again, not even from anyone around you, you may be in some spiritual dark time. Pray through it my friend. God is good!

Your often dreams point in the direction or situation of your life. Pray it through my friend. God is for you! You cannot change the dreams you keep having about a fellow, situation or place until the spiritual circumstances over such change! This is very Serious!

To many people, every bad dream is from Satan and all good ones are from God. Not true! You always need diligent proving of each accordingly! Don't give dreams time to either not come true or come true. Pray them through; diligent praying my friend. Never wish a dream away! Bad dreams may become realities very speedily and good ones may never see the light of life if you don't go to God very quickly and often times over them. He rewards diligent seekers. Don't keep quiet!

In any case at any time of life, never play down any dream. Deal with it wholly until you have rest in your spirit. Amen.

I see God activating you again and more clearly in the place of dreams, visions and revelations in Jesus name. Amen.

*** Word from Mirella...

*** How desperately we need the Holy Spirit, the sevenfold Spirit of the LORD: the Spirit of wisdom and understanding, the Spirit of counsel and might, the Spirit of knowledge and of the fear of the LORD (Isaiah 11:1).

That's should be the core of our cry unto the LORD: *"...how much shall the Father give the Holy Spirit to them that ask Him?"* (Luke 11:13). Beloved, this is our Need, day after day!

What's wisdom? It begins with the fear of the LORD (*"The fear of the LORD is to hate evil: pride, and arrogancy, and the evil way, and the froward mouth, do I[Wisdom] hate."* - Proverbs 8:13). What's understanding? It's the knowledge of the holy (that is, to depart from evil (Job 28:28)). All this mentioned is of and is the Holy Spirit. Thus, the deepest need to receive Him.

Ask such of the LORD this day for Proverbs 2:6(KJV) declares, *"For the LORD giveth wisdom: out of his mouth cometh knowledge and understanding."*

"Fill us, o LORD God, with Your Spirit and power!"

The true route of and to the fear of the LORD, holiness, wisdom, understanding, knowledge, counsel and might is the HOLY SPIRIT.

Shalom! ***

Chapter 76

Looking Beyond the Errors

No matter what happens in the process of time, never ever lose sight of the real personality you've known of the erring fellow.

Maybe your spouse is obstinate now, your pastor is distant from you, your friend has disappointed you, your parents have hurt you ever so deeply, your business or ministry partners, associates or caucus members are in variance with you or maybe now you've met new people, found new love or enjoying the fellowship of a new church, pastor or lover or a new companion and you're basing your decision on an event of pain or a bad twist in the turn of event. That's a bad decision. Reflect back of who the person was to you, did to you, what they brought to you and the care they gave to you when you first knew them.

Jesus went back to Peter and other apostles even after they deserted Him, reneged on their commitments and started out on a wrong track. He came to them to restore them even preparing food for them because He knew their heart. He knew they loved Him.

"Jesus saith unto them, Come and dine. And none of the disciples durst ask him, Who art thou? knowing that it was the Lord. Jesus then cometh, and taketh bread, and giveth them, and fish likewise." John 21:12-13.

The future could be difficult for a fellow who throws out the baby with the dirty water.

There are many people we've thrown away because of the pain they caused us unintentionally at crucial times whom God still counts as part of our destiny. Just imagine Jesus saying 'bye' to His disciples for letting Him down at the most needed time of His life on earth. How could they have become who they're? There might not have been the Acts of the Apostles. But He knew they could falter and told them so before they did and He already prepared a plan of restoration.

Making a plan of restoration for people even before they falter o fail you is a way to live for all kingdom champions!

Many of those you've neglected are dying to hold your hands again. Your church objected to your marriage, your pastor refused to release you properly when you needed to move, your friends called others to deny you of that acutely needed favour...it might have been done in love to keep you because you meant so much to them. Don't for some unpleasant turns push away those God puts there as building blocks for your glorious future.

Mistakes do happen and they have to happen. Reach out again and be ravished in the love, care, counsels and kindness you both enjoyed beforehand. Reach out to your pastor again. Reach out to your leaders again. Reach out to your friends again. Although Paul rejected Mark for being a lazy missionary before but a turning point came when he said,

"Only Luke is with me. Take Mark, and **bring him with thee: for he is profitable to me for the ministry.**"2 Timothy 4:11.

Though your spouse was once unfaithful and was chased out, but remember what actually brought you together before and the genuine time shared together. Hurts happen. Bad times happen. Errors and blunders occur, but people do truly repent like Peter and need to be restored. Reach out again dearly beloved!

"Wherefore lift up the hands which hang down, and the feeble knees; and make straight paths for your feet, lest that which is lame be turned out of the way; but let it rather be healed." Hebrews 12:12-13.

Blessed day ahead.

Love you!

Chapter 77

Eternity in Heaven

One great error you can make on the case of where to spend eternity is to stay stuck to just one pastor, church or ministry's visions, revelations or doctrines without checking thoroughly with the Bible and others who have something to say about it.

"Now the Berean Jews were of more noble character than those in Thessalonica, for they received the message with great eagerness and examined the Scriptures every day to see if what Paul said was true." Acts 17:11.

Major reason a lot will be surprised at the gates of eternity is that they've not searched the bible thoroughly on what they've been taught or never allowed others' teachings to instruct them.

Going to heaven requires an uphill diligence. My heart bleeds when I look at many Christians who have believed wrong or watered-down gospel and are delusional just because their church is large or their pastor is very powerful. Ah! Many powerful pastors with large congregations are already in hell while some will soon join them.

Don't dance to hell with social pastors and churches where just anything goes in the name of winning the world for Christ by socialising. Neither should you be under all bondages of super spiritual pastors and churches who for reasons of heaven hate other folks around and live life of a recluse; always bringing one confusing error or the other. Just search the word, listen to sound- teachings that bother on the things above and not the ephemeral ventures of the motivational greed, then stand on the truth, the word and well established route to the kingdom. I search daily as a folk who has not fully comprehended but who doesn't want to end up in hell for unreasonable errors.

You need to search the bible and listen to others very diligently and carefully to make it. This is a very serious matter my friend.

"And beside this, giving all diligence, add to your faith virtue; and to virtue knowledge;And to knowledge temperance; and to temperance patience; and to patience godliness;And to godliness brotherly kindness; and to brotherly kindness charity. For if these things be in you, and abound, they make you that ye shall neither be barren nor unfruitful in the knowledge of our Lord Jesus Christ." 2 Peter 1:5-8.

Love you.

Chapter 78

Discerning God

There are so many things done these days that folks put the name of God on which God doesn't have anything to do with. Very serious matter! "God spoke to me: God asked me to marry her, God made me do the album, God told me to move to America, God told me to do that business, God told me to break out of that church (and also go with the members?), God started this church and etc." We are so confused that we don't know God's voice different from ignorance, greed and flesh any more.

This generation is so confused. And the world just laughs at everything. Everybody says God says when God never says nothing most of the time. You need to die to the flesh (ambition, strife and greed) to recognise the voice of God. It's not a common commodity. Although God is near but not common. No!

"The LORD said, "Go out and stand on the mountain in the presence of the LORD, for the LORD is about to pass by." Then a great and powerful wind tore the mountains apart and shattered the rocks before the LORD, but the LORD was not in the wind. After the wind there was an earthquake, but the LORD was not in the earthquake. After the earthquake came a fire, but the LORD was not in the fire. And after the fire came a gentle whisper (a still small voice). 1 Kings 19:11-12.

Chapter 79

Open Your Heart

Why should anybody be afraid to share what dream, vision or revelation seen with you that concerns you? No matter how close you might be to God, there's still something you don't know yet (negative or positive) that He might bring to your attention via another vessel (of any level). Nobody ever yet boxed God, not even the prophets of old. Open your mind to other streams so grave may not be open to you too soon.

Prophet Elisha said, "Leave her alone! She is in bitter distress, but the LORD has hidden it from me and has not told me why." 2Kings 4:27.

If you believe you've relationship with God, then go to Him to sort out things or ask him questions if the thing seen is negative. You may have an uncovered area of life unawares. Or maybe you've recently dipped in form or slipped downward without noticing! Stuff happens. Achan could snick into the camp unawares to Joshua.

"Examine yourselves, whether you are in the faith; prove your own selves. Know you not your own selves, how that Jesus Christ is in you, unless you are counterfeits?" 2 Corinthians 3:5.

*** Word from Mirella...

*** Beloved ones in Christ,

How pertinent is it for us to bear and be the Voice of the LORD! Lo, His voice carries power and authority; Hebrews 1:3 says, "Who [Jesus Christ] being the brightness of his glory, and the express image of his person, AND UPHOLDING ALL THINGS BY THE WORD OF HIS POWER, when he had by himself purged our sins, sat down on the right hand of the Majesty on high:"

What does it mean to be and have the voice of God?

It means to bear witness of what He bears at and in heart! John the Baptist, speaking of his divine mandate, said: *"I am the VOICE of one crying in the wilderness, 'make straight the way of the LORD'..."* (John 1:23).

Thus, to declare the voice for the LORD, you must be a sent one...not necessarily an apostle! To be a sent one signifies that the One that sent you gave you a MESSAGE to declare unto the people you are sent to (simply, being a messenger). Meaning? The message given unto the sent one carries the power and authority of the Person that sent him/her!

Beloved, let's put aside every form of uncleanliness, let the coal of heavenly living fire touch our lips of clay and earthen vessels and set us on the course of being God's messengers.

Remember, when Isaiah encountered the LORD of hosts, he perceived how unclean and unworthy he was - and then - was PURGED of uncleanliness and, finally, SENT of the LORD, upon heeding the call (see Isaiah 6).

The same applied unto Jeremiah: the LORD put His words in Jeremiah's mouth, when sent unto the house of Israel (Jeremiah 1:9).

The reason why most of supposed God-given words... prophecies don't carry power and, thus, don't materialize is because they aren't from God! God doesn't perform what He doesn't say. He is the One to declare and perform His word... not men declaring what He ought to perform and expecting Him to do so. That will never happen.

Beloved, be a sent one! John 3:34 says, *"For he whom God hath sent speaketh the words of God: for God giveth not the Spirit by measure unto him."*

Praise the LORD! It's so a privilege and honour to be a voice for the LORD upon the earth. See how excellent and majestic is the voice of the King of glory: Psalm 29:3-9 says,

"3 The voice of the Lord is upon the waters: the God of glory thundereth: the Lord is upon many waters.

4 THE VOICE OF THE LORD IS POWERFUL; THE VOICE OF THE LORD IS FULL OF MAJESTY.

5 THE VOICE OF THE LORD BREAKETH THE CEDARS; YEA, THE LORD BREAKETH THE CEDARS OF LEBANON.

6 He maketh them also to skip like a calf; Lebanon and Sirion like a young unicorn.

7 THE VOICE OF THE LORD DIVIDETH THE FLAMES OF FIRE.

8 THE VOICE OF THE LORD SHAKETH THE WILDERNESS; THE LORD SHAKETH THE WILDERNESS OF KADESH.

9 THE VOICE OF THE LORD MAKETH THE HINDS TO CALVE, AND DISCOVERETH THE FORESTS: AND IN HIS TEMPLE DOTH EVERY ONE SPEAK OF HIS GLORY."

Be a Voice, not an echo!

Shalom! ***

Chapter 80

The Church in the Wilderness

There's a great gap, a gulf, between the revelation of purpose and the manifestation of its reality. In this gap, you will have "the church in the wilderness" and "the tabernacle of witness in the wilderness" Acts 7:38;44. Meaning, a time of real test, a time of nothingness, a time of heart-deep trouble, neglect and rejection. Real limitations. This may be marital, ministerial, material, immigrational or otherwise. Anybody can talk to you or deal with you as they deem fit while in this process. It's a time people cry like Jesus, "Father, why hast thou forsaken me?"

Only a handful of people get out of this still totally ready for the next stage. It's not a child's play, God proves people before He approves them. He will use anything and everything.

"Yea, and all that will live godly in Christ Jesus shall suffer persecution (ridicule or what have you)." 2 Timothy 3:12.

Nobody has immunity from this. Nobody, not even you! There's a time for this in every great purpose and move of God. Abraham had it and Jesus did not escape it. Maybe you're in it already. It's a season of God's silence! Church in the wilderness!

Three factors that contribute to the wilderness experience...

1. God does initiate it. He led Israelites into it. Jesus was led into the wilderness to be tempted by Satan.

"Then was Jesus led up of the Spirit into the wilderness to be tempted of the devil." Matthew 4:1.

2. Humans can initiate and or elongate it by means of sins, disobedience and rebellion to God. All led by Moses from Egypt including Moses himself died in the wilderness except Joshua and Caleb. That's not God's plan but human factor. It can happen to anybody except we examine ourselves critically moment by moment.

"God setteth the solitary in families: he bringeth out those which are bound with chains: but the rebellious dwell in a dry land." Psalm 68:6.

3. Satan can orchestrate it. He is the master planner of frustration and limitations. He likes to cage and humiliate God's purpose or plan over people.

The way of Escape

Only God remains the way of escape from whatever He brings on you, you bring on yourself or Satan attacks you with. Humble yourself before God, repent of any stain on your garment, re-commit yourself to eternity and His eternal plan, then pray all manners of prayers at all times without ceasing asking for mercy and strength. Ask Him to step in. Plead profusely for His mercies and reject vehemently any short-cut Satan brings to you. Don't turn stone to bread. Don't indulge in sex to be married. Don't go diabolical for breakthrough. Just face God like Joseph, Job, David and Daniel.

"If my people, which are called by my name, shall humble themselves, and pray, and seek my face, and turn from their wicked ways; then will I hear from heaven, and will forgive their sin, and will heal their land." 2 Chronicles 7:14.

Keep at God with all you've got and you will get Him. Sure!

"Whoever shall call on the name of the Lord shall be saved." Acts 2:21

Chapter 81

Marriage 101

Who you're recklessly pursuing without restraint for marriage may have an undisclosed and or undiscovered defect that you're not built to handle in life! Stay under deep word-based prayers and submit to 100% will of God to discover what God wants. Romans 12:1-2.

Who you call trash and loathe may turn out to be a heap of treasure a little while after you exited! Naomi and family left Israel before they discovered that's where they'd be.

"We walk by faith and not by sight". 2 Corinthians 5:7.

Tame your senses with the word!

What you fall for as great treasure may become a heap of rubbish in the nearest future! Lot chose the well-watered land before realising that's where he'd lose all he ever had, including dignity -Sodom and Gomorra!

"The things seen are temporal while the unseen are eternal". 2 Corinthians 4:18.

You cannot give God your list and expect Him to follow you. He had a list before you're born. Ask Him for His.

"Before you're formed in the womb of your mother, I knew thee and ordained you as..." Jeremiah 1:5.

Find out what He ordained; don't give Him list. He had a plan before your birth!

You're already in a deep romance and sex with somebody even if he/she is already married and you're asking God for His will to be done in your marital life or to show you who you should marry! Eh? Please, don't let me talk!

"Do not be deceived God is not mocked, whatever a man sows, he reaps." Galatians 6:7.

You're going to his house to sleep overnight even though you're not yet married and you're praying, "Oh Father, take control tonight and let me not fall into temptation"! You yourself you're the TEMPTATION of the highest order. Anyway, don't abort once you're pregnant and don't blame God once you're infected!

You know how you got into marriage...how formication led to your settling down even though you're a professing believer that time, but now you're a father of faith or mother in Israel when your children start their own like Solomon multiplied David's weakness. You need to sit down with your wards instead of shouting and battering. Let them know you sinned and reaped its consequences. Pray together with them and uproot the trends. Shouting doesn't remove a systemic trend and time does not terminate it...it only hides it for a period. Your children are you! Eh?

If you're a true child of God and anybody engages or marries you even it's for three months, something different must have happened to such no matter what level of wickedness is upon his/her shoulder! Saul prophesied in the camp of Samuel!

"Oh baby, I love you...I miss you...I need you here right now"... If these are only things you hear from him after a period of being with him and your spiritual, mental and physical life has not improved, leave him otherwise you will soon be nursing a baby alone without a husband. He's probably saying the same thing to many girls at the same time!

If he/she doesn't have respect for your parents, you might soon become a punching bag for him or a baby sitter husband (as she jumps from one outing to another)!

If all you have as foundation to get into marriage is the lovy-dovy feeling or the love of the physical beauty or liking, you're not going to last!

If who you love to marry is somebody who appeals to you and attracts you 100% of the time, no flaws. First, you have issues with lust. Second, you're looking for an angel.3rd, they only live in heaven or spirit realm. Lastly, if such lives with you in the house, that's a fallen Angel-Nightmares!

He/she is so sexually appealing and socially relevant, so you must marry such by every means. You think those are lasting factors? He would soon eat very well and looks exactly the way his father is and she will soon have to cope with children forgetting early morning fix ups!

The foundation of real, durable and excelling marriage is God and His will alone. All else soon fade into insignificance! Praise the Lord!

He/she may or may not have all in your list, but must be Born-Again, God-fearing, zealously committed to God-things, the church and must not be lazy at life! If these exist in him/her, others are latent on the inside!

If all he/she wants anytime you meet is kiss or touch, that's a porn star. Go back and ask God for another fellow. Life is more important than such frivolities!

You're not married yet but sex has been involved? Eh? God has moved out! The relationship can stop at any time and just about anything can happen except you both truly and thoroughly repent before the Lord!

Laziness is as addictive and destructive as any other substance abuse. Don't marry the lazy! Such is a lifetime dreamer without any action!

May God Himself guide your life in Jesus name. Amen.

Peace!

*** Word from Mirella...

*** Seeking FIRST the kingdom of God and His righteousness (Matthew 6:33) can't be the topmost priority of a believer with a natural/carnal mind. This latter is crowned with self and crowded with all self-related issues, ambitions and goals.

It is written, let this mind be in you as was in Christ (Philippians 2:5). That mind enabled Christ Jesus to bear the crown of thorns and, consequently, the crown of glory (Philippians 2:6-11), according to the divine will of God. This mind is selfless; this kind of mind is wherein the LORD works both to will and to do, according to His good pleasure - that is the same mind bore by a soul that works out his/her salvation with fear and trembling.

There's thus a need for the mind of Christ at work in us for the carnal mind can't discern the will of God nor work out his/her salvation effectively, not to speak of receiving the crown of righteousness - at Christ's appearing, after all said and done. ***

*** The plan of Salvation is to raise a CHOSEN generation, a ROYAL priesthood, a HOLY nation, God's own people, whom He has brought out of darkness into His marvellous light.

Beloved ones in Christ, there's no guarantee of tomorrow. Thus, live for and in God. The LORD God bears eternity in His very hands... He was before the beginning and the end!

Let's humble ourselves and retrace our steps to the place of repentance and holiness. Shalom!" ***

*** "Poverty is one of the two possible destinations of the long journey of life, stride by stride...thus, travel wisely." ***

Chapter 82

Revival Starts with Just One Person

Revival doesn't need many people to start. It starts from one person; one person who's repentant, who cries to God, who wants God to move, who refuses to be comforted, complacent or compliant with what everybody around rejoices over: One person who will stop at nothing "until the spirit be poured on us", one persons who weeps until God moves!

"Until the spirit be poured upon us from on high, and the wilderness be a fruitful field, and the fruitful field be counted for a forest." Isaiah 32:15.

One person like Enoch, one Person like Elijah, One person like Nehemiah, one person like Deborah. "I, Deborah, arose as a mother in Israel." One person like Habakkuk, one person like Paul.

Another W.F. Kumuyi. Another E.A. Adeboye. Another Benny Hinn. Another Smith Wigglesworth. Another one of a rare kind!

ONE PERSON who refuses to let go, be normal or follow the flow. One person who himself becomes the flow. One person who's tired of ceremonial church. One person who's tired of the coldness all over. Just one person.

ONE PERSON in a community, in a generation, in a nation, in a state, in a church, in a college, on campus, in a university, in a company.

ONE PERSON moved by God. One person who says "here I am". ONE PERSON...Are you the one?

"Lord, I have heard of your fame; I stand in awe of your deeds, Lord. Repeat them in our day, in our time make them known; in wrath remember mercy." Habakkuk 3:2.

May you that one person today in Jesus name. Amen.

Chapter 83

Want God-given All-round Fulfilment and Greatness in Life?

It's not much of the inspiration or prophecy but trust in God and undying perspiration.

Many are oftentimes inspired or have prophecies over their lives but never really come to fruition. If life were to be by prophecies alone, then every Jewish man will be a super success as a result of prophecies innumerable even directly from the mouth of God on them. But alas, life is beyond that.

Some book I once read many years ago put success like this: 10% inspiration and 90% perspiration.

Are you always down that prophecies don't favour you and you don't have the inspirations talked about by the high-sounding spiritual brothers and sisters? What you may not know is that nobody ever became a giant in any field by prophecies alone. As a matter of fact, there are many people who don't know whether prophecies or prophets exist and have made good of their lives by perspiration (unflinching dedication and diligence).

Impossible is a thing of the mind. If you have possibilities in your heart, don't sit down for people to dump on you notions, dreams and prophecies of impossibility. If you can say "No" in your heart in agreement with God, then nothing changes that.

"If you have faith as a grain of mustard seed and say this mountain [or mulberry tree], be removed and cast into the sea and you do not doubt in your heart, it shall be so", Jesus said in Mathew 17:20 and Luke 17:6.

How can you have possibility internally and submit to impossibility externally? Nothing is greater than the power of a highly internalised faith expressed in all things. God is good.

I grew up with some folks who kept talking of the foreign land where God was going to use them powerfully according to prophetic dreams they've had. I didn't have such prophecies but believed greatly in "go ye into the world and preach the gospel". So I only always prayed to God, then went out to preach to others. It didn't take more than five years of that before the door of many nations began to open.

What many people don't know is that "the more sure word of prophecy"- the word of God already favours you.

I have seen brothers who married who everybody prophesied to be impossible just because they stayed put on persistence. When I first moved to Ireland, I had not less than 20 dreams and prophecies from others of deportation, but that's a thing of the past now. You can determine to refuse evil dreams and prophecies. You can look a mountain in the face and reject it. The word of God is your prophecy.

How could you neglect God's word and start searching for high-sounding prophets and prophecies around? Sheer ignorance.

Ask many great ones in God, they will tell you, "it's a walk of faith, a fight of faith on daily basis".

Almost everyone who said to me, "You can't have that or you won't get there. I had a dream about it", was proved wrong by means of importunate stay on God who hates to see us cry.

I don't know what bad dreams you're having or they have for you, they won't come to pass. Are you facing strong resistance in the place of academics, marriage, ministry, finance or immigration? Just stand in God and fight the good fight of faith...you will win because you've won. Faith (determination that you won't bow out) is your victory.

"Whatever is born of God overcometh the world (all spiritual & physical obstacles) ; and this is the victory that overcome the world, even our faith." 1 John 5:4.

Amen.

*** Word from Mirella...

*** It's time to alight from those heightened unfounded revelations and return to basics, people of God. In the innermost chambers of your heart, you so know that those mere confessions aren't changing a comma of your present state...thus, it's time to reconsider and be repositioned.

The greatest undoing of believers is living in sin (which is, holiness in their sight but false in God's eyes) and concomitantly expecting the best from the LORD. What a mentality! The kingdom of God is founded on clear and unwavering eternal principles and only those that align unto such shall eat the good thereof.

Proverbs 16:6 says, "by MERCY and TRUTH iniquity is purged: and by the fear of the LORD men depart from evil". How clearer can His Word be?

People of God, the fear of God brings genuine repentance; and genuine repentance means to depart from evil. Genuine repentance comes by, and is as a result of, mercy and truth. Isn't written, "let's therefore come boldly unto the throne of grace, that we may obtain MERCY, and find GRACE to help in time of need"? What does that mean?

Genuine repentance and subsequent uprightness is birthed by mercy and grace: mercy forgives and grace gives truth, to help you walk before the LORD (that is, to be separated unto the LORD). John 1:17b says,"...*grace and truth came by Jesus Christ*". Praise God. Jesus said, praying unto the Father before His death, "*SANCTIFY them through thy truth: THY WORD IS TRUTH. As thou hast sent me into the world, even so have I also sent them into the world. And for their sakes I sanctify myself, that they also might be sanctified through the truth. Neither pray I for these alone, but for them also which shall believe on me through their word*" (John 17:17-20).

Thus, grace is received through the Word, which is the truth: "*If ye continue in my word, Jesus speaking, then are ye my disciples indeed; and ye shall know the truth, and the truth shall make you free*" (John 8:31-32). However, you have to continue in the Word, before you can experience the freedom in Christ.

So, drop those man-made definitions of grace for they can't connect you indeed with the Giver of grace! The law doesn't set free, only the Truth can! The truth is greater than the law (for the Truth made the law!) because it endues a man with divine power to do even beyond the marked and discrete commandments, for Jesus said," think not that I am become to destroy the law, or the prophets: I am not come to destroy, but to FULFILL. For verily I say unto you, Till heaven and earth pass, one jot or one tittle shall no wise pass from the law, till all be fulfilled"(Matthew 5:17-18). Romans 8:3 declares, "for what the law could not do, in that it was weak through the flesh, God sending his own Son in the likeness of sinful flesh, and for sin, condemned sin in the flesh: that the righteousness of the law might be FULFILLED in us, who walk not after the flesh, but after the Spirit".

Thus, the Truth is [in] the Word: righteousness is fulfilled in us by the price paid by Jesus Christ for mankind (that is, the condemnation of sin in the flesh for our sake), even unto as many as receive Him and walk in the Spirit (and according to His Word) - see John 1:12. Seek the truth by the Spirit and ye shall find it (see Proverbs 20:27).

Beloved, it's written, *"wherewithal shall a young man cleanse his way? By taking heed thereto according to thy word"; "Thy word have I hid in my heart, that I might not sin against thee"* (Psalm 119:9,11).

...and Jesus said, *"I am the way, the TRUTH, and the life: no man cometh unto the Father, except by me"*.

Further reading: Proverbs 8.

Shalom! ***

Chapter 84

Think Again!

I need to say this: You find it very easy to sleep over at the guy's house and do stuffs that all nonbelievers do(everything). The only excuse is: we're in a relationship and my parents want me to finish my degree or I want start working before getting married. What you don't know is that, with the trend you're in, you're married already joined by Satan in the synagogue of immorality. You're married and God is out of the whole show, left out and busy with someone else who needs Him. In your being the choir leader, prayer warrior or youth executive or in the ushering unit at this period, you're indirectly working for the enemy oozing out the spirit of lusts on all you're in contact with in the church, especially those of weaker faith or spirit within the body.

"... I have this against you: You tolerate that woman Jezebel, who calls herself a prophet. By her teaching she misleads my servants into sexual immorality ..."Rev 2:20.

Meanwhile, when you now think you're finally ready to marry getting to do so called "Introduction", "Traditional marriage/ engagement" and "Church or Court wedding", changing into different clothing articles like chameleons, you're just involved in practically empty ceremonies full of the words of men, orgies, revelling, superficial excitement, waste of money, time and resources without the blessing of God the only true "Father", because you've lost Him a long time ago just like the parents of Jesus who embarked on journey with Him left back without any knowledge they didn't have Him with them.

"And he said unto them, Ye are they which justify yourselves before men; but God knoweth your hearts: for that which is highly esteemed among men is abomination in the sight of God. And He told them: "You are the ones who justify yourselves in the sight of others, but God knows your hearts." Luke 16:15.

The generation we are in have more joy in what physical trends dictate and what mortal man says than what the word of God stands for. If you're happy enough to start sleeping over in his house, then you're ready for marriage. But are you not a derelict to be at peace to continue to sleep in a man or boy's house, have sex with him but continue to claim you're not ready for marriage?

If you're not ready for marriage, you don't need a relationship or sleeping over in a guy's house, let alone have sex or sex-related activities.

This is where a lot of youths sell out their calling, anointing, future, ministry, move of God over their lives and destiny only to hopelessly search for it later with no reality of it anymore. Then they continue the curse or the lifestyle of their parents they once frowned at.

"See that no one is sexually immoral, or is godless like Esau, who for a single meal sold his inheritance rights as the oldest son. Afterward, as you know, when he wanted to inherit this blessing, he was rejected. Even though he sought the blessing with tears, he could not change what he had done." Hebrews 12:16-17.

As a young man who left Islam for Christianity years ago, if what I see in the church today especially among the youths and also the "I don't-care/cold/ just-come-to- church- attitude" of the pastors today are what I saw then, I would have been long discouraged. Truly, we are in the end of the end time when traditions of men and church membership have precedence over righteousness and peace with God.

Just imagine, what will the next generation look like? Prostitutes even on the pulpits telling others, "God is love"!

Chapter 85

3 Things You Need to Give Attention to if God Must Bless or Use You

1. Prayers (often with fasting of different sorts). "We will give ourselves continually to prayers..." Acts 6:4.

2. Study of God's word (not once off but consistent intake via various forms of it)." We will give ourselves to...and the ministry of the word." Acts 6:4.

3. Outreaching with what you know or have (not being a dam but a flowing river). God only goes with go-ers and not idlers) - "Then the disciples went out and preached everywhere, and the Lord worked with them and confirmed his word by the signs that accompanied it." Mark 16:20.

Chapter 86

Who is a False Prophet or a False Christian?

"Many false prophets will arise to deceive many...", Jesus warned in Mathew 24:11.

If many false prophets, false christs will arise, many of them may be false christians first. There are false Christians as much as there are false prophets and false christs.

Although the word "many" is massive, but that's not my concern for today.

I see many people tagging even well-meaning servants of God false, not because they're sent of Satan, but for other reasons: because the word "false" simply means "not genuine, not real or fake".

Therefore, there's a thin line between being a true servant of God (true Christian) and a false one, especially for those who think they've genuinely come to the Lord. This line must be watched very carefully. If not watched, you will have a tag you don't think you should wear and also be on your way to eternal damnation, bearing the blood of many who have been misled on your hands unknown to you.

In dealing with this subject a few years ago in a bible study, we came to this understanding that false prophets are either: 1. Those directly sent of the devil or 2. Those who have of a truth come to the Lord, but now involved in Christian sharp practices or malpractices. "Not everyone who says to me "Lord, Lord" shall enter the kingdom of my Father. Many will say to me in that day, "I cast out demons in your name, prophesied in your name and in your name did many miracles", but I will say, "depart from Me you who work iniquities, I know you not." Mathew 7:21-22.

I know a lot of well-intentioned servants of God or Christians who have towed this line. Many of us have had our hands at some time soiled in so much as to give the enemies the chance to drag the glorious names of God in mud and got Him blasphemed bitterly.

"He that does righteousness is righteous... He that commits sin is of the devil..." 1 John 3:7,8.

I know many who are born again Christians or pastors all over the world that have asked people to abort pregnancy, duped them, falsely promised to marry folks and ran away, had immoral affairs with them and absconded with people or company's funds or got involved with other unreadable acts with people who will call telling of their experiences. Loads of these people were born again but got involved in issues beyond the reach of Christian integrity.

When you list the characteristics of false prophets, many of the vices mentioned above will be there.

Many of the people talked about here have these continued habits un-repented of. Which other name befits such than "false prophets", even if it were Peter or Paul the Apostle?

Some people's problem is that they are under the teachings of those who use grace to cover up for unrighteous living. The works of the flesh are clearly listed by Paul in Galatians 5:19 downwards. Grace does not cover anyone who makes a habit of any of them. If a prophet or a Christian falls into a sin or any unrighteous act, but instead of repenting and moving out of it, teaches either with his habit of continuity in such or in its communication which misleads others that such doesn't matter, let it be known unto such fellow that: "All unrighteousness is sin", Paul said.

"Can we continue in sin and want grace to abound? God forbids!", Paul argued in Romans 6:1-2.

Masturbation is a sin. If you do it and teach others by any means, you're false. We sometime slip into spiritual slumber and fall in errors, but we're not false yet if we cry out to God and also let others know we've erred.

I have encountered many who have fallen headlong and teach glorious messages that make people relax as if nothing is amiss. They're false Christians or prophets. They make people double children of hell. They mislead innocent people.

I have erred many times. I have been in bad situations not befitting a child of God, but I will own up and move out, up and on. What a glorious walk will it have been for me never to have erred ever since my conversion 24yrs ago from Islam? But many times the angels must have covered their faces in shame looking at me wallowing in dirty mud like Samson or David of old, but to teach others that nothing was wrong by any means is to be considered a false Christian, a false prophet. Sin is sin and has no other name.

Some with wrong teaching will say, "It's my flesh and not my spirit", "Where sin abounds, the grace of God abounds much more". They're warped, false and in spiritual slumber...maybe to only wake up in hell. God forbid!

The Christian girls who dress to seduce or put themselves out to act as Delilah are false Christians. False Christians and false prophets are at the same level and in the same group as they both mislead people. They profess to be something else whereas they mislead people.

"Examine yourselves, whether ye be in the faith; prove your own selves. Know ye not your own selves, how that Jesus Christ is in you, except ye be reprobates?", Paul said in 2 Corinthians 13:5.

But the good news is if Bar-Jesus, called the great power of God in Samaria, could repent at the preaching of Philip the evangelist, the false Christians and prophets lured into falsehood by means of sins that crept in unawares by the satanic beguiling CAN REPENT, make amends, return to the Lord, turn a new leaf and lead a righteous life following the Lord all the way to eternity again.

"Let him that steals steal no more, rather let him work with his hands..." Paul admonished in Ephesians 4:28.

The thin line must be watched. "Watch and pray", Jesus said.

"He who does righteousness is righteous."

This generation needs to be taught that watchfulness of each step we take is not childish nor a child's play. The greatest message or mission work so far is to preach to thyself o preacher.

Things are spoilt enough under irrational interpretation of God's most simple law, the gospel of Jesus.

What's important in this this life is to know that one day, death will take each of us to eternity where judgement will be meted out on all that our life revolves around. Nothing could be hidden anymore and no one will be able to hide under grace (the supernatural ability of God so talked about but unused in our daily holy living but only employed for things earthly). We will be naked before God with nothing to help us. I have seen a glimpse of this and I will be a liar to keep silent... God's word and our conscience are great tools for personal scrutiny and judgement now before the appointed day for each of us. As I write now, many are keeping this unchangeable appointment. It could be your turn next.

"It's appointed to man once to die and after then judgement." Hebrew 9:27.

Check your ways.

God is good.

*** Word from Mirella...

*** We are either the products of God's mercy or vessels of dishonour and shame (Romans 9:22-23). It's pertinent to understand that our lives depend wholly on the very mercies of the LORD, for He Himself said unto Moses in Romans 9:15-16 KJV, *"15... I will have mercy on whom I will have mercy, and I will have compassion on whom I will have compassion. 16 So then it is not of him that willeth, nor of him that runneth, but of God that sheweth mercy."*

Beloved, when we encounter the mercy of God, favour follows. Yes, the LORD will build us up and appear in His glory; He will regard the prayer of the destitute, hearken to the groanings of the prisoners and release those appointed unto death (Psalm 102:16-30)! That's the magnitude of God's mercy. Yes, when we obtain of Him that showeth mercy, we receive grace to prosper. Hear this: freedom comes through truth; truth comes through grace and grace cometh through mercy.

Mercy is the key that re-positions men to God's designed high places uniquely for them. Thus, it's time to come unto the throne of Grace and obtain mercy, so to receive grace to be helped!

I pray for you this day, in the name of Jesus and laying precious hold of the blood of the Lamb and God's mercies, that God will be merciful unto you; that the LORD will hear you out of Zion and cause His face to shine upon you; that the LORD will set you free from every prison and redeem you from every death-sentencing and hopeless situation; that the Almighty hand of God will pick you from every valley and dunghill, and set you among princes for He owns the pillars upon which the earth was founded! I decree over your life this week, "go forth and receive divine favour; receive divine liberation; divine speed; divine visitation; divine supply; divine strength; divine insight; divine increase in the name of Jesus, amen!"

I await your testimony! God bless you; shalom! ***

Chapter 87

Three Keys to Overcoming Sexual Temptation and Falling Headlong

Many unsuspecting Christians have their hands soiled by or are neck-deep in the mud of immorality without any premonition that they will ever be in this state of life ever. There're people who deliberately look for this Satan-induced pleasures and I am not talking about such people here because they might need an atmosphere of a burden-removing and yoke-destroying power of God (a strong deliverance anointing) to get set free. But for people who just slip into it unawares from time to time, coming out of it with deep regrets, deep sorrows and wondering what ever went wrong with their life, these keys are for you.

1. Pray deeply against temptation always. Pray that you will not be led into temptation and be always delivered from evil. Pray this prayer even when you think you're very strong and don't feel any temptation is looming. Pray. "Pray... so you will not enter into temptation", Jesus said. Pray deeply my friend like a man who needs a miracle to raise the dead.

2. Talk with your spouse, an accountability partner or a trusted friend. "Two are better than one, because they have a good return for their labour: If either of them falls down, one can help the other up. But pity anyone who falls and has no one to help them up." Ecclesiastes 4:9-10.

You must have somebody you talk everything to that can talk you out of the nonsense Satan or Situation has talked into your heart. You need somebody. Anybody who doesn't have somebody around him/her can fall no matter how well graced or anointed.

"For she has been the ruin of many; many men have been her victims. Her house is the road to the grave. Her bedroom is the den of death." Proverbs 7:26:27.

3. Keep boundaries. Boundary-less men and women are easily accessible to all kinds of temptation. Why would you keep a girl you like in your house to be your maid when you know you check her out wittingly at your libidinous moments? "Watch...so you don't enter into temptation", Jesus said. Everyone has libido and it's wisdom to remove your kegs of Petrol from any fire or inflammables around. Your Postman smiles broadly with you while delivering your mails and you still stay there every day waiting for him. You're a done-deal. Many people don't have need of the maids they keep in their house or people from their spouse's family who love to live with them. Saying no today will prevent you from the press conference of tomorrow where they will be questioning you to explain how it happens. Stop visiting people alone whose spouses are not around.

Great men lose their great success for lack of boundaries or restraint.

It's better to be careful than to be sorry.

May the God of Israel be our fortress and shield us from the arrows shot to slay us or bring us down from the enemies in Jesus name. Amen.

God bless you.

*** Word from Mirella...

*** We dwell in the ⎾Presence of the King when we are in sync with the living waves of His glory and holiness.

My strength fails me to praise Him that is truly great: Whose greatness is unsearchable; Whose works & mighty acts are declared and praised from one generation to another (Psalm 145:4)!

Worship Him with all your whole being; empty yourself before Him. Bow down in adoration to Him, despite the staring issues of life. Yes, for He is the GOD OF ALL FLESH...nothing is too hard for Him to handle!

Turn to the LORD...turn to Him with shouts of praise and thanksgiving; then shall He turn again your captivity like the streams of the south (Psalm 126:4)!

Shalom! ***

Chapter 88

Know This Deep in Thy Heart Dearly Beloved

Great men are designed from the crucibles of seeming impossible.

It's just to test their resolves and build their mental muscles to know impossible is nothing! Okay?

Talk less, build internal resolves more. Be resilient on the inside. Give no room for weakness. Pray, Fast and Study the word to build internal structures upon which you can acquire external infrastructures.

Meaning is: God will never give anyone He's to greatly bless a project physically possible. No. Never. It never occurred. Never.

So, all great people you have ever seen or will ever see are made from the hot furnace of obviously seeming impossible projects...but with God, nothing shall be impossible. Amen.

Have a great day!

Chapter 89

Three Keys to Put Your Life in Focus

1. In your life, relationship, business or ministry, let only those sent of God be the ones that you're labouring on. Don't pamper, parade nor patronise people who God doesn't count on for you.

* You will recognise those God has for your life by the peace they have with you and their contentment with you cum truth-based corrections they give to you.

* Your God-given agents of change and partners in progress fight for you even when you're not there. They don't necessarily cover your errors but they book you for another chance, another opportunity to correct the errors.

* Don't keep resuscitating a relationship of often resentments, misunderstanding or ill-wishes otherwise you will grow old investing on wrong soils amounting to wasted destiny! Rest and Let God have His way.

2. Give yourself over to God when people give up on you. People may give up on you and they may be right, but if you give yourself, your time and focus over to God, you will be right (in time).

3. Never kill yourself over what man did to you, it might be the next step to your destiny. Let your attention be on what God

is doing always. There's always something God is doing...
always

Check it out. Give yourself over to it.

"Meditate upon these things; give thyself wholly to them; that
thy profiting may appear to all." 1 Timothy 4:15.

Chapter 90

Three Keys You Need in Life

1. Just pray regardless of your feelings...Many people who found God also did not know they could get Him, but they kept praying, pleading for mercy, they were not without fault as such (they didn't stop purging themselves either) and suddenly God came through for them. God delights to help each one of us. Keep praying..."I am the God of flesh, is there anything too hard for me", saith the Lord. Jeremiah 32:27.

2. Don't beg anybody if you know won't give them what they demand of you. Be at peace with everyone and live your life as much peaceful as you can. Don't put yourself under duress to meet someone's else demands that are not part of your word-based lifestyle. That will make you an entertainer. Live straight, simple and sincerely. No matter the situation, stand firm on the truth you know. "Speaking truth one with another." Ephesians 4:25.

3. Don't look for fame around; you don't need it in heaven nor to enter there and God doesn't need it to bless you. Be committed to your one talent and use it well if that's all you have. Smile, for God lifts in due season when He sees fit. Just follow God one step at a time with peace in your heart.

Check your **peace-o-meter** all the time. It is important. It's a sign God's there.

"And the peace of God that passes all understanding will keep your heart in Christ Jesus." Philippians 4:7.

Amen.

Chapter 91

Three Things So Important

1. Be determined to get to heaven. "Work hard to enter the narrow door to God's Kingdom, for many will try to enter but will fail.", Jesus said in Luke 13:24. Work on the grace available to be there. Hell is horrible and it's for ever.

2. Pester heavens till you're truly handpicked of God for use as a vessel of honour. Importunity is the word. God has need of humans, but only the persistently importunate stand to be really used.

   "Those that make mention of the Lord, give him no rest until he makes Jerusalem (you) a praise in the earth..." Isaiah 62:7.

   It doesn't matter how many times you have failed; you can trust God to raise you again. He doesn't give up on men until they're finally tied down forever in hell.

3. Live in truth and utmost sincerity with all you come across at whatever cost. You might be the only contact somebody have to God for life. Represent God well at every moment of life to any and everybody. Give the whole truth whichever way at all times. You might be somebody's last chance. "You're the salt of the earth", Jesus said in Mathew 5:13.

Happy day to you.

Chapter 92

Genuine Training and You: Three Types of People in Life and Ministry

1. Those who never had training or never had genuine trainers or training but who could be great if given the chance of good training.

    Examples: A. People of Nineveh in the book of Jonah who quickly repented at the prophetic warning of Jonah the prophet B. Apollos- Acts 18:24-28 C. The 12 disciples Paul met in Ephesus in Acts 19:1-7.

2. People who have access to genuine training or trainers but who are stiff-necked. Examples: A). Gehazi - the servant of Elisha. B). Judas - disciple of Jesus. C). Demas - An associate of Paul. These ones could be under the most serious Pastor, Parent or Partner but they already have their mind made up whatever is said or taught is tantamount to a waste of time, energy and resources. The word will never mix with faith in them.

3. People who have the privilege of genuine training or trainers and make good use of it by means of listening, searching things out to establish the truth firmly and practising the trainings one concept at a time. They may or may not make mistakes along the way, but they eventually produce fruits accordingly. Examples: A. Joshua-Servant of Moses. B. Elisha- Servant of Elijah. C. Peter and other ten disciples of

Jesus (excluding Judas the betrayer); Timothy and Titus also (associates of Paul).

Action Question: Where are you in these three categories?

Prayer Focus: Father give me the privilege of genuine training, trainers and open my heart to be submissive to and profitable with it in Jesus name. Amen.

Chapter 93

The fire must not go out

Life is very tough when God's fire has departed.

I have watched many fiery young men grow up and lose the fire. Then they start scheming how life must be lived. They want to build house, buy car, live nice. Things they once knew that being on fire will produce without scheming!

Fire preserves. Everything you have fear about is secured when you're on fire for God. After Moses saw the fire, Pharaoh faded in significance to him. God is that fire.

"Our God is a consuming fire." Hebrews 12:29.

When a man loses his fire, he starts pursuing his fear -The shadow (what shall I eat, drink and wear? My family, my career, my dignity, my reputation!).

When you lose fire, fear multiplies. Things of no importance before become very big. You start looking for money to do big funeral for deceased parents or your baby naming ceremony!

God's quickening fire in the bone of a man will attract the best of God's choice wife without manoeuvring and produce great quality ministry void of scheming. Acts 6.

Fire from above makes you laugh at what people want to die to achieve. You're already positioned in authority, so you don't look for the position of authority.

If you retain God's fire, you will be preserved. Your fear will be allayed always (Table before you in the presence of your enemy-fear-because your head is anointed-it's on fire - Psalm 23).

When we missed our steps as young men years ago, I saw how we began to frantically look for how life will be good. We began to propound theories of greatness instead of staying in the vision that makes great. Many I thought had the trappings of very great men of God are still running around to make ends meet today. Losing fire can run anyone mad. Ask Samson.

Retain your fire or you will have to maintain your fear for life. Many are in that valley now. Just maintaining life. Chai!

Fire opens doors because it burns, melts, consumes and eats up any and everything on its way. Fire doesn't fear nothing. Nothing! Stay on fire for God. If you've lost it, you can return to the Altar right now...I feel an anointing coming back on you now...Hallelujah!

You don't need more scheming, you need an increase in fire and all things will take shape.

When you're on fire, your life depends on nothing else except God. And He is more than enough. Nothing ties you down anymore because nothing is for economic reasons but for God alone...Hallelujah!

I see many do ministry to sustain life. It is as a result loss of the original fire. There's life in ministry without looking for it. For your life is hid in Christ with God...wow!

You don't put God first while on fire for Him, you seek Him first. Nobody on real fire puts God first. No! God is sought first and you follow. When people lose touch with God, then they start stuff and put God's name on it. Wrong! Tower of Babel instead of Altar of fire! Seek God first.

One great feature of God's fire is: It sets your heart on God all day long. When worries take root in you, then you need to go back to the altar.

Many are begging God in long prayers to help them with what He didn't create them for because fire has gone out of their altar.

One great power of God's fire in a man's life is: It kills the flesh, it kills ambition, it breaks man down, it purifies your intention, it melts your heart. You're sold out to God alone!

Securing and preserving fire is only by Seeking God first in Every case on Everything at All time. Mathew 6:33.

Don't put God first. He doesn't line up with anyone's programme. It's wrong. Seek Him first rather, checking out what His plans are. Then walk in them.

You will run after men a lot if you lose your fire. Fire attracts. See the Apostles. Men ran after them always. They refused to serve tables. They refused to run after men looking for favour or help around. Dignitaries sought for their help. They barraged them with helps and gifts of all sorts. Men on fire are men of glory, great substance!

When your fire is blazing, your future is bright. If your fire is dull, your future is down.

Fire only goes out where there's no wood. Proverbs 26:20. When it's not fuelled. The wood for God's fire in you is to seek and abide in Him only.

I have never really struggled for many things of life. My world is contained in ceaseless prayers and walking in the known will and word of God. Once anything becomes a struggle, I turn to God only. I have joy trapped in my soul than I can express to anyone. No inferiority feeling. His Fire burns in my bosom for years.

When all your aspirations are based on things of this life, check your fire level. Colossians 3:1.

One great way to lose fire is to base your life on groundless motivational. God has perfect plan for your life that can be revealed if you truly seek Him. You can only be fulfilling-ly faithful in what He raised you up to be. Jeremiah 29:11-13.

There are so many people who used to be fiery evangelist, teacher, prayer warrior, Bible Student, pastor or counsellor. They lost the fire and couldn't find their way back. May your name never be on that list when the story of your life will be read in Jesus name. Amen. Return if you've lost the fire! You can go back to your first love right now. God's door is opened. Amen.

May God keep you and Bless you. May He cause His face to shine on you and be gracious to you. May He lift His countenance upon you and give you peace. May He set you on and keep you in His holy fire from now and forever in Jesus name. Amen. Peace be upon you.

Chapter 94

Three Major Important Points to Living (God Planned and Ordained You Before Existence)

1. You can only do all things within the confines of your divine coding. You've been coded before birth like Jeremiah. You've been detailed-ly sewn up by the divine Master Planner-God!

You will always be a great failure in the lines not of His choosing. You cannot become another Apostle Paul, not even Timothy was. You cannot be Pastor Adeboye. Cease from the struggles! Just be normal.

Have you ever seen another Pastor Kumuyi? He is in his own class. You may be with Paul and God fashioned you to reach the Jews complementing his commitment to the Gentiles. Bazallel was with Moses but in a different stream to bring to structured reality the prophetic revelations of Moses.

Luke was although a medical personnel by training but a circumspect writer under the Apostles. He made us know what they did by his writings. He's equally an apostle (but of writings and documentation)-fantastic servant of Christ. Key man, crucial in the gospel much more now after all the fiery apostles rested in God.

Matthew 23:34 (ASV) "Therefore, behold, I send unto you prophets, and wise men, and scribes:"

Some are prophets, not all. Some are wise men, not all. But equally some are scribes (powerful writers), not all. Jesus sends all of them equally and none is greater than another. They can all be under one roof like the apostles of old if they have crucified ambitious greed and competitive jealousy.

You're important, beloved. Your style, work or system is indispensably important.

You cannot be anything God has not made you successfully. Uzziah, a prosperous king died a leper trying to be a priest!

"But when he was strong, his heart was lifted up to his destruction: for he transgressed against the LORD his God, and went into the temple of the LORD to burn incense upon the altar of incense... and while he was wroth with the priests, the leprosy even rose up in his forehead before the priests in the house of the LORD, from beside the incense altar." 2 Chronicles 26:16,19.

Everyone with his divine coding. You will flow unhindered in the code you're earmarked for. Who you are is on the inside of you. Let it flow! Don't change it. Importantly also is the fact that you don't have to find that code. You're already in it. That's why you struggle when you want to preach or act like Morris Cerrullo or twist your tongue like Chris Oyakhilome. There's an unknown flavour God is bringing out through you.

"And(God) hath made of one blood all nations of men for to dwell on all the face of the earth, and hath determined the times before appointed, and the bounds of their habitation; "Acts 17:26.

To be continued...

Chapter 95

Three Important Points to Living (Continued)

2. To continue with what or who God already moved from no matter how precious is an eternal waste. God wants us to do what He does per time.

I understand that for many people, you may never need to change any person around you, move away from your location nor embark on any different project in your life like in the case of many people in the Bible or our time. But for many others the world over, there are so many friends, church members, pastors, locations, relationships, projects, ministries, or churches God is done with (for you) and you must line up with Him in His direction of operations for now. Not knowing nor doing this is the greatest undoing of this generation.

God could've anointed Saul as your king yesterday, but today God already moved to David, so for Samuel to keep praying over Saul is none of God's business.

There are many people, places and projects you will like to continue investing on, but for you, God's time over that has elapsed.

"The tribe of Issachar supplied 200 leaders, along with all of their relatives under their command. They kept up-to-date in their understanding of the times and knew what Israel should do." 1 Chronicle 12:32.

There are some churches we are pastoring that God has moved from. Some of us stay with the name of a ministry because of the name of the big boss there not because God's intention for us still lingers on there.

Relationships God has left; Projects God has done with; Locations God has moved from: Intentions God has dropped. Many such things cripple our movements. They stop our progress; age us fast and milk us dry!

We merry-go-round over them for years and grow old without any major effect and impact in life nor honour with God.

'But God has revealed them to us by his Spirit: for the Spirit searches all things, yes, the deep things of God." 1 Corinthians 2:10.

The Holy spirit searches all things, so must we re-examine all people, places and projects moment by moment to know God's mind about such to redeem the time for the days are evil.

You don't want to be 80yrs old to know you're not supposed to have ever lived in Dublin, New-York, London or Lagos. You don't want to have the Third child before knowing that one month before your wedding Heavens already cancelled the relationship. You don't want to finish signing the name of the other fellow as a ministry, company or project trustee before knowing he or she is sexually disoriented!

Signs of sorrow, dissatisfaction, crushing burdens, cautions or outright suspicion could be a red light to danger about that place, person or project. Check with God in deep prayers. God doesn't pay for the places, projects or persons He moved from.

Jeremiah 33:3 'Call to me and I will answer you and tell you great and unsearchable things you do not know.'

Some people, places or projects will always age you, cause you pain and sorrows till death.

But...

Remember: God wants you to always be at peace, at least inside of you, then make progress to fulfil His will on the earth as it is in heaven. He is the God of all peace!

"And hath made of one blood all nations of men for to dwell on all the face of the earth, and hath determined the times before appointed, and the bounds of their habitation;" Acts 17:26.

To be continued...

Chapter 96

Three Major Important Points to Living (Conclusion)

1. You can only do all things within the confines of your divine coding. You've been coded before birth like Jeremiah. You've been detailed-ly sewn up by the divine master planner - God!

2. To continue with what or who God already moved from no matter how precious is an eternal waste. God wants us to do what He does per time).

Conclusion...

3. Don't struggle with Nobody over nothing (even if it's your right), just learn to personally pray enough to the God of heaven. He has more than enough to satisfy you.

"And he removed from thence, and digged another well; and for that they strove not: and he called the name of it Rehoboth; and he said, For now the LORD hath made room for us, and we shall be fruitful in the land." Gen 26:22.

No matter how precious anything or anyone maybe in your life, never physically strive over such, just pray to the God who can fight for you.

Anytime you rise in defence of yourself fighting over things or humans by whatever emotional, physical or psychological warfare, God sits back, leaving you to your fate.

"Be worried over nothing, but everything by prayers..." Philippians 4:6.

Why should somebody not wanting to be with you in marriage, relationship or ministry become a physical tussle? If you've totally submitted to God, the easiest thing to do on earth is to release things and people the pain sustained notwithstanding. Pain is part of this life and God is always able to sooth all pain. Releasing Isaac was nothing to Abraham, painful though, but He got the blessings.

"He shall wipe away tears from the faces of people..."

Human heart is really deep and many times very cunning. Thus, to fret yourself over this is to invite going to the grave early.

There's nothing you can ever do over a determined mind. Nothing. Every precious effort from you to such seems a bribe. Don't stand in the way, just stand with God. Cease from thine own wisdom. Only God wins soul.

Jesus said, "No one can come to me except the father draws him..."

"All the ways of a man are right in his own eyes."

While working in the ministry of the great servant of Christ Bishop Francis Wale Oke in the '90s (oh,I love that Prophet of God), some of those who led us there had their personal agenda of launching independent ministries. They talked to us loads about starting their church, recruiting some of us and buying instruments already. It's a shock to me as I never saw this in the Deeper Life Church where I was prior to then. Some of them died in the middle of the plan while some were able to actualise it but without much significance in life. It's a painful trend to the servant of God but committing things to God via much prayers had always been the reason for his stability and continued relevance in the scheme of things.

Your spouse's determination to dump you in search of a new illusion cannot be stopped by your fretting and fighting but only by your praying to the one who can stop his/her heart.

Prayerful people also go through much pain, but always win in the end.

Don't run from pillar to post trying to hold things together. No! Run deeper and deeper to Him who's got the whole world in His hands. He's your pillar!

Read Psalm 24.

God bless you and all yours now and ever more. Amen.

Love you!

Chapter 97

Is Your Life Prepared for God?

A prepared message is useless from the mouth of a fellow with an unprepared life. Just like the staff of Elisha in the hand of Gehazi!

God seeks for prepared lives. Peter on the day of Pentecost was a prepared life without any prepared message but got thousands for the Lord on the spot. Put your life out for thorough preparation. That's all we need.

Amen.

*** Word from Mirella...

*** "We are only worthy in His mercies and grace...

Worthy to come to the Throne of grace by Christ Jesus

Worthy to stand before Him by Christ Jesus.

Worthy to ask and receive in Christ Jesus."

The standards of God aren't humanly attainable. Thus, despite how much effort we put to measure up, let's not lean on such. Only whom is accounted worthy in His sight is truly is! Humility demands that we receive His mercies and grace, wherein we are accepted in the Beloved.

No man is truly worthy by his efforts! We're worthy solely in Christ - by His blood, by His death, by His resurrection, by His stripes, by His love, by His mercies and by His grace - before the Father.

Jesus, in John 14:13-14 KJV, declares:

"13 And whatsoever ye shall ask in my name, that will I do, that the Father may be glorified in the Son.

14 If ye shall ask any thing in my name, I will do it."

We are quick to make demand in the name of Jesus, based solely on the authority accrued to Him, and expect the supernatural to happen...that doesn't always yield positive results, especially when we count ourselves worthy before God based on our righteousness and spiritual efforts. However, the reason why we ask in the name of Jesus and receive thereof has two major foundation layers: the first one being on the basis of being worthy by His mercies and grace and the second based on His sovereign authority.

Leaning on His mercies and receiving His grace quicken us to walk to the Father's pleasure: that's true holiness.

Have a blessed day ahead; shalom! ***

Chapter 98

Praise or A Show?

Much of what is called praise now is just pure exhibition of flesh and never connected to God. Just pure entertainment of the body with no iota of eternity focus. God is not reached!

It's each person's duty to put a line of divide as a true seeker of God.

"God is spirit, and those who worship Him must worship in spirit and truth." John 4:24

*** Word from Mirella...

*** You Can Still Prevail!

I Samuel 17:40, 45-51 declares,

"40 And he took his staff in his hand, and chose him five smooth stones out of the brook, and put them in a shepherd's bag which he had, even in a scrip; and his sling was in his hand: and he drew near to the Philistine.

45 Then said David to the Philistine, Thou comest to me with a sword, and with a spear, and with a shield: but I come to thee in the name of the LORD of hosts, the God of the armies of Israel, whom thou hast defied.

46 This day will the LORD deliver thee into mine hand; and I will smite thee, and take thine head from thee; and I will give the carcases of the host of the Philistines this day unto the fowls of the air, and to the wild beasts of the earth; that all the earth may know that there is a God in Israel. note

47 And all this assembly shall know that the LORD saveth not with sword and spear: for the battle is the LORD'S, and he will give you into our hands.

48 And it came to pass, when the Philistine arose, and came and drew nigh to meet David, that David hasted, and ran toward the army to meet the Philistine.

49 And David put his hand in his bag, and took thence a stone, and slang it, and smote the Philistine in his forehead, that the stone sunk into his forehead; and he fell upon his face to the earth.

50 So David prevailed over the Philistine with a sling and with a stone, and smote the Philistine, and slew him; but there was no sword in the hand of David.

51 Therefore David ran, and stood upon the Philistine, and took his sword, and drew it out of the sheath thereof, and slew him, and cut off his head therewith. And when the Philistines saw their champion was dead, they fled."

Spiritual battles can only be won by the help of God! When the root of an issue is revealed to you of the Lord and the specific weapons are delivered into your hands: you receive the emblem of the authority of the LORD!

As seen in the biblical passage above, specifically verse 40, David CHOSE five smooth stones by the brook, which bore the saving strength of the LORD, that killed Goliath! That's the secret of victory: the spiritual significance of the word "chose" means, specific...definite...and accurate weapons of warfare were taken to confront Goliath!

Secondly, we need to develop a living relationship with God (that is, hearing ears, and an obedient and ready heart). When we get to a junction in life, it's pertinent to seek the root of every setback! Lo, God isn't a free 'take-away' centre: wherein we come to grab what we want and snap away - in the place of prayer! Some answers to prayers are steps that need divine instruction unto us to handle: for example, Joshua's defeat at Aia due to Achan's sinful act, and the three-year doom of Israel during David's reign as a result of his predecessor's breach of covenant with the Jebusites.

God, other times, directs us with divine weapons that target and defeat that particular obstacle!

How important it is to know God truly...those vague prayers would come to a halt! Knowing God directs our feet upon the right path to take. Ignorance of God sets our lives on the course to the pit (also due, sometimes, to sinful habits in our lives) and God remains silent: meaning God can't truly intervene... He can't exercise the word of His power in that situation troubling you. Thus, ask Him for mercy, that He may wash and sanctify you wholly to Himself; then, ask Him to reveal the root of the particular problem confronting you. Surely, He will reveal such to you and instruct you upon the path of divine victory: David declared, *"For by Thee I have run through a troop; and by my God have I leaped over a wall[...]He teacheth my hands to war, so that a bow of steel is broken by mine arms"*(Psalm 18:29,34). That is the saving strength of God to those that fear Him!

Prayer Points

- Father, have mercy on me: wash me in the blood of the Lamb and sanctify me wholly to You.

- Father, cleanse me from all form and nature of unrighteousness by the precious blood of Jesus.

- LORD God, reveal unto me the root of every mountain challenging me in the name of Jesus.

- LORD God, reveal unto me the weapons of warfare that You have in store to defeat this particular mountain in my life (name it - as revealed unto you by the LORD) in the name of Jesus.

- LORD God, teach my hands to war; set my feet upon the path of victory over every battle of life in the name of Jesus.

- LORD God, thank You for hearkening unto the voice of my supplications this day in the name of Jesus.

[Pray upon these lines till God reveals and directs you]

Amen, amen and amen! Keep seeking the face of God and He shall surely be found of you in His tender mercies.

I pray for you this day: may the LORD hear you from Zion, may His face shine upon you in the name of Jesus, amen! Alleluia!

Finally, meditate upon Psalm 18.

Shalom! ***

Chapter 99

My Revelation

On the 15th of February,2015, I was dead in the vision of the night (just after 3am) and was having my record shown me at the transit between hell and heaven. Many other born again Christians were there with me.

I argued with the angel at the gate when heaven's gate was shut and we were billed for hell. I told the angel I had confessed all my sins before dying. The angel showed me the record with my mistakes on it and I cried in a such a deep way as I could see hell waiting with Satan ready to torment for life. I told the angel that nobody ever told me all of these before I died.

The angel was too peaceful but very firm. I woke up back to life and I know there's a serious problem not only with me and the present church, but many servants of God also.

One of my major mistakes is that God said I am an entertainer. Entertaining all ideas from all and sundry. Being flippant with standard.

Hell is fearsome dearly beloved.

Chapter 100

You Have More Than Enough

The men of old including prophets and apostles only had prayers at their disposal through which they called God for everything they needed, faced or got involved in and God heard them.

Both humans, earthly resources and situations respond to prayers because God hears humans and controls things via prayers.

If all you have today is prayer (having lost all things, pushed to the wall, deserted by people, disappointed by situations, hedged in a non-productive location, thrown down by sickness or other issues), just pray! What you have is more than enough!

Hannah couldn't talk again as a result of a heart-rending situation, but she went to God broken hearted with nothing but pain & roaring cry of the heart alone, and she was answered in that she prayed.

You don't need prayer warriors or elderly prophets to help you out. You NEED GOD ALONE through your heart and mouth expressing your pain.

THERE'S NOTHING GOD CANNOT DO.

He may change your location to change your situation or he may change your association to bring your elevation.

He may change your affinity or vicinity to break you out of invisibility. Whichever way, God arranges life for divine touch and deliverance through prayers.

Take time out to personally pray and take this very seriously because your whole life depends on it without an alternative.

You will be sorted out. Amen.

"During his life on earth, Jesus prayed to God, who could save him from death. He prayed and pleaded with loud crying and tears, and he was heard because of his devotion to God." Hebrews 5:7.

Blessed art thou.

Just pray. How many things can you share with humans before you're tagged "Box of troubles"? Pray to God with all heart poured out in all manners of ways. Pray...

When answers to your prayers will come, it will be like you did a magic. Pray, answers are coming. Halleluiah.

"Be careful for nothing; but in everything by prayer and supplication with thanksgiving let your requests be made known unto God. And the peace of God, which passeth all understanding, shall keep your hearts and minds through Christ Jesus."

Philippians 4:6-7.

*** Word from Mirella...

*** God is God; He needs nothing to be Who He is! Beloved, it's high time we "released" God from the box of our minds: for with God, nothing is impossible. Without faith it is impossible to please God: for he that cometh to Him must believe that He

IS, and that He is the Rewarder of them that diligently seek Him (Hebrews 11:6)!

The question of the day is: "HOW do I come to the LORD God?"

We ought to come to Him recognizing Who He is: true knowledge of Him births faith!

It takes believing Who He is and standing thereupon to walk with Him. Lo, understanding Him isn't the duty of our finite mind, but of our regenerated spirit by the Holy Spirit! God is too deep to comprehend by mere human insight. The depths of life are hidden in Him. The deep things of His are unveiled by His Spirit unto us through our spirit-man.

How often we've erred by lacking true knowing of God. Today can spark a new beginning!

Believe in God because He is God, the I AM! He that defines and gives entity and identity! Believe His counsel; believe His Word! Concerning that situation, believe His words.

"Blessed is she that believed, for there shall be a performance of those things spoken to her from the LORD" (Luke 1:45)! Amen.

Shalom! ***

Chapter 101

Live in Love

Don't wait or watch evil dreams, visions and prophecies made either by you or others come to pass on anybody even if such don't have Jesus as saviour and Lord yet.

To do this amounts to heart-seated wickedness. No matter what bad you see or hear about another fellow, it is a test from heaven over your life with God watching if you have enough love to partner with Him in reaching out to humanity or not. Even God hates the death of a sinner, but He looks for every means to bring all to salvation purchased with the precious blood of His Holy Child Jesus Christ.

Let God judge His creatures or saints as He wants but you stay in His presence as a peacemaker between God and Man. Be an intercessor. Be a holy watcher. Pray for people even if they're going through the consequences of their misdeeds. You cannot create any human neither can you save your own soul in the day of evil if the Lord does not send help. The evil people watch to happen to somebody may be on them first.

"Whoever shuts his ear to the cry of the poor will call and not be answered." Proverbs 21:13.

He who wins a sinner covers multitudes of sins. Be this person. Persevere with God to see evil judgements averted. That's how to be light in this dark world.

"And the Lord turned the captivity of Job, when he prayed for his friends (who earlier on had been the worst nightmares of his life): also the Lord gave Job twice as much as he had before." Job 42:10

Don't wish (even in the inner recesses of your heart) that an evil prophecy, dream or revelation comes to pass on another human fellow or a church or other Christians. Cease from this wickedness.

Be blessed.

Chapter 102

Take it to God

No matter how big or small a matter, a decision to make, a need, a form of fear, a point of pain or difficulty maybe, please take it to God in committed prayers.

He delights to help us in all things. Big things are not big deal with Him and small things could negatively affect our lives if we're too proud to involve Him.

Take people's names to God. Take what they say to Him like Hezekiah. Take what people decide about you, the letter you got, the new attitude of your spouse, business partners, ministry associates or church members to God. Take the names of your spouse friends and children peers to God.

"...But in everything by prayers and supplications with thanksgiving let your requests be made known unto God." Philippians 4:6.

Make a commitment to talk Him through everything in deep prayers. Don't be afraid. Answers are coming. God is great. Keep praying all forms of prayers in all ways by every possible means.

"Whoever shall call on the name of the Lord shall be saved."

Great breakthroughs are on the way. Praise the Lord.

God bless you immeasurably.

Chapter 103

The Faithful Remnant

When failures meet, they discuss events; but when success meet, they talk ideas. (Author unknown). But better still...when kingdom giants meet, they discuss God and the fear of the Lord only! In what category do your friends fall please?

"Then those who feared the Lord talked with each other, and the Lord listened and heard. A scroll of remembrance was written in his presence concerning those who feared the Lord and honoured his name. On the day when I act," says the Lord Almighty, "they will be my treasured possession. I will spare them, just as a father has compassion and spares his son who serves him. 18 And you will again see the distinction between the righteous and the wicked, between those who serve God and those who do not." Malachi 3:16-18.

*** Word from Mirella...

***Jeremiah 17:5-8 says,

"5 Thus saith the LORD; Cursed be the man that trusteth in man, and maketh flesh his arm, and whose heart departeth from the LORD.

6 For he shall be like the heath in the desert, and shall not see when good cometh; but shall inhabit the parched places in the wilderness, in a salt land and not inhabited.

7 Blessed is the man that trusteth in the LORD, and whose hope the LORD is.

8 For he shall be as a tree planted by the waters, and that spreadeth out her roots by the river, and shall not see when heat cometh, but her leaf shall be green; and shall not be careful in the year of drought, neither shall cease from yielding fruit."

How blessed it is to trust solely and wholly in the LORD! God is angry...and hurt when His people... His children choose to trust in men and in themselves, rather than Him; upon such folks He deemed them 'cursed'. Many times, the commonest wrong of the people of God is trusting in men, rather than God. We've to repent of such: let's ask the Father for mercy and, thus, the removal of the corresponding curse from our lives.

To trust in God comes by knowing God. As usual said by me, "only God can reveal Himself to a man to be really known". Thus, ask the LORD to impart the revelation knowledge of Him unto your heart this day.

Oh, when you truly know God, you shall be strong and do exploits (Daniel 11:32b)!

Additionally, when you know God and, thus, trust in Him, you will always wait on Him: *"those that wait on the LORD shall renew their strength, they shall mount up with wings as eagles. They shall run and not be weary, they shall walk and not faint"* (Isaiah 40:31).

Lastly, to trust in God means to rely totally on Him, to lean on Him, to look unto Him. *"I will lift up my eyes unto the hills from whence cometh my help. My help cometh from the LORD Who made the heavens and the earth. He will not suffer my feet to be moved: He that keepeth thee will not slumber."*(Psalm 121:1-3).

Psalm 125:1-2: *"They that trust in the LORD shall be as mount Zion, which cannot be removed, but abideth for ever.*

2 As the mountains are round about Jerusalem, so the LORD is round about his people from henceforth even for ever."

"Many trust in chariots, some in horses: but we will trust in the LORD": will you join this last category today? Choose to trust in the Lord!

God bless you; shalom! ***

Chapter 104

Three Serious Observations of Life I Have Made

1. It's always an unneeded headache or an impossible task of a pursuit for those inside whom God has not put hunger or pain for that target. Therefore, stop wasting your time, energy, saliva and life over such, otherwise your hunger and enthusiasm will soon be overthrown. There are many possible things looking so obviously impossible waiting for those who have enough pain and hunger. Rhetoric or many words lead to vanity. Separation and consistent action with much resilience is the key.

2. Failures create unquenchable anger, then overheating hunger for success. God sometimes allows some breakdowns to deepen our roots for routing onslaughts. All greats were many times knocked out and off course, but God raised them up again and they moved on more strongly. All of the great people you know are part of this list. If you must succeed, you will be on this list.

3. Prayers look very ordinary, but do pray. God listens to prayers. God hears prayers. God answers prayers. God waits for us to pray out all our pains, tragedies and requests all the time. Just keep praying over everything and anything in all kinds of prayers anyway and anyhow you can pray 24hrs a day,7 days a week. Just pray to God and keep praying nonstop. This is the greatest of life's secrets- talking to God through the Holy ghost in the name Jesus. Pray always on all things please. Pray!

Chapter 105

Over The Years I Have Come to Know One Thing

I may be facing the worst turn of life events(as I have been in many) and do not know what's going to happen to me; humans may have deserted me or keep saying about me things that can even make the dead to rise to defend him/herself against the fabrications or just unchecked errors(a real child of God doesn't do many of the things people will allege us of but nonetheless because loads of folks are like unturned cakes-presuming to be children of God-they will go ahead assuming and saying stuff); and being in the midst of nowhere a lot of time not knowing how God may come through but really praying and telling God of the pains, tragedies and the need for His help, I just found a new channel, another phase, a higher place - new reality... Undeniable answers to prayers that only divine interventions can bring!

Of a truth, in the last 24 years of walk of faith with the Governor of the universe, He has proven time and again that "He does hear the voice of mortal man." He can hear you! He can pick you up!

No matter what you're facing today, don't be afraid, just pray to God in the name of Jesus. He will hear you; He will come and save you.

"Whoever shall call on the name of the Lord shall be saved." Acts 2:21.

Amen.

Chapter 106

Sundry Thoughts

In the kingdom of God dressing matters. God doesn't only judge hearts but also your acts involving your dressing. People outside of the kingdom can do what they like, but not the joint heirs with Jesus. There's priestly /royal proper dressing of the kingdom and there is a careless dressing of the kingdom of the prince of the power of the air, Satan himself!

You don't lose anything by humility. You even gain what who you humble yourself under has to offer while retaining what you have in you already. It does not take anything away from you. Nothing. It only adds.

Do everything you can do about everybody around you- help, enlighten, pray for, correct and do everything necessary (never stop doing all these for life), but be sure it's not at the expense of your relationship with God and peace.

Don't love people for who you want them to be for you. No, love them as they are and as they love to be each time. Celebrate God's uniqueness and decision in every one. Antagonism could be pregnant with an eternal truth and easy support could be based on vanity. You must let God move individuals to do unto you what's written concerning them for that period. Only God is God and no one else on earth. Recognise and respect people's individuality and live your life too without bulging.

Lastly, don't be always angry at life or folks, there are serious truths in every turn of event and behavioural trends of people. Just open your mind. God is good!

It's not preaching, teaching or singing the gospel that's the issue, but doing the gospel (walking in holiness is the key to see God in heaven). I had a revelation of multitude of born again Christians going to hell owing to one sin or the other not dealt with. No matter what you believe, heaven and hell issue is a grave matter. Really serious!

Everything is a test for another phase of life. Disrespect or outright dishonour could be allowed to happen by people who never meant it to test the level of the pride, self or anger remaining in us to be dealt with.

I failed this test in 2004 when I was flown to Congo from Nigeria by a group of ministers and we had to move through terrible war territory to preach in a conference. Materials were printed bearing my name and all that. But on the main day of the programme, a local preacher was brought in to just introduce the programme but he went on taking over 80% of the programme time preaching and conducting deliverance, leaving me with just few moments to preach and round off. I was too enraged to preach. Anger got the better of me. That's the end of my contact with that part of Congo till date. Little did I know that such will still occur time and again.

I failed the test then, but now things have progressed. I go to services, including where I am invited to preach, prepared to enjoy God and listen to what He will tell me through others. If I am called to do anything, it's a privilege and not a right.

I am prepared to be used by God anytime but if God has another agenda, I am honoured enough to be in His presence. He is God.

"Before honour is humility." Proverbs 18:12.

It's not as easy as I have said it here, because growth is a process and does not happen like snapping fingers. Each person has his or her style earmarked by their relationship with the Holy Spirit.

Be blessed.

Chapter 107

Divine Dealings Are Inexplicable

You may try, but you will never be able to fully explain the dealings, the way and the purpose of God concerning you to any human fellow.

People who need to know it will not need much explanation and people who will not understand it may occupy you with questions forever, but they will not still understand it.

Only your spirit fully understands it and no one else. That's why you alone will be held accountable how you go about it.

There is 'joy unspeakable full of glory and that passes all understanding' in fulfilling it. YOU MAY NEVER BE ABLE TO FULLY EXPLAIN IT. So, do not waste too much energy and time on articulation. It's a lone way.

'The natural man cannot receive the things of the spirit; they're spiritually discerned.' 1 Corinthians 2:14.

Chapter 108

Prayer Push

After hearing and prophesying about the 'sound of abundance of rain" in 1ˢᵗ King, Elijah went on top of mount Carmel to pray, sending his servant to watch out until it poured heavily on earth.

Many call themselves students or teachers of revival rocking their chairs in the church office or shoving through piles of book in the libraries of revival without getting down to doing real praying. All you can have with these is head full of history and expectation that never becomes manifestation.

Elijah put his head between his knees. Revival occurs and it's sustained in the place of non-stop prayers.

The move of God, real revival is birthed in real deep prayers.

'The effectual fervent prayers of a righteous man makes tremendous power available...Elijah was a man of like passion but he prayed to shut heaven and to again cause rain.'

"...The effectual fervent prayer of a righteous man availeth much. Elias was a man subject to like passions as we are, and he prayed earnestly that it might not rain: and it rained not on the earth by the space of three years and six months. And he prayed again, and the heaven gave rain, and the earth brought forth her fruits." James 5:16-18.

Revival is fulfilling your God-given purpose in your life, home, ministry, church or community.

You can pray down the manifestation really quick big time. God hears and answers prayers. Jeremiah 33:3.

God's ears are opened to you today, go in unto Him just as you're. Amen.

I love you.

Chapter 109

Turn to God Alone

Pray deep and put your total trust in God alone; watch every other thing, person as an educative comedy.

Never be wise before God nor man. Never lean on your understanding for it may be obsolete, totally out of date.

Trust in God alone, but He will send things and people your way that must teach, bless and guide you in the places you must go.

Pray! But don't lay things or people to heart, so you may live long.

"For thus saith the Lord GOD, the Holy One of Israel; In returning and rest shall ye be saved; in quietness and in confidence shall be your strength: and ye would not."

Isaiah 30:15.

Amen.

Chapter 110

Heart Attack and Sudden Death... God Forbid!

I first experienced this in 2003 or thereabout when I was in the midst of very strenuous phase of life. I just knew what it's as it started though I was very young.

My middle chest gave me such heavy pains than ever imagined. It's as if little darts were thrown at my heart and thick drawly saliva began to come through my lips. The pain was so intensely heavy I couldn't move anywhere but had to sit on the spot. I knew I was dying. I knew this is how many have died or developed stroke just immediately.

Little did I know that I was taking too much of stress and strain to heart that I was not supposed to, although I was really in deep troubles of life-very many with little or no help.The pain was a timely check before either stroke or death.

A word came to save me then and it's needed even now not just for me, but everyone passing through traumatic experience of life..."Don't ever let it get into your heart."

Challenges of life abound and they may never cease, but there's no part of it that must be directly allowed to affect your heart.

From time to time I still feel such pains and I just know there must be an action immediately otherwise I will never be alive to handle the challenge anymore.

These three action steps will help you:

1. Stop everything else and take the troubles to God in deep prayers. Philippians 4:6-7.

2. Don't cover up a real trouble. Talk to appropriate people who could help.

3. Avoid people, places and projects that remind you of such or breathes fresh air into it. It's your duty to know what breaks you down and avoid it totally. You're responsible for your life.

I have discovered stress gathers overtime and turns to serious heart condition leading to sudden death. Many are gone and hundreds are joining them daily via heart failure. It's your responsibility to know yourself and when your heart has had enough. There's no replacement for life.

We shall not die untimely in Jesus name.

"Keep thy heart with all diligence; for out of it are the issues of life." Proverbs 4:23.

Love you.

Chapter 111

Don't You Know It Is the Same?

I am not talking of people of other faiths, but don't many of the professing Christian women know that there's no difference between leaving their breasts out in dressing and guys leaving their balls out walking around?

How would feel seeing a guy coming to the altar to lead worship, give testimony or just talking with you with the balls all out? How? Very obnoxious.

Cover up please! You're more of a satanic distraction leading to people's destruction and yours too dressing that way! A true child of God doesn't dress such way! No way...

Circle of Fame Magazine

Chapter 112

The Mandate

Number one killer of the call of God is ambition. Number one killer of ministry is ambition. Number one killer of the hand of God and the anointing of the Holy Spirit is ambition.

Ambition hides or surfaces many times as what is popular held as "motivation or motivational"... e.g. "You can do it if somebody did it before".

Ambition tells you which city you must live in, the person you must marry and the kind of way you must talk cum the kind of dressing you must wear.

The Antidote to ambition is SUBMISSION to the Will of God! You can be asked to stay in the wilderness or move from your father's house like John the Baptist and Abraham. Jesus submitted His will(ambition), so you must.

Ambition resides in the will of man. The antidote to it is the will of God...vision from His heart to yours.

"And he(Jesus) was withdrawn from them about a stone's cast, and kneeled down, and prayed, Saying, Father, if thou be willing, remove this cup from me: nevertheless not my will, but thine, be done." Luke 22:41-42.

The hand of God is spiritual...carnally minded people cannot stay under it a long haul! Got it?

Chapter 113

To Help the Young Ones, Connect First (My heart Burden)

I talk with loads of young people on several platforms and my heart is burdened about the ever widening gap between the church, pastors, parents and the ever bubbling young people. I love God to use me bring a paradigm shift so faith is not lost with the old generation. I feel pressed spiritually!

To solve a person's problem, there must be a communication line.

The young people are in one hand with their issues hiding everything they do off parents and iron-pastors while the parents and pastors are - on the other hand - making laws, orders and principles that must not be defaulted by anybody.

The problem will continue for as long a communication bridge is not built. Parents and pastors disdain the young people for being naive, unable to make sound decisions, flippant and non-cooperative, the young people look at them as archaic, unreasoning, mentally congealed, too outdated and out of trend. Until there's a is common ground for communication, aluta continua!

You may never be able to solve the problem of a person that doesn't communicate with you or you don't communicate with.

Condescension for communication is indispensable: the experience of the elders should be merged with youthful exuberance and new revelations of the young, to be useful. Combined with prayers, this will produce dynamic homes, churches and communities.

*** Word from Mirella...

*** No man owns anything for God is the Possessor of heaven and earth. The secret of blessedness is belonging to God... being wholly "owned" by God (that is, being totally sold out to Him unreservedly): then shall you be prosperous indeed...spirit, soul and body.

A man truly possessed of the LORD has his all (if ever anything pertained to him) placed in the hands of God, his soul set at the bosom of the Father, his spirit in sync with the Holy Spirit and, as long he tarries upon the earth, he remains eternally-minded.

Genesis 14:18 - 24 depicts true blessedness, as seen in the life of Abraham:

"18 And Melchizedek king of Salem brought forth bread and wine: and he was the priest of the most high God.

19 And he blessed him, and said, Blessed be Abram of the most high God, possessor of heaven and earth:

20 And blessed be the most high God, which hath delivered thine enemies into thy hand. And he gave him tithes of all.

21 And the king of Sodom said unto Abram, Give me the persons, and take the goods to thyself.

22 And Abram said to the king of Sodom, I have lift up mine hand unto the Lord, the most high God, the possessor of heaven and earth,

23 That I will not take from a thread even to a shoelatchet, and that I will not take any thing that is thine, lest thou shouldest say, I have made Abram rich:

24 Save only that which the young men have eaten, and the portion of the men which went with me, Aner, Eshcol, and Mamre; let them take their portion."

Shalom! ***

Chapter 114

The Three People You Don't Need in Your Life

1. People who pity you to be with you or do things for you.

2. People you have to always beg to be included in your team or to help you

3. People who believe others are better than you and they're just around you waiting for the next flight to the better land.

These all make you look less than human. They never see who God made you to be. You need less of such to progress. Take yourself off them before they run you into suicide. You're created with dignity deserving of all moments of celebration.

"That the communication of your faith may be effectual by the acknowledgment of every good thing that's in you." Philemon 6.

Chapter 115

Witchcraft Operations

Somebody is going through stuff and needs this now, so here you go...

Witchcraft attacks happen to everyone, Christians or non-Christians alike. IT HAPPENED TO ADAM and EVE, it happened to Elijah, it happened to Paul and Silas.

When it occurs, a long term battle or storm could ensue. The aim is to defeat the purpose of God in somebody's life, home, church, ministry or community.

Witchcraft attack does happen to individuals, families, churches or communities.

Three Sublime ways witchcraft operates:

1. An outright attack from a dare devil like Jezebel on Elijah. Straight, face to face battle. A demonic enterprise, a front door battle with the enemy. JESUS WAS CONFRONTED STRAIGHT ON BY SATAN. Everybody does experience this at some point in life. Even as an unbeliever, my mother was physically confronted by a witch telling her, 'I will take your life.' This became one of the major reasons she ran to God in 1985 when all else failed. It's not a hidden battle, but front line confrontation without hidden clause. Jezebel told Elijah, 'I am ready to finish you dear prophet.'

"Ahab told Jezebel all that Elijah had done, and how he had killed all the prophets with the sword. 2 Then Jezebel sent a messenger to Elijah, saying, "So may the gods do to me and more also, if I do not make your life as the life of one of them by this time tomorrow." 3 Then he was afraid, and he arose and ran for his life and came to Beersheba, which belongs to Judah, and left his servant there." 1 Kings 19:1-3.

2. Incitement of those in your circumference to slowly but sublimely induce an attack. Eve was gotten by friendly conversation by subtle serpent and Adam lost his throne and crown to words from a lover. Many people have committed suicide, run away from their homes, ministry or calling as a result of either actions, non-actions or reactions from those who have access to them. Many things done by folks around you may be a trigger to arrows already shot in the spirit. There's nothing ugly enough that David's brother did not say as a vocal cord for the attack of Satan on his soon to be realised destiny. Many things around, like a little rumour, some comments from a fellow church member, some form of looks or hissing from your friends, spouse or parents and so on could be pregnant with heavy witchcraft capable of detonating a major destiny.

3. Dreams, visions, revelations are means by which God communicates to us all, believers or non-believers alike, all His creations. Satan hijacks this flow a lot. A major battle of life can start from a minor dream laden with the enemy's tricks. Many lives, homes, churches, callings, ministries and communities have been overthrown by some uncensored dreams thrown directly from hell but rapped with the most spiritual undertone. Anybody can be attacked this way.

Way of Escape...

Resort to the word of God. Only God's word, breathed on by the Holy Ghost is able to dispel any devil. Don't be afraid, victory was accomplished on the cross by Jesus Christ shedding His blood to disembody Satan and his team. Amen.

'Having spoilt principality and power, he made a show of them openly, triumphing over them... overcame them by the blood of the lamb and the words of our testimony...we are than conquerors through him that loved us.' Amen. Praise the Lord!

If you don't know Jesus, there's a serious satanic canopy over your soul, your life and your witchcraft torments are unending. Come to Jesus today asking Him to wash your sins and save your soul. He is the Saviour and the Lord. TELL HIM LIKE I DID 24 years ago, 'Jesus,save me.' Amen.

Write, call or Inbox me for further helps.

*** Word from Mirella...

*** The only revelation you need, and that bears life-giving reality, is GOD. Don't search the Scriptures to attain a higher level of "spiritual" knowledge! Seek Him, also through His Word, to know Him. God is known via experience, not strenuous and sweat-ful study: therein is true knowledge. Lo, only the revelation of God unto a man, pertaining to any facet, really works and propels a living relationship with God.

We have laboured in vain all through the hours of ignorance; let's give heed to the voice of the LORD this day. With God all things are possible.

Thus, before you rest from this day's activities, ask God: "O God, reveal Yourself unto me that I may truly know You."

John 17:3 says, *"And this is life eternal, that they might know thee the only true God, and Jesus Christ, whom thou hast sent."*

Daniel 11:32 says, *"And such as do wickedly against the covenant shall he corrupt by flatteries: but the people that do know their God shall be strong, and do exploits."*

See also Jeremiah 9:23-24.

God bless you; shalom! ***

Chapter 116

Guide Against Dishonour

Nothing waters down the grace and anointing of God on a man like disrespect or dishonour. While we're not to look for our own honour, but being dishonoured could shut down the flow of grace in the direction of the perpetrator.

They said to Jesus, 'Is this not Jesus son of Joseph the carpenter ...? And He could not do much miracle there...' Mathew 13:54-58.

Three factors could bring dishonour:

1. Satan could incite a fellow to just dishonour a person of grace for nothing evil he's done, just to make him little in his eyes and to the detriment of the perpetrator.

2. Being too close to people could make you stink to them. Familiarity breeds contempt. Hence, to guard the grace, you have to be circumspect. Reserved people can guard the grace better. King Solomon warns,

   "Be not too frequent in your neighbour's house, otherwise he would be weary of you and hate you." Proverbs 25:17.

   Being easily accessible by people and easily accepting of people could make you loathsome and dishonourable.

As an outgoing person, I regret a lot of contacts I make with people till date. Everything must be measuredly done. Humans are deeply funny!

2. Some people come from background where disrespect is a way of life and they're raised up like that. Paul warned Titus of a certain people call Cretans saying,

"One of themselves, even a prophet of their own, said, The Cretans are always liars, evil beasts (cruel criminals), lazy gluttons." Titus 1:12.

This people called liars and cruel criminals disrespect could do just anything including disrespecting anybody at any point in time.

How to curtail it...

A. Walk in wisdom always. You must know when your presence, touch, contact or connection with people, places or projects is enough, then leave God to do the rest.

   "Don't sing anymore where you're already disdained"- **African Idiom.**

   Don't keep feeding the filled, look for the hungry. Don't let folks vomit on you. Overfeeding makes people constipate and or throw up. There's a time when enough is enough!

B. Rebuke all sorts of demonic avenues to cast you down through dishonour.

C. Carry the presence of God in abundance around.

God bless you.

*** Word from Mirella...

It Takes God to Know God

*** Among the greatest undoings of the present Christians is obeying the traditions of men, at the cost of the precious Word of God...thereby generating veiled hypocrisy, which is deemed "normalcy" among men.

God isn't happy at that. Lo, what is greatly esteemed among men is abomination in the sight of God. Thus, let's get our principles right once and for all!

In the present age, man can set out to act in the way well-pleasing to his fellow men just to obtain acceptance and to be judged a "wise & righteous" person. However, during the course of his performance, such one has angered the LORD!

Choose this day whom you shall live for: God or man? Whosoever you live to please clearly defines who really is your lord.

Choose God: live for Him...please Him. Luke 16:15 says,

"And he said unto them, Ye are they which justify yourselves before men; but God knoweth your hearts: for that which is highly esteemed among men is abomination in the sight of God."

~ Mark 8:8-9 says, "8 For laying aside the commandment of God, ye hold the tradition of men, as the washing of pots and cups: and many other such like things ye do.

9 And he said unto them, Full well ye reject the commandment of God, that ye may keep your own tradition."

Shalom! ***

Chapter 117

Check Around... the Gold May Be There!

After you have looked above calling on God, look around for what He might have put there, and be wary of looking abroad because what God wants to do doesn't have to come from far.

Many overlook those around them to look far for help when God has touched their surroundings to help them.

"They said, "Is this not Jesus, the son of Joseph, whose father and mother we know? How can he now say, 'I came down from heaven'?" John 6:42.

Chapter 118

Change Does Happen by Encounters

Change has many ways it happens with people. Three of the prominent ways are:

a) An encounter with God.

Nathaniel's mind about Nazareth changed at the instance of a word of knowledge from Jesus. Paul was blinded to change (He was made blind to encounter change). Moses encountered the burning bush and Nebuchadnezzar turned to Animal. You cannot but change after an encounter with God.

b) Inspiring information.

Faith comes by hearing. People's lives change when they acquire new light on issues. Appropriate pieces of information could induce a change of way. New understanding brings new direction.

c) Personal experience.

Bereavement, troubles of life, watching others go through stuffs, failure, and other happenings of life have impactful power to visibly shake and change a man.

Of all, positive encounters with God have the greatest power to change the cause of a man permanently.

I pray you will encounter God today for a great change in Jesus name. Amen.

Blessed season.

Chapter 119

Divine Processes

If God will use, bless or pass through you greatly, He will make you go through great processes. Most of these processes will come and go without much of your knowing what they are for.

God will strengthen you to succeed in all in Jesus name. Amen.

Love you!

Chapter 120

Only God Changes People

For long I was in the college of those who think they can and must change people, but after many years now, I know only God changes people by means of heart-change. Nobody can change nobody (not even your own biological or spiritual children) either by draconian laws, heavy preaching or prophetic threats. After major crusades, many still go back with their concubines or boy/girl friends for night shifts.

Just talk the truth and leave God with the rest while watching your own very life!

"Behold, all souls are mine; as the soul of the father, so also the soul of the son is mine..." Ezekiel 18:4.

*** Word from Mirella...

*** Pray this day: *"Show me Your ways, O LORD; teach me Your paths"* (Psalm 25:4). Therein, is life... holiness, peace and fullness of joy!

Shalom! ***

Chapter 121

Nobody Moves Forward Without Sacrificial Giving... NOBODY!

You must do all you can at all times to the fullness of your capacity to all people without looking back. God freely gives us all things for onward release to others. "It's more blessed to give than to receive," God's word says.

You have not truly known God and cannot be fully blessed or used of Him if you have the good of this life, either spiritual or physical, but you hoard it from those who need it.

"...there is that withholds more than is meet, but it tends to poverty." Proverbs 11:24.

Unseen forces help givers because "A liberal heart must be made fat" no matter the situation on earth.

By giving, some have hosted angels unawares like Abraham in Genesis 18.

"Be not forgetful to entertain strangers: for thereby some have entertained angels unawares." Hebrews 13:2.

There must never be a circumstance whereby you should not give any more except you do not have any more, but God is too faithful to leave you destitute or without having anything!

"There's he who scatters, yet increases..." Proverbs 11:24.

Giving is a spirit, so if you're always in pain to give, you need that spirit. It's called grace.

"...the grace that God has given the Macedonian churches. In the midst of a very severe trial, their overflowing joy and their extreme poverty welled up in rich generosity." 2 Corinthians 8:1-2.

No matter who has needs around, you will not have a heart to reach out except the giving grace is on your life. A giver has his life opened unto all good things because his hands are opened, God knows he can trust him for onward releases to others without coercion.

A giver has his life opened unto all good things because his hands are opened, God knows he can trust him for onward releases to others without coercion.

I am not sure God's purposes can be fulfilled in the life of a fellow who does not give even in pain. God tests our love by our giving!

"Those who sow with tears will reap with songs of joy. Those who go out weeping, carrying seed to sow, will return with songs of joy, carrying sheaves with them." Psalm 126:5-6.

When God would eventually release His eternal covenant blessing on Abraham, He asked for Isaac to be given Him. Abraham was tested and He passed. Giving is a test!

There's nothing anybody could have done to you that you can't help them in their time of needs if God has so endowed you. We've been hurting God for thousands of years, yet He remains our greatest helper in time of need or trouble!

"For we have not an high priest which cannot be touched with the feeling of our infirmities...Let us therefore come boldly unto the throne of grace, that we may obtain mercy & find grace in time of need." Hebrews 4:15-16.

If you always rationalize, you will remain earth-bound in the things of life. But you need to be up above to rule earthly circumstances.

Giving is not talking. It is not preaching neither. It's doing. You're the priest of your environment as a believer. Start the giving chain. Let people touch you with the feelings of their infirmity.

If the resources finish, God will replenish you. Don't turn down anybody when anything still remains. Give it out. It will come back in many folds!

"Withhold not good from them to whom it is due, when it is in the power of your hand to do it." Proverbs 3:27.

If God will make you great, you will be tested in giving, nothing can excuse you from this! "Peter,do you love me more than these",Jesus asked, "feed my sheep". It's a proof of your love!

When there's a vacancy at the top and heavens want to promote a man into another phase of life, your resources are tested, your giving is pruned mercilessly. "Abraham, give me your only son", God asked!

The test of giving is done in very subtle, silent ways many times unknown to us. Ask yourself, "when did God test Eliab, the eldest brother of David, that God told Samuel," I have rejected him" when a king was needed? Ask yourself the question!

If you're called of God and it's hard for you to give, the calling may die off! Your gifting does not determine your future as much as your giving.

Your future (your whole life) is tied to your giving! Give your time, money, space, strength, skills and whole life to those who deserve or non-deserving of it. Forgive and give!

Selective giving is not motivated by God and is not done unto God. If you can only give to your family, business, ministry, church, friends, those you love, those who love you or your pastor, you have not started giving. Pharisees did the same. Even the wicked do the same according to Jesus.

Give to those who cannot repay. Feed those who cannot say thank you. Reach out and pastor those who cannot honour you back. "If our hope is only in this world, we're of all men most miserable", Paul warned.

If you will learn to open your hand (as your heart opens to freely give and be of help to humanity, especially those of the household of faith), God will fill it up.

We brought nothing into this world and it's certain we will take nothing back. So, it's of great importance to use all our resources and worldly goods to serve the purpose of Him who "is not unrighteous to forget our labour of love".

"For God is not unrighteous to forget your work and labour of love, which ye have shewed toward his name, in that ye have ministered to the saints, and do minister." Hebrews 6:10.

May God's ever flowing grace for giving that opens up destiny freshly flow our way this season in Jesus name. Amen.

Peace be unto you my friend. Peace!

Chapter 122

Facing Obstacles and Handling Rejection...God is Able!

When the one sent of God into your life comes in, your mistakes do not matter to such. You're just unquestionably loved. You deserve this!

The coming of your spouse may be taking time so you may appreciate such as sent from God when it happens. But it will happen. You won't be denied!

I have experienced what humans call rejection before, it pains, but it's because God doesn't want such in your life. The people God sends cannot leave you. They find you too pleasant not to be around.

Many times rejections pave way for grand receptions. If Joseph's brothers didn't do what they did, he wouldn't have got to the throne of Egypt. Glory to God!

Brothers in Christian fellowship, pastors and fathers in the faith have said unbearably un-hearable things about me before, but they later changed because God turned the tide!

One strong thing I have come to know is: You're only rejected if you reject yourself!

You don't have to look like an animated Barbie to be married or accepted. It takes internal inferiority or rejection to be doing everything physical to please people!

Internal rejection is a reason why a lot of you open your breasts around. You don't believe you're beautiful enough without a showcase. You don't have to be window-shopped to be loved. God made you beautiful and you're beautiful! Amen.

If you've really met with God, you can't be a weakling nor a self-rejected person. You're so confident that words of men matter a little to you. Psalm 125:1-3.

God definitely will send people into your life that will take care of you and help you up into a new season.

I have never seen the righteous forsaken nor his seed begging bread. You will not be forsaken neither will you be begging around for help in Jesus name. Amen.

Look up to God and be confident He will do it because He will!

It takes internal defeat to accept rejection of any form as the end. Many are highly honourable people of substance but internally defeated. That's why Paul prayed that our eyes of understanding to be enlightened.

"A man with valuable possessions but without understanding is like the animals that perish." Psalm 49:20.

Most depressed people have issue with personal acceptance. You have to be a person of unconquerably impregnable spirit. You're accepted in the Beloved and you're complete in Christ who's the head of principalities and powers.

Yinka Peters [a friend] came to sympathise with me for being kicked out of a place we had school, church and home in 2003 only to find me on the street of Ikeja, Lagos excited about life. Nothing conquers you if you don't submit yourself. "Greater is He that's in us…"

No book can contain the rejections and un-hearable treatments doled out to me when I came to Europe, but in the words of Paul, "None of these things moved me neither count I my life dear unto me." The unconquerable one lives within us. His name is Jesus!

"You will meet with many obstacles on the way, Jesus told His team members, "but be of good cheer, I have overcome the world, you're lifted above them and higher than them all." John 16:33 Paraphrased.

Rejection sometimes points to what you can do. David's brethren chided with him for making enquiries about Goliath. He ended up lifted dealing with him.

The Lord is the strength of your life, of whom shall you be afraid? None! Be strong, keep moving, the Lord is with you. Peace be unto you and all yours now and forever in Jesus name.

Amen.

Chapter 123

Get This Deep into Your Spirit

If you sincerely pray to God to reverse a trend in your life, a project you're about to dabble into, a relationship you're involved in if it is not His will, He will reverse it if He's not in it. I believe this word is sent for somebody.

Pray sincerely about it with your heart out. God will hear and intervene in Jesus name. Amen.

The fastest way to throw Satan out is to clean sin off your tabernacle or your coast. When there's no sin in your shores, the devil will be far.

"Submit yourselves, then, to God. Resist the devil, and he will flee from you." James 4:7.

Did you stop doing good because many you've helped disappointed you? It's just like he who stops praying because he felt his last year's prayers weren't granted. May be you don't know the purpose of doing good yet... It's from God and done unto God alone. It changes everything when you see God in who you help!

God may be leaving it late to strike a deal with you. Don't lose hope. Lazarus died before Jesus arrived not because his sins were too many, but "Known unto God are all his works from the beginning of the world". Acts 15:18.

God will still move over your life if you don't stop your parts of the deed! Keep probing...troubleshooting; keep moving!

"Let us not become weary in doing good, for at the proper time we will reap a harvest if we do not give up." Galatians 6:9.

You may enter London to reap the harvests of your Lagos seeds. Keep at what you're doing for God. He's everywhere.

You gave all you can (your time, skill, resources and life) in that church. You're left high and dry. But you should know that the body of Christ comprises of many churches of which that church is included. You're not losing out. Your reward is approaching. Now, it can be from any church. Even the one where you think you never sowed! Amen.

You can be preaching around and not be doing God's work. Preaching is not necessarily God's work. Stop burning personal, family and church money on unnecessary ventures. God's work is to do what God really asks you to do.

Rid your heart of all un-forgiveness and misgivings no matter what anyone has done to you, because these may become the undoing of your life if not. Joseph forgave his brothers who connived against him longest time before they showed up, giving birth to two boys and naming them 'forgetiveness (forgoing the past) and Fruitfulness (moving ahead with life)! Forgiveness leads to fruitfulness!

With lies, pretence and boasting you do not only quench the Spirit of God, you forfeit precious relationships on earth. Faking doesn't have a place in God's kingdom!

"Wherefore putting away lying, speak every man truth with his neighbour: for we are members one of another." Ephesians 4:25.

God certainly does not write cheque for the projects He doesn't have hand in, but He does bail us out of any ditch we put ourselves or allows Satan put us in once we're ready for Him. He will save you if you turn to Him. Isaiah 30:15.

May God open our eyes of understanding today. May His grace and wisdom be multiplied unto us all in Jesus name. Whatever the situation of your life, may God's mercy be made known showing the way out. Amen.

Peace be unto you.

*** Word from Mirella...

Watching at Night with the Father

*** As I journeyed with some people I knew well in the earth realm, I started to distance myself away from the rest, along with one of the fellows. We kept on chatting on some giggly issues. All of a sudden, we began to run so fast, that we became far apart from each other. Running, a vain word came from my mouth - still being in the spirit of the conversation that I was engaged in not too long ago.

Immediately, my spirit man spoke clearly to me," how could such a word come through you and expect spiritual victory?". I quickly corrected myself and, all of a sudden, I began ascending into the sky. As I flew upwards, I was declaring the Word of God. I quoted three biblical verses (two of them I recall vividly), namely: "I can do all things through Christ that strengthens me"(Philippians 4:13) and "...greater is He that is in me than He that is in the world" (I John 4:4).

Upon quoting the third and last verse, still ascending in the heavens, a demonic resistance arose and attempted to draw me downwards. However, I withstood such by rebuking it outspokenly with the blood of Jesus Christ, and it withdrew - I literally shook it off (just as Paul shook the viper into the fire).

Then, I looked around me... I wasn't alone. There were many other people that were ascending into the heavenlies too. As I cast a panoramic gaze beneath me, I beheld the whole earth (speaking of humanity) at rest... asleep; it was NIGHT. However, as I looked, I saw some people curled up in their deep sleep, and some others kneeling upon their beds in prayer.

Then, a person (that apparently looked like a man, dressed in red top and trousers) carried me back to earth and placed me on my bed. Amazingly, as I journeyed back to the earth, the personality that bore me and placed me back on my bed was the same that carried and put to bed every other person that travelled in my company back to earth, at the same time.

Then and there, the Word of the Lord came unto me, "THE LORD KEEPS RECORD OF THOSE THAT WATCH AT NIGHT WITH HIM".

After a few scenes in the dream, I woke up. As I pondered upon the dream, two biblical verses shone upon my heart, so to confirm the origin of the dream. They are:

"It is vain for you to rise up early, to sit up late, to eat the bread of sorrows: FOR SO HE GIVETH HIS BELOVED SLEEP" (Psalm 127:2);

"BEHOLD, bless ye the LORD, all ye servants of the LORD, WHICH BY NIGHT STAND IN THE HOUSE OF THE LORD" (Psalm 134:1).

Beloved, the night is truly a time of renewing encounter and time with God. Thus, don't take it lightly.

Until you prevail through the night in the place of communion with and prayer unto God, your upcoming day can't be blessed. Arise at night in the place of prayer and find rest for your soul.

Shalom! ***

Chapter 124

God's Way of Loving...Your Key to The Next Phase of Life!

God's love compels us to halt undue criticism of others, even those that are not of our faith, but to look for ways to help them. "The goodness of God leads to salvation."

Reaching out to people could be big or small but the quality of love and sincerity put in it makes it acceptable no matter the size!

We can do good to others without loving them (Pharisees did so just to be seen as confirmed by Jesus in Mathew 6) But we cannot love without doing good!

Loving people doesn't start by doing things physical, but spiritually offering sacrifices on their behalf in the place of prayers, asking God to help them first, so whatever we do will go a long way. Jesus prayed for Peter.

Only things done in true love reaches God. He searches the heart. Everybody can talk about others, but only people whose heart is driven by the love of God do something about such.

Criticizing others never changes them but helping them out does. You don't know what who is going through to be like that. People need more help than you think.

If you truly love your church members, your children, your friends, your co-workers, it is not gifts you will lavish them with as the heathens do to buy people's heart or cajole them first, you will bend your knees to deeply pray for them.

"I travail again until Christ be formed in you", Paul prayed for the foolish Galatians. Galatians 4:19.

The greatest legacy you can lay down for people is to secretly deeply pray for them without them knowing. Men praise you for what they know and you may lose your reward with God for this as Jesus warned in Mathew 6. Pray for people without them knowing.

If all you pray for as a pastor is for people to come to church, maybe God didn't send you. Coming to church is useless if people's lives are not changing. Pray for them to have God step into their cases and they will come to church unforced!

Take charge of your wife's and children lives in the spirit realm before they wake up, commit them to God. Don't wait for problems to start for you to be running around. Take charge spiritually first. That's how to love!

As soon as you notice that people have issues of life, take it upon yourself first in deep committed prayers (not lips service as many do), then do other things you can. Don't help without praying to God for help for those in need.

"Except the Lord builds the house, they labour in vain that build it." Psalm 127:1.

Don't create the habit of talking ill and talking bad of others in your home. Children of God don't do that. It will open your home to all kinds of troubles. Rather assemble your children and family members to pray with you over people. They will all grow up loving God.

It will be difficult for you to not love and care for those you truly pray for. Heart gravitates towards what it's invested on.

Pray for those who curse you and despitefully use you. That's a higher life. That's the life of God. That's how to love. Jesus gave Himself for the salvation of the whole world.

You won't win with hate, retaliation or revenge, because God will oppose you. You will only win with love. Leave vengeance for God. It's His business.

Sometimes it's very difficult for me to continue with large percentage of those I know because of serious damages done, but that's flesh. I love them, pray for them and want to see good happen to them more than humans can comprehend. You can't keep bending people down and grow up!

You can't be bitter and be better at the same time. It will surprise you how much God loves those people you're bitter about.

Do good to all excluding none. Start with what you can: Your heart, Your prayers, Your word, then your deed. Start today. Start now. Do it. It will open your life to another phase. God is good!

Love is a test of how much you live in God and want your prayers answered. Anything outside of true love voids your fasting and prayers. God is love!

May God's peace be multiplied unto us, may His love for Him and others increase in soul in Jesus name. Amen.

Blessed love day! Look for somebody to pray deeply for showing the love of God.

I love you!

*** Word from Mirella...

*** Dear sister in Christ, don't dampen the resounding discernment of your inner man and accept a marital proposal as God's will, all because you believe that brother is much and more spiritual than you. Are you genuinely saved? Filled with the Holy Spirit? In a living relationship with God? Then, you've the true witness of the Holy Spirit in you and, thus, He will lead you aright. Follow Him! ***

*** Holiness births purity and chastity. Until you're purged and set apart unto the LORD, you cannot be truly pure nor chaste! ***

*** Dear Sister in Christ, bearing yourself with dignity is made easily possible by having the fear of God: being obedient to His Word. ***

*** You've been struggling with sexual immorality...and you so desire to break free from it but to no avail. I come to you with the answer: THE GOSPEL OF JESUS CHRIST. Paul declared, "I am not afraid to preach the GOSPEL of our Lord Jesus, for IT IS THE POWER OF GOD UNTO SALVATION."

God has made such provision in Christ Jesus and, thus, is set to save you. Come unto Him today! ***

*** Genuine salvation eradicates the seed of sin, for such a fellow is born of God and, thus, has the seed of God in him/her. The seed of God births holiness. Decide to water it with the Word and prayer, till wholesome manifestation of the life of God in you. ***

*** Spending eternity with our heavenly Father is part of our inheritance as sons and daughters of His. In fact, it is written that it is His desire to give us the kingdom (Luke 12:32). It's clearly part of Salvation agenda: that we may be saved to the uttermost (Hebrews 7:25, 5:9).

Don't give up your eternal and glorious birth-right for crumbs and gnashing of teeth in hell fire! **

*** When God's good pleasure to give you the kingdom meets your obedience unto His Word from a pure heart, He will surely deliver His kingdom unto you. Meaning? He'll endow you with His power and glory. Remember, every kingdom has its power and glory (see Matthew 6:13, Luke 4:6). ***

*** The call to seek first the kingdom of God is because it is our heavenly Father's good pleasure to give us the kingdom.

However, the gate of His kingdom is NARROW. Thus, strive to enter through it (Luke 12:24)! ***

Chapter 125

Your Life Will NOT Be Locked Down if You Will Pray Enough...Pray!

Satan paints a picture of total defeat and a bleak future to your face, but you can reverse it in the place of prayers because Jesus dealt with it already!

"...blotting out the handwriting of the ordinances written against you and contrary to you..." Colossians 2:14.

Many people who have testimonies of great success have also been to the valley you're now, but was brought out as they engaged God in deep prayers!

"He brought me out of a miry clay and horrible pit, he placed my feet on the rock..." Psalm 40:1-2.

Your worth is incurred by acquisition of the breath of the Almighty you got in the place of prayers.

"Those who wait on the Lord will exchange their strength..." Isaiah 40:31.

Sometimes Satan doesn't only paint a picture of defeat, you yourself know this is a major trouble, but Prayers to God can turn the tide. I don't know how it works, but it works all of the time everywhere.

"And call upon me in the day of trouble: I will deliver thee, and thou shalt glorify me." Psalm 50:15.

If you play with prayers, you may end up a prey to all kinds of situational forces and demonic manoeuvres.

Can't forget years ago how a madam who operated a food canteen called me to pray over her shop. She had low sales for some period. We've only started singing about the blood of Jesus when the canteen worker began to confess their witchcraft activities over the business when arrested by God's power.

Sometimes I wonder why Jesus took prayers so seriously. After all, He's Jesus, the Son of God and God Himself, but His prayer life was an intense one. It's to tell us that many things will go wrong in our full glare if prayers are not taken seriously.

"But Jesus often withdrew to lonely places and prayed." Luke 5:16.

There's no lasting minister or ministry that plays with prayers. None. None. None. None ever. None. None!

I was in deep trouble early 2004 in Lagos, Nigeria. I went to Redemption Camp to pray on the first altar near the road for three days. It's so bad that I couldn't take a room there for privacy and the security men harassed us not a little in the middle of the night. On one of the afternoon while the Sun was scorching I fell into a trance of a son that'd be born unto me, I was surrounded by servants of God who said the name will be Answer. The prophecy is fulfilled now. It's fulfilled word for word late last year when Answer Samuel Was born on the 2nd of NOVEMEBER,2015 and christened by at least 25 pastors in attendance praying over him.

Don't just sit around to watch your problem continue. It might even be cancer. Don't keep arguing with men. Separate yourself to pray. There's a God in heaven who hears and answers prayers. Pray. Turn your face to the wall and cry to Him. Amen.

"Hezekiah turned his face to the wall and prayed to the LORD (to deliver him from death and he lived) ..." Isaiah 38:2.

You may not know when, you may not know how, but God will do it again. Just pray. Separate time out and pray.

"For thus saith the LORD, Ye shall not see wind, neither shall ye see rain; yet that valley shall be filled with water, that ye may drink, both ye, and your cattle, and your beasts." 2 kings 3:17.

I have passed through many troubles than I can number. Many from the devil. Some I caused by myself inadvertently but deceived of Satan. In all, I don't look for people or prophet, I look for God. And now so far, I can't complain.

"Call unto me, I will answer you. I will show you great and mighty things that you know not." Jeremiah 33:3.

Everybody is doing things and calling all to know of it. You go ahead exposing what God is doing with you also without serious prayer back up. It may be devastating in the end. Don't take any step without deep prayers.

"Be alert and of sober mind. Your enemy the devil prowls around like a roaring lion looking for someone to devour." 1Peter 5:8.

You can lose your call if you become prayer-less. You just become administrative and ceremonial minister going out visiting people, eating from house to house, doing naming ceremonies and burying the dead without any major impact in life. Somebody else will be called by God to handle the original purpose! Remember: Many are called but few will be chosen as worthy to continue with the call.

"Hold on to what you have, so that no one will take your crown." Rev 3:11.

God does answer all peoples prayers somewhat, I believe, but only the prayers of the righteous make tremendous power available all the time. Therefore, be born again and live in holiness always so you can see God in action always in your prayers.

"Therefore confess your sins to each other and pray for each other so that you may be healed. The prayer of a righteous person is powerful and effective." James 5:16

Combine your prayers with fasting. Don't just be eating around like Yokoshuna paying others to fast for you or waiting for magic prayers from prophets. Hannah prayed herself. No lasting success story without personal involvement.

Life is a spiritual warfare, if you don't pray enough, you may lose it at all levels.

"And he (Jesus) spake a parable unto them to this end, that men ought always to pray, and not to faint;" Luke 18:1.

"The LORD hear thee in the day of trouble; the name of the God of Jacob defend thee; Send thee help from the sanctuary, and strengthen thee out of Zion; Remember all thy offerings, and accept thy burnt sacrifice; Grant thee according to thine own heart, and fulfil all thy counsel in Jesus name. Amen. Psalm 20:1-4.

Peace be upon you! Amen.

*** Word from Mirella...

We Are Strangers on Earth!

*** We are indeed STRANGERS on the earth and, thus, the obvious necessity to anchor unto spiritual leadership to navigate unscarred. No wonder David declared, "I am a stranger upon the earth; hide not Thy commandments from me" (Psalm 119:19).

The spiritual realm is governed by principalities, powers, spiritual wickedness in the heavenly places; and the greatest of all, the kingdom of God. If we won't remain wanderers in the spiritual realm, we must come to the knowledge of spiritual realities - which clearly calls for identifying with spiritual entities (either with God or Satan). Many believers are stranded, others are wandering aimlessly and endlessly in the higher network that constitutes the spiritual realm.

Beloved, it's time to cease to wander and come into Zion, that we may SEE AND KNOW! Spiritual contention so exists, believe me or not. Principalities and powers are at work, laying hold and at stale cities and nations. That is why the Body of Christ must ARISE in the place of prayer to contend for the land. Rejoice, because *"the earth is the LORD's and the fullness thereof; the world and they that dwell therein"* (Psalm 124:1). The LORD Almighty, the mighty terrible warrior, owns the earth. Thus, arise and declare His lordship over that city...nation!

Daniel fought against the forces contending for the lordship of the territory wherein he was, till his answers came. Beloved, until you declare vehemently and significantly the lordship of Jesus Christ over that city, answers to the prayers of the saints therein will be withheld, and angels sent to minister to the needs of the Church within that territory will be resisted. This clearly depicts the dynamics and power of prayer!

Spiritual victory is constituted of holiness, the Word of God, and prayer and fasting - this threefold cord can't be broken, being powered by the breath and life of God, even the Holy Spirit.

If you desire to strike a significant and resounding chord in eternity, you need to ask the LORD to open your eyes, that you may behold wondrous things out of His Word (Psalm 119:18). Beloved, this is pertinent because life is spiritual. Until you've seen it indeed, you don't know it! The first step to overcoming, even in spiritual battles of life, is to be able to see into the occurring happenings in the realm of the Spirit. The other aspect of this twofold requirement is that it enables you to mine out wondrous, terrible and precious treasures out of God's Word - this speaks of mind-blowing, Spirit-filled secrets and keys.

That brings us to the vitality and power of prayer. This latter acts as the *locos* for seeking the Father to open your spiritual sight. When your eyes are opened, you'll become quickened to see into spiritual realities and find out the secrets of the LORD.

Oh, God has secrets. Won't it baffle you to know that there's a SECRET place of the Most High? When you embark on the right route, as led of the Holy Spirit, you'll surely stumble upon His secrets in His secret place.

The opening of spiritual sight lays such responsibility upon the shoulders of the concerned fellow: to give himself/herself continually to the ministry of the Word and prayer (Acts 6:4).

Above all, the Word of God revealed and the living state of one's prayer and fasting life produce the very life of God in such a fellow: HOLINESS ! In such dimension, your perspective of God and His kingdom become ever accurate and clear, transforming you from glory to glory. Amen. Shalom! ***

Chapter 126

Five Ways God Talks

With Regards to Marriage, Ministry, Business or Other Events of Life

Firstly, God speaks primarily through His word-The Bible.

"In the past God spoke to our forefathers through the prophets at many times and in various ways, but in these last days he has spoken to us by his Son [the word], whom he appointed heir of all things, and through whom he made the universe. The Son is the radiance of God's glory and the exact representation of his being, sustaining all things by his powerful word. After he had provided purification for sins, he sat down at the right hand of the Majesty in heaven." Hebrews 1:1-3.

Anything God's word says is said already. This is to make everybody get access to God's voice. Anything that agrees with God's word is God's voice. Joshua 1:8; Deuteronomy 28:1.

So the most basic way God speaks in these last days is through His written word. Therefore, if any ignores the word but is looking for the voice [like so many christians do], he won't get anything. God's word is God's voice

Say after me: God's word is God's voice!

Secondly, God speaks through dreams.

"When a prophet of the Lord is among you, I reveal myself to him in visions, I speak to him in dreams". Number 12:6.

He spoke to Joseph son of Jacob through dreams. He spoke to Joseph father of Jesus through dreams. He spoke to Jacob through Dreams. He has spoken to me clearly numbers of times through dreams. Although this is not the primary way He speaks, because the devil manipulates this a lot. God wants you to seek Him through His word first! Okay?!

Thirdly, God speaks through audible voice.

Clear word from heaven like that of Jesus in Mathew Chapter 3 while He was being baptized. God does speak unequivocally on distinct issues audibly without mincing words. Again, this is not His primary way of speaking to His Children. He speaks audibly enough through His word, the Bible. When you are in the presence of the Bible, you are in for the voice of God.

"With him[Moses] I speak face to face, clearly and not in riddles; he sees the form of the LORD. Why then were you not afraid to speak against my servant Moses?" Number 12:8.

Fourthly, God speaks through your personal liking or taste.

"For it is God who works in us both to will and to do of His good pleasures". Philippians 2:13.

God does put a right taste or liking in the heart of a Christian so when you see it, you just know this is it. This is what the Bible mostly calls desire.

"The desire of the righteous ends only in good, but the hope of the wicked only in wrath". Proverbs 11:13.

And also

"...but the desire of the righteous shall be granted". Proverbs 10:24.

This is what we call sudden and or settled upsurge of a strong urge in the way of righteousness which God always grants It takes on all your motions and emotions, you can't drive it off. You are restless about it until it's accomplished. A great example is when David went to give his brother food in the army camp and then suddenly started asking about Goliath. It was a clear directive in the spirit as David had a taste to see God's enemy disgraced! He was restless until he saw it done. Glory to God!

Lastly, God speaks through keen and inexplicable insight into a matter, person, church organisation or community. We call this physical/spiritual sight. You can't tell how you know it, but you know this is it. You just know this is it. The confidence is there.

Overall, the word of God must be consulted profusely in all cases. It is the final authority on all matters.

"I will worship toward thy holy temple, and praise thy name for thy lovingkindness and for thy truth: for thou hast magnified thy word above all thy name". Psalm 138:2.

God does speak through Prophets also...any available child or servant of God can be used to speak to you. He might be talking based on any of these five pillars.

"Despise not prophesyings".1 Thessalonians 5:20.

Be Blessed. Peace.

Chapter 127

Quick Lessons on Choosing
a Marriage Partner

Take unusual steps beyond normal praying to really praying about the person and digging into known facts about his/her life vis-a-vis the foundation and personality.

Yes, foundation and personality. Two very important matters in any relationship be it marital, organisational or otherwise.

Foundation corresponds with the word track records in professional arena and personality resonates with the person's make up which could be easily found out by what the person speaks and does repeatedly and while under pressure or duress.

"We are what we do repeatedly." - Aristotle.

Study the person's community origin. Study about marital procedures and conflicts resolution among the people. Check the similarities with your family/community backgrounds and dissimilarities.

Check detailed-ly through pages of the person's Facebook reading through what people posted to him/her and or what he/she posted and responses. Query what you see!

Last but not the least, severally call and spend time with him/her to know who he/she is.

Pray to know him/her more. Our God reveals. He has all secrets with Him.

On the issue of final decision for marriage, please do not be much emotional. Marriage is 90% directives from heaven coupled with personal decision and 10% emotions. Emotions are like roller-coaster. They come and go!

"Do two walk together unless they have agreed to do so?" Amos 3:3.

PRAY PROFUSELY AND REALLY SEEK THE FACE OF GOD BEFORE ANY DECISION IS MADE AND TO YOURSELF BE TOTALLY TRUE!

Why? Because proverbs 20:6 declares thus: Many claim to have unfailing love, but a faithful person who can find? NIV and Amplified version puts it this way: Many a man proclaims his own loving-kindness and goodness, but a faithful man who can find?

Proverbs 19:14 b also says, "...but a wise, understanding, and prudent wife is from the Lord."

Remember, Marriage is an investment. Do it wisely.

Be blessed.

Chapter 128

The Greatest Secret of Success Ever!

Over the years of curious and vibrant personal relationship with the Almighty God [and it is really the only thing I live in and for...we live, move and have our being in Him], coupled with personal observations [like Solomon always did as discovered in the Bible book of Proverbs] of the lives of very influential servants and children of God the world over, I have come to really understand the root of real and lasting success: **The move of the Holy Spirit**.

Jesus said "The flesh profits nothing, only the Spirit gives life". King Solomon in Ecclesiastes said "Whatever the Lord doeth shall be forever, nothing can be added to it nor removed from it". King David in Psalm submitted in both chapters 127 and 110 "Except the Lord builds the house, they labour in vain that build it" and "in the day of His power, His people shall be willing". The Gospel of John opined "no one receives anything except it comes from heaven"

When the Holy Spirit moves over a soul, a home, an organization, a community, a city, a nation or over a situation, the repel effects of the move become what we call success, breakthrough or turning of captivity.

Consequent on the foregoing, the quest for fulfilment ends in futility until God in the power of the spirit moves. You remember" it is not by power or might, but by my spirit says the Lord" in Zechariah 4:6. Therefore, nothing moves until God moves!

Get back to the root. Get back to the foundation. Psalm 11:3. Get back to the place of real result-The presence of the mighty God of Jacob, the God of Jeshurun who rides on the wings of the wind to help His people.

Remember, those that be planted in the house [the presence] of God shall flourish in courts of our God! When you are rooted in God, you become like a tree planted by the rivers of water whose fruits are borne in their season and their leaves don't wither and whatever they do will PROSPER. Psalm 1:1-3. Glory to God!

I am persuaded of better things this season, things that accompany salvation...but not by power nor might, but by My spirit, says the Lord!

Chapter 129

Bible's Stand on Marriage and Relationship

You cannot, in the name of "honour your father and mother so it may be well with you", buy or send money for Muslim festival ram or idol or traditional festival paraphernalia to your parents as a duly born again Christian. No! Otherwise you partake of their sins and block their way to salvation. I know many believers do this ignorantly, but it's a lopsided interpretation of God's instruction.

Your wife or children don't have to go and stay with your Muslim or pagan family to represent you or appease them during their festival, for it's not Christ-based. If God has saved you from such, seek for others to come out of it. Don't appease them. Christ is the way, the truth and the life! John 14:6.

There's no difference between giving somebody alcohol or giving them money to buy it. So, if you're taking a wife from a family that insists you must do either, take your leave. If the lady is yours, she will follow you. What blessings will alcohol influenced parents-in-law give a child of God?

Why must your wife have to dance with family masquerade for marrying the first-son or giving birth to twins if you're a true believer? What accord is between light and darkness? Can you sing Christian worship songs while the masquerade parades? Stay with one. Christ or family god (goddess if there be any)!

Your spouse to be doesn't have to be an object of church-wide prophetic analysis. Are the analysts the ones you want to marry? Your personal conviction based on the conclusion between you and God as His child is your blueprint for your marital destiny!

A true child of God in Christ Jesus cannot under any circumstance be married to a person who's not a true child of God (maybe a Mouth-Christian, Muslim, Buddhist, animists, Jehovah witness and so on), just like Light and darkness cannot live together. No!

Your friends, family, pastors and parents can influence who you marry by ways of examples, instructions, guidance and counselling but have no right to impose who the person should be as that's your destiny duty. If you're being beaten, bullied or abused to cringe against your will, run before you're killed. If living in the West, report to authority for protection!

Profuse prayers to the God of heavens with your own mouth, thorough study and standing on God's word and down to earth sincerity are all needed in your search for a God-given spouse!

May God guide in your life in Jesus name. Amen.

Chapter 130

Do I really Love Him/Her?

Love matters...

Love is best shown in actions such that if the person does not understand your language, but can experience what you mean. Love is action, not much of words. The trouble of our generation is that much is said, less is done! The change can start from you!

Love is to pray for those going through difficulties, bereavements, troubles, look for how to help them without judging them behind and afterwards speaking good to them while with them. Love is to help the erring, calling him to talk to him and saving him from his sins without condemning him at the back, speaking evil of him even at church meetings and putting up plastic smiles when you see him.

"Knowledge puffs up, but love builds", Apostle Paul Said 1 Corinthians 8:1.

As a true believer in Christ Jesus, if all you could think about while in courtship/relationship is to rob bodies together indulging in lustful activities, calling it love, be ready to cry later on in your marriage. "He who sows into the flesh will reap corruption...for whatever a man sows, he shall also reap."

You want to show love in relationship before marriage? Go on prayer walk together, do real study of the bible and make sure the anointing or ministry [life assignment] given to spouse-to-be does not start dying as a result of your ungodly activities!

If the grace or the presence of God in the life of a person doesn't increase as a result of your involvement, it's not God's will for you to be together, the dreams you had notwithstanding.

Love in relationship is not missing each other and wanting to go and spend nights together in secluded place or hotels, THAT'S LUST of the first class order.

If you're really meant for her, you will find yourself groaning night and day before God for His will to prevail over her and God's grace to increase on her.

Otherwise, if you just want somebody to rob body with. Why don't you then go to paid prostitutes?

There are many folks roaming around like ravening wolves, hungry lions now, they also even speak in tongues and quote Bible. All they want to do is mess you up sexually and terminate God's assignment for your life. Delilah is a spirit and can be on anybody.

You give your life for whom you love, NOT YOUR SEX!

SEX before marriage in any form [romance or actual deed] is not love, it's LUST operated by a daemon spirit that ruins marital future. You may never know the will of God in marriage once lust creeps in!

A true believer may fall in the devil's booby trap of lust, but will immediately experience hell and do everything to run out. It's a test of if you're truly saved or not.

"He that's born of God does not [deliberately or stay in] sin, for the seed of God remains in him." 1 John 3:9.

Chapter 131

God Talks; You Too Can Hear Him

If you seek the Lord with all sincerity, you will find Him big for He's not far from any one of us. Amen. God's in near!

It's not a sin to have believed people for who they said they're but it's foolishness to stay glued to such even after you have insight into the truth that proves them otherwise.

If you stay with God, the creator, long enough you will have deep insight into people's life even before they open their mouth. They call it word of knowledge, wisdom or discerning of spirits! Stay with God! "Did my spirit not go with you?", Elisha asked Gehazi!

If you ask God about a situation, He will tell you His mind. This is for all children of God. God is near to us!

This doesn't make me a prophet, but when I was finding a wife, any Christian girl I liked and prayed about God usually told me His mind (vision, revelation, dream or outright prophecy from someone I never told) about each in few days of praying (for some, that same night). One lady in particular was resiliently on my case, so I separated myself to pray as I went to preach in a friend's church. The first vision of the trip was of her showing me her husband. Case closed. God speaks. Talk to Him. Mathew 7:7.

There's nothing too big, serious or too small or trivial that we cannot talk to God about. He is so near, dear and loving. He is God. While talking with a precious Lady the other day, she opened up about not having her period as at due date (she's chaste and don't mess around as known to me). She feared a demonic infliction. I took the matter to God. A vision showed up of her washing herself. I called and told her that within two days, you will flow normally. She called the second day that she's now on. All I could say to God is, "You're involved in every human case."

Talk to Him beloved. Answers will come. Amen.

Chapter 132

Important 3's You Need to Know

3 Peoples are needed to get to where God planned for you [Jeremiah 29:11]: 1. God, 2. Yourself, 3. People God will bring into your life (Not the ones you force yourself on or forced be with you). Very important!

3 People to submit to: 1. God. 2 People who love you with all sincerity and truth. 3. Godly people who live to please God alone, hide no sin, cover up no unrighteousness and talk no ill of any created by God (these could be Pastors, Parents, Partners or any person).

3 funny things I always muse over: 1. You're single for some time, people say, "he's probably not in for marriage because he's problem nobody knows or he's comfortable masturbating himself". 2. They happen to see people of same gender always visiting you, staying long or overnight, people say, "He's gay." 3. Finally, they see you with a person of opposite sex and they say, "Wow, these Christian people also enjoy...wow, wow!" If you're tossed around by opinions, you will soon die a non-entity!

3 lines you must reject: 1. The line people want you to be in against your innermost conviction. 2. The line people draw as the boundary you must never cross in life. 3.The line God told you never to be in! Only you in God your maker is You and nobody else!

3 ways to true integrity: 1. Do everything to please God and walk in His word. 2. Do everything to make sure you're sincerely true to the word of God even in your most secret private life. 3. Do everything possible to please humans with all your power and leave the rest to the Judge of the universe, the Almighty God!

3 type of people around us all: 1. People who want things to work and they will stand with you to make things work [Just like genuine mothers to their wards]. 2. People who stand aloof judging every step you take even if you give them your head to eat. 3. People who're indifferent to either your success or failure.

3 most likely things people do in ministry: 1. Many do everything they can while waiting on God to move through. 2. Many just do it as normal personally owned business with all human energy. 3 Many hang down their hands waiting for when God will move without doing anything!

3 things to know about ministry: 1. God doesn't pay hurriedly, but He is faithful at due times. "Godliness is not a way to gain, but godliness with contentment is a great gain", Apostle Paul Said. 2. Many times you will be really going through much pain and people will chide at you or desert you thinking you're making much gain. 3. A lot of the times the people you suffer pain over may not be the ones God will give you gain from. But God is faithful, so do everything as unto God alone! Amen.

3 kind of life that people live: 1. Life Submitted to God totally. 2. Life submitted to Satan blatantly. 3. Life submitted to God to an extent and yielded to devil's tactics sometimes-Satan prefers this and it's lived by many so called believers. Not too cold and not really hot life. Jesus said, "I will spew you out."

3 people you don't need in your journey to what God planned for you: 1. People who always say yes to what you say. 2. People who say No or the truth to you like God. 3. People

who never apologize to you for hurting you! They hurt you without apology!

3 important pillars of divine relationship: 1. Only God truly puts people together for His purpose. God alone makes relationship [true relationship] happens. 2.God designed each of us for the relationships suited for us. That's why Paul's message could be boring to you and Pastor-David Richman's message is delicious! 3. You can frustrate divine relationship by the force of flesh e.g. Jonathan and David and Barnabas and Saul.

3 important facts about prayers: 1. Even when the answer is coming, sometimes you feel God has forgotten you. 2. Prayers are prayed because only God can truly help man. 3. Persistence is the only secret strength of prayers. Luke 18:1-8.

3 things people don't know about daily decisions: 1. Your decision is either for God or Satan. 2. Your decisions DECIDE your destiny. 3. Your decision is formed by your knowledge and relationships!

3 things you do daily without knowing: 1. You're ageing. 2. You're moving closer to death. 3. You're getting closer to God or Satan. The decision is yours!

3 forces that have the greatest interest in you on moment by moment basis: 1. God. 2 Satan 3. Flesh!

3 facts to know about the Holy Spirit of God: 1. He does not argue like your pastors or mentors will do with you. He teaches, guides and reveals, leaving you to make the choice. 2. He does not force anybody to do anything, not even in the Garden of Eden. No, He doesn't force. 3. He is called "Holy-Spirit" because He only stays in vessels of holiness. You can still be speaking in tongues, doing praise jamz and making all the noise even when He's no longer there and you think He's like the Bible time Samson!

3 forceful principles of God's kingdom: 1. Anything can be changed by faith- a firm conviction that you're tired of that trend. 2. Real prayers change situations no matter how terrible. 3.You will never be the same or small in life in the practice of faith and prayers. Never!

3 things you must learn about people: 1. People can be good. 2. People can be bad. 3. People are humans after all!

3 things you must never do: 1. Don't regret your making- You can't change how God made you, either white or black, tall or brief, having robust head [too long or too big] or an under-size one! 2. Don't retreat from your life-don't surrender to pressures of life or Satan's lies. 3. Resist all temptations to relapse into the conquered sinful habits -It may be harder to get out of!

3 things you must do daily to get to where God planned for you: 1. You must pray through a point of need like Hannah each day- Pray through, all kind of prayers. 2. Daily intake of God's word in whatever form possible is critical to your daily journey to the promise. 3. Sow a seed, take a step towards your destiny daily!

Chapter 133

Important 3's You Need to Know - Part II

3 ways to look at people hurting you too deeply so you may enter where God planned for you: 1. They don't know better- "Father, forgive them, for they know not what they do", Jesus said dying. 2. God is testing you through them. 3. You made a mistake of being with them in the first place. Move forward!

3 Burdens too heavy to enter where God planned for you with: 1. Pride-God resists the proud. 2. Immorality of any form-Your body is the temple of the Holy Spirit. 3. Un-forgiveness - no un-forgiver will ever be forgiven by God!

3 danger points you must run from to get to where God planned for you: 1. Anger [for it can be traced to your rights [your pride] ... I, me, myself – It cost Moses the Promised Land. 2. Comparison -You will never be another person. No! You're unique in God's plan. Paul and Peter are different. You will never be Pastor Chris Oyakhilome. No! 3. Wasting time in other people's business. It wastes life!

3 things are needed to get to where God planned for you: 1. Faith in God and His plan for you; 2. Patience of Character in everything; 3. Peace within your heart based on God's word about each step you're taking. Only you and God can ensure this! Hebrews 6:12.

Chapter 134

God Reveals Himself and Any of Us Can Find Him!

There is no other way to know God except by staying with Him personally. Only Him can reveal Himself to somebody else.

"And we shall know if we follow on to know the Lord..." Hosea 6:1-3.

God wants to use everybody, but He only uses who He can reveal Himself to.

There's nobody used greatly of God that does not have a personal experience of Him. This include real divine drilling, screening, scrutiny and tests!

God can reveal Himself to whoever really needs Him and searches for Him. Jeremiah 29:11-13.

Many want to know God through men and women of God, but nobody can reveal God to you except Himself.

"All things have been committed to me by my Father. No one knows the Son except the Father, and no one knows the Father except the Son and those to whom the Son chooses to reveal him." Mathew 11:27.

When God wants to reveal Himself to a man, He will first reveal yourself to you.

"Woe to me!" I cried. "I am ruined! For I am a man of unclean lips, and I live among a people of unclean lips, and my eyes have seen the King, the LORD Almighty." Isaiah 6:5.

When you know God [When God reveals Himself to you in an area], you become a god in that area. You become men like Joshua, Elijah or Elisha who command other men and nature at will.

"If he called them gods, to whom the word of God came" (and the Scripture cannot be broken) John 10:35.

The revelation of God is the end of the frustration of man.

"The light of the eyes rejoices the heart, and good news refreshes the bones." Proverb 15:30.

Your mouth is open widely and accurately on a matter when the revelation of heaven has entered your heart. Revelation puts you in charge.

"A false witness shall perish: but the man that heareth speaketh constantly." Proverb 21:28.

We learn of men when we stay with them [I can speak like Pastor W F Kumuyi, Bishop Francis WALE OKE or Bishop Oyedepo because I stayed with them for some time]. So also you can only learn of God in time when you stay with Him! Mathew 11:29.

You can know more than others do when you spend more time with the Father more than others do.

"I have more insight than all my teachers, For Your testimonies are my meditation." Psalm 119:99.

Thank God for the books, tapes, YouTube and television messages of holy men of God the world over, but for you to truly know God for real, you will have to spend real time alone in prayer-talking to God and studying of His words.

"Jesus answered and said unto him, If a man love me, he will keep my words: and my Father will love him, and we will come unto him, and make our abode with him." John 14:23.

You cannot confront the world until you really know God for yourself (Not the God of any servant of God, but the Almighty God). Without this, you will soon be brought to your knees.

"And such as do wickedly against the covenant shall he corrupt by flatteries: but the people that do know their God shall be strong, and do exploits." Daniel 11:32.

Many go about teaching or acting in the name of the God of the pastor they know, like the seven sons of Sceva, But God is not known of them. Satan and situations of life know those who have known God or encountered Him.

"One day the evil spirit answered them, "Jesus I know, and Paul I know about, but who are you?" Acts 19:15.

If we seek to truly know God, we will find him, for He's not far from any of us.

"His purpose was for the nations to seek after God and perhaps feel their way toward him and find him - though he is not far from any one of us." Acts 17:27.

Bow your head where you're and say to God," O Father of heaven & earth, the Almighty God, I love to know you...I submit to follow you through Christ Jesus the only Saviour of the world. I am here Lord."

"But if from there you seek the LORD your God, you will find him if you look for him with all your heart and with all your soul." Deuteronomy 4:29.

Amen.

Chapter 135

All Rights Are Privilege-Based

Yes, she's your wife and must submit at all times, but not when you're sleeping around but still want her to answer to your sexual needs. WHAT IF YOU'RE ALREADY INFECTED? You need to be godly to enjoy the God-given rights over another. It's a privilege!

As a woman, you make money and send all of it to your family members everywhere and never accountable to your man but want him to take care of all your needs, YOU MUST BE A LEARNER! "Iron sharpens iron; so a man sharpens the countenance of his friend." Proverbs 27:17.

There's no reason for you not to stand up and find work as a man to contribute to your family living, but you're using authority over your wife's income and what it must be used for. That's abuse!

If as a parent you failed in your responsibilities to your children, you cannot threaten them with a curse. If all curses said stand, do you think anybody in the world will still be blessed?

Before you can curse somebody as a husband, pastor or parent and God will make it stand over a Christian fellow who's your wife, church member or child, the fellow must have clearly sinned against God with no willingness to repent!

Christian people are afraid of humans for nothing and most of the time never have an iota of the fear of God. You hear them say, "My parents blessed my marriage". They blessed it does not mean God blessed it. You messed up for years even till your wedding night, angering THE ALMIGHTY, but never pregnant for your parents to praise you. YOU DON'T KNOW GOD!

The leader is abusing or molesting you and you can't breathe an air of freedom, growth or appreciation but you cannot move on because he's apostolic authority to curse you. That's not true. He doesn't!

You must honour everybody, Parents, Pastors, Husband, BUT YOU MUST NOT DISHONOUR GOD TO HONOUR THEM. "Children, obey your parents IN THE LORD", Not against the Lord!

The Gospel of Jesus is very simple, Jesus Christ is very simple, BUT HUMANS HAVE BROUGHT IN THE CORRUPTIONS and COMPLICATIONS OF cultures and traditions of men into it!

"This only have I found: God created mankind upright, but they have gone in search of many schemes." Ecclesiastes 7:29.

The more I withdraw to observe people, the more I see many who actually serve more of culture than God. The word 'Culture' starts with 'cult' which could evolve into cultism! That's why you see a 35-year old woman who sleeps around but cannot be simply married and made settle down because anyone that wants to marry her must follow her to the village to observe certain traditions of elders costing huge amounts, so all men just sleep with her and run away!

Your parents belong to another religion as a BELIEVER IN CHRIST, but you'll have to buy all their festivals paraphernalia or be present there so you can be blessed and not cursed. You're simply making covenants with other gods or goddesses!

You need to go back into the scriptures to see things for yourself the way they're said. Jesus took over the life of John, Andrew, Peter and James while with their fathers fishing. Did they go back there and say, "Father, please bless my follower-ship of Jesus"? The parents were obviously angry, may be until years later when they now became apostles to whom people referred, "These are the men that turned the world upside down".

A lot of believers have secret sins that make them afraid of humans, human institutions and traditions of elders. They'd have been cautioning Jesus not to talk against Pharisees, Sadducees and obsolete laws of MOSES if He were to have lived in our generation!

All authorities wielded by leaders (Pastors, Parents and Husbands) are based on privileges with attached conditions. AND THEY ONLY EXIST TILL THE FATHER OF ALL steps in to truncate the trendy flow! God will not just give authority to anybody so everybody can be afraid of him.NO!

Believers are not to do anything under the fear of man. The fear of man brings snare!

"Serve wholeheartedly, as if you were serving the Lord, not people, because you know that the Lord will reward each one for whatever good they do, whether they are slave or free. And masters, treat your slaves in the same way. Do not threaten them, since you know that he who is both their Master and yours is in heaven, and there is no favouritism with him." Ephesians 6:7-9.

No curse from your leaders (parents, pastors or husbands) can stand on you if you've done all within your ability to make things work properly and you've walked in the word of God.

"As the bird by wandering, as the swallow by flying, so the curse causeless shall not come." Proverbs 26:2.

As for anyone working in God's kingdom anywhere and you're not the top leader, it's wrong to have a notion that you're serving Pastor so and so. If it's a man you're serving, your reward is limited to what that man can do. You're serving the Lord and fulfilling your own calling. If that's not the case, then find a way to serve the Lord as we all work among and with men.

"But none of you should be called a teacher. You have only one teacher, and all of you are like brothers and sisters. Don't call anyone on earth your father. All of you have the same Father in heaven. None of you should be called the leader. The Messiah is your only leader." Mathew 28:8-10.

All rights are privilege-based. If the privilege is abused, the right may be voided.

Peace be unto you.

Chapter 136

God and You Alone!

Don't be afraid. Just pray. Pray to God about each thing and everyone. Mention the case as it is in your best language of expression. Don't be afraid, Just pray. God will do it. Philippians 4:6-7. Amen.

You can't give up on yourself no matter how many have given up on you once God has not given up on you!

Today, just like every other day, clear every debris between you and the Father of heaven. He is our very life, our source and sustainer. Let your life be a vessel that can always accommodate His presence and glory.

Anybody's story can change. There's no timeline with God. He's not constrained by time or age. Anybody's story can still change. God created time and He's not under its auspices! There're things to do and God's glory shall appear unto you.

"Then Moses said, "This is what the LORD has commanded you to do, so that the glory of the LORD may appear to you." Lev 9:6.

The easiest way for the lazy is giving up. In Christ Jesus [who Himself is our strength and by whose strength we can do all things], we don't give up until we give up the ghost!

"Now the just shall live by faith: but if any man draw back, my soul shall have no pleasure in him. But we are not of them who draw back unto perdition; but of them that believe to the saving of the soul." Hebrews 10:38-39.

No matter what God is saying to you (directly or through men, hard or comforting), He just wants to bring you close to Himself so He can fulfil His plan for your existence. You're His investment and He doesn't want to finally lose. God doesn't mind prodigal children; He wants you back!

"For I know the thoughts that I think toward you, saith the LORD, thoughts of peace, and not of evil, to give you an expected end." Jeremiah 29:11.

There's no human case that's impossible with God. No place you're where God cannot reach you anymore.

"I am the LORD, the God of all mankind. Is anything too hard for me?" Jeremiah 32:27.

Humans are the principal agency of God's communication with humans. Therefore, consider very wisely what each human brings to your table. There may be wisdom even in hateful words; truth may be locked in oppositions!

"Yet I sent you all My servants the prophets, again and again, saying, "Oh, do not do this abominable thing which I hate." Jeremiah 44:4.

God always has a way of getting across to us but in ways we cannot dictate. Thus, humility of heart to receive with simplicity the engrafted word of His voice through His own appointed means is imperative.

"In order that the many-sided wisdom of God might be made known now..." Ephesians 3:10.

Understand this, God is doing everything to reach you where you're right now. He is moving things off to get you up and out. He is a good God!

"...He makes the clouds his chariot and rides on the wings of the wind." Psalm 104:3.

There is a grand solution to the predicament you may be in right now. A glorious way out made by, of and from God.

"...will provide the way of escape also..." 1 Corinthians 10:13.

Don't look down on yourself, because even God is looking up to you to handle major projects for Him. Amen.

"What is man that you are mindful of him, the son of man that you care for him?...and crowned him with glory and honor. You made him ruler over the works of your hands; you put everything under his feet: all flocks and herds, and the beasts of the field..."Psalm 8:4-7.

Many times some people will hurt you so deeply trying to pass across a point to you. The point is for your good, but the pointer maybe an irritant. Take the content without minding the container because your life may depend on the point. God is reaching you anyhow!

"For precept must be upon precept, precept upon precept; line upon line, line upon line; here a little, and there a little..."Isaiah 28:10.

There's a voice of God to help you hidden away in your morning prayers, time of devotion, one chapter-a day bible reading. Don't play with it.

"...and the gathering together of the waters called he Seas: and God saw that it was good." Genesis 1:10.

God can never leave you alone until a man is in hell finally. His breath is trapped in our lung and nostrils. His hand followed the prodigal son around till he came back home. Praise the Lord.

"...and my delights were with the sons of men." Proverbs 8:31.

If you do not remember anything in this life anywhere you're, always remember this: YOU CAN CALL ON GOD ANYWHERE. He's ready to come to us!

"For whosoever shall call upon the name of the Lord shall be saved." Romans 10:13.

You can boldly return to the throne of grace to obtain mercy again even if you've been pushed off by sins before. God wants you back there. Mercies exist for you. Grace is available for you. Don't run elsewhere.

"For we do not have a high priest who is unable to sympathize with our weaknesses...Let us then approach God's throne of grace with confidence, so that we may receive mercy and find grace to help us in our time of need. "Hebrews 4:15-16.

Amen.

For more information on the authors, prayers or counselling, please call these lines:

Pastor David Richman or Sis Mimi: +353-879230934, +353-899534714,richlayink@yahoo.com, directorate.powerhouse @gmail.com or follow us on the links at the back cover.

If you live in Ireland or just visiting, you can enjoy worship and Bible Teachings in any of our centres in Galway, New-Bridge, Kildare or Dublin as could be seen on our website.

If you like to surrender your life to Jesus Christ today, say the following prayers:

"Lord Jesus, I believe you with all of my heart and confess with my mouth that you are Lord.

Wash away my sins by your blood and write my name in the book of life today.

I decide to follow you with my spirit, soul and body from henceforth.

So, help me Lord.

In Jesus name. Amen."

We pray for you today that your sins be forgiven, your sicknesses healed and your diseases be cured in Jesus name. Amen.

With this prayer, your journey with God has started or been renewed. Find a church where the truth of the Gospel of Jesus Christ is being preached and practiced to be a part so you can grow thereby.

We will see you in heaven on the last day in Jesus name. Amen.

We're open to invitation to preach, teach and minister the Gospel of Jesus in Conferences, Seminars, Church worship, Revival or crusade events the world over. If you are led to call us, please use the means above.

Peace be unto you and all yours!